Abstracts from

The New London Gazette

*Covering
Southeastern Connecticut*

1770-1773

Richard B. Marrin

HERITAGE BOOKS
2008

HERITAGE BOOKS
AN IMPRINT OF HERITAGE BOOKS, INC.

Books, CDs, and more—Worldwide

For our listing of thousands of titles see our website
at
www.HeritageBooks.com

Published 2008 by
HERITAGE BOOKS, INC.
Publishing Division
100 Railroad Ave. #104
Westminster, Maryland 21157

Copyright © 2008 Richard B. Marrin

All rights reserved. No part of this book may be reproduced or transmitted in any form or by any means, electronic or mechanical, including photocopying, recording or by any information storage and retrieval system without written permission from the author, except for the inclusion of brief quotations in a review.

International Standard Book Numbers
Paperbound: 978-0-7884-4552-1
Clothbound: 978-0-7884-7331-9

Table of Contents

Introduction. 1

Abstracts 3

End Notes 237

Indices 249

Introduction

Volume II of *Abstracts from The New London Gazette* covers a rather peaceful period – 1770 through 1773 - in the history of colonial New London and the other towns of Southeastern Connecticut. On a weekly basis, the *Gazette* demonstrated that business and trade were flourishing – better than in the late 1760s when notices of bankruptcy were frequently seen in the Public Notices part of the paper. Relations with King George and Mother England, anxious to make the Colonies pay for themselves, which had become strained the decade before with the enactments of the Sugar and Stamp Acts, grew a little bit better. But the undercurrents of American seeking liberty, expressed by gestures like the non importation agreements, never went away. Toward the end, a massacre and a tea party, both in Boston and both reported in the *Gazette,* gave a hint of things to come.

Otherwise things went on as usual. The *New London Gazette* reported first hand on the region's activities, the marriages and deaths of its citizens, news of accidents, fires and crimes, a yen in some of the colonists to the West, changes in the weather, maritime matters ranging from ship arrivals to shipwrecks, what the merchants had to sell, and on a hundred other threads that, woven together, present us with a tapestry of the day to day life of the citizens of Southeastern Connecticut in the days just before the Revolution.

Come. Open the *Gazette* and read along.

1770

From *The New London Gazette,* January 5, 1770

thefts

Last Monday, se'nnight, a goldsmith shop in town was broken into and some books stolen out of the same. The stock of the shop had been removed the preceding evening. This and a number of other articles, which had probably been acquired the same way, were found in a bag on board a boat, but the thief, supposed to be one Taylor, has absconded.

Last Tuesday night, the cabin of Capt. Latimer's sloop, lying on the beach, was broken open and a quantity of wearing apparel stolen out of a chest.

fire

We hear from New Haven that the old wooden college there was last Saturday evening discovered to be on fire, but was soon extinguished. By some discoveries, it appeared to be the premeditated action of some malicious person.

ox

We hear that an ox which was fattened by Mr. Jacob Baldwin of Canterbury was last week killed and weighted as follows:
beef: 1,113 pounds
hide: 117 pounds
rough tallow: 163 pounds
total weight: 1,393 pounds

obituary

Last Friday morning departed this life, Mr. Simeon Wood of Lyme, after a long and tedious illness of a malignant fever in the 31st year of his life. He left a sorrowful wife and four small children. He was a man well respected by all, both for his Christian values and piety and also as a kind husband, a tender parent, a good neighbor and generous to all.

slave for sale
To be sold, a likely Negro man, 23 years old, understand the farming business well. Enquire of the Printer.

just imported via Philadelphia
and to be sold by Dr. Thomas Fosdick in New London a choice collection of genuine patent medicines: viz: Turlington's Balsam, Walker's Jesuits drops an infallible cure for the venereal disease [1], balsam of honey for cure of consumption, colds and all complaints of the breast.

post
The Western Post has not returned, supposed to be owing to the ice at Saybrook ferry.

List of letters at the New London Postoffice

Obidiah Bayley Jr.. - Groton
Benjamin Bancroft & Sons - Groton
Ebenezer Beebe - Nahantiuck River
Zebulton Butler - Lyme
John Coleman - New London
Nathaniel Coit Jr.- New London
Singleton Church - New London
Colonel Cheseborough - Stonington
William Carr - Colchester
John Dyer - New London
Margaret Duffy - New London
Ebenezer Eames - Norwich
John Elderkin - Groton
Nathaniel Eels - Stonington
Ezra Fuller - Lebanon
John Frank - Southold, Long Island
Daniel Foot - Colchester
William Foster - New London
Starr Archibald Greenfield - Lyme
Nathaniel Gardiner - Stonington
Benjamin Hancock - Norwich
George Howe - Groton
Richard Harris - New London
Noble Hinman - New London
Joshua Hempstead - New London
Edward Latham - Groton
Jon Lee - New London
James Mumford - New London
George Mumford- New

London
Mr. Miner, Jr. - New London
Elisha Miller - Lyme
Nathaniel Miner - Stonington
Temperance Reed - Saybrook
John Rogers - New London
Thomas Robinson - Scotland

James Shouls - Groton
Nathaniel Saltonstall - New London
Manuel Starr - New London
Anne Thompson - New London
Jesse Teagus - New London
Joseph Wise Jr. - Lebanon

real estate for sale in Norwich
    Notice by Mr. Benjamin Huntington of Norwich, to be sold at public auction at the dwelling place of Joseph Peck, inn holder of Norwich, all the real estate lately belonging to Mr. Joseph Tracy of Norwich, consisting of sundry small lots of land, a dwelling house on almost every lot; said lands are all in Norwich, two in Chelsea and the rest in the First Society, near Town Street.
    All those indebted to Mr. Tracy are asked to settle accounts with Ebenezer Baldwin.

ran away
    from Benjamin Sharpe of Pomfret, a servant man named Charles Cada; about 22 years of age; five foot five inches high; well set; has a small forehead; his hair of a brown color and thick, newly cut off on top.
              ****

From *The New London Gazette,* January 12, 1770

Stamp Act
    From the papers from the last Packet[2] [from London] there is not the least appearance of a design to repeal the acts imposing a duty upon goods imported into America or to change the Ministry or to dissolve parliament, although petitions from all over England for a dissolution either have been presented or are preparing. The *North Briton* [an English newspaper] of October 28th says it is impossible to imagine anything more cold,

uncivil or forbidding than the receptions these petitions met with from the Sovereign who has never uttered a single syllable to any of the Gentlemen who have attended on these occasions. Hence the writer considers that we should absolutely despair of any success - at least for the time. One comfort only remains to us as Englishmen. Our History tells us that whatever Minister has dared to act against the general sense of the People has in the end fallen, the unpitied victim of his own insolence and rashness.

a curiosity

We are credibly informed that nearly twenty three years ago, a child was born in the southern part of Massachusetts Bay, who bearing a similarity to both sexes, it was disputed it what apparel it should be dressed in, but it was at last agreed to dress her in women's and it was baptized by the name Deborah. This woman grew up and till lately passed as a woman but having for some time lodged with one of that sex, the latter found herself to be with child and swore the former to be the father of it. The consequence of it is that they are married together and the father, instead of his former name Deborah, was married Francis Lewis.

obituary

Preston: Last Friday night departed this life from consumption[3] Samuel Morgan of this town in the 65th year of his life. He had for some years served the Town and colony in a number of public characters, he being for some years a captain of the militia among many other positions. His funeral was attended by a large concourse of people. He is left by his widow and ten children.

administration of estates

Notice to the creditors of insolvent estate of Capt. Azel Fitch of Lebanon, by commissioners Ichabod Robinson, William Williams and Samuel Hide, appointed by Probate Court, will be held at the house of Mrs. Elizabeth Alden, inn holder in Lebanon.

land for sale in Lyme

To be sold at public auction at the house of Josiah Mack

of Lyme, administrator, all the estate of Jonathan Mack of Lyme, excepting the widow's dower. Said estate includes seven acres of land, three of which are in Champion meadow and four acres in weed land, both in the Northern Society of Lyme.

strayed or stolen
   from Samuel Fox of the North Parish of New London, a young steer.

   from John Hughes of Norwich, two heifers.
      ****

From *The New London Gazette,* January 19, 1770

call for meeting among merchants
   Inserted at the request of the Merchants. The great importance of trade and commerce of every state and especially to this colony is too obvious to need enlarging upon and equally evident it is that a good understanding, harmony and frequent intercourse among those engaged in trade, are essential almost to it very being – at least to make it flourish to any considerable degree. The great unhappiness of this colony in this respect has long since been observed to consist in not having a capital, in which a center of the mercantile interest might be formed, which would prevent many and great inconveniences as well as losses, both private and public. This has occasioned our neighboring colonies to become both our factors and carriers in the more profitable branches of business and to avail themselves of many great advantages which would otherwise have centered among us. To prevent this entirely must be a work of ours to do it as far as our present situation will admit. It is with great deference to the Gentlemen Merchants of this Colony, proposed:
   THAT a meeting of the principal Merchants and Traders of this Colony be held in Middletown town on the 20th of February next, by themselves, or a Committee from each town, to take the above into consideration and conclude upon such measures as they shall judge be best for the encouragement of Trade and Manufacture among us and to form themselves into a Body Chamber, or Society, for those purposes and under such regulations, as, upon full confirmation of the subject, shall

appear best for the Community in time.

floods

    We hear from Hartford that last Monday se'nnight[4], there was the greatest freshet[5] ever known at that season of the year.

    We also her that the same flood has entirely destroyed the Furnace at Simsbury, in the occupation of Messrs. Charles and George Caldwell. Three buildings being entirely demolished thereby and a fourth that would have shared the same fate, was with great difficulty removed. The damage occasioned hereby is estimated now at 1,200 pounds.

body found

    Southold, Long Island: Sometime last week as a number of "moon cursers"[6] were employed in getting on shore the logs and drift wood that had come from the mainland in the late freshet, they discovered a man drowned and drove on shore near Oyster Pond Point, his flesh much torn off and nothing to describe him by, but his having on two pairs of stockings, a pair of shoes with buckles that were not mates; likewise a horse, saddle and bridle came ashore at Plum Island about the same time.

stolen

    A pair of saddle bags were taking off the horse of Amos Babcock of Branford as it was tied up outside Capt. Coit's tavern in New London. It contained sundry notes on hand from a number of persons, of several hundred pounds, payable to the subscriber, a number of deeds, a pair of calfskin shoes and a pair of plain silver buckles.

goldsmith

    Advertisement by Robert Douglas Jr. of New London, gold smith and jeweler, next door to Capt. Titus Hurlbut, that he has employed Mr. James Watson, clock and watch maker, who makes repairs on all kinds of clocks and watches in the neatest and best manner. He will warrant his work for two years.

****

From *The New London Gazette,* January 26, 1770

post delays
   The eastern and western mails that were due last Wednesday and Thursday se'nnight did not arrive under Monday last, owing to the difficulty of traveling.

fire
   Last Monday, a dwelling house in the occupation of Mrs. Moses Fargo in this town [New London] took fire upon the roof, it and the house of Capt. Nathan Douglas, contiguous thereto, were in eminent danger, but the fire was happily extinguished without much damage.

hats for sale
   Aaron Cleveland acquaints the public that he has a felt manufactory in Norwich where he sells felt hats of all sizes, singularly or by the dozen.

****

From *The New London Gazette,* February 2, 1770

news of other vessels
   The snow *Peggy,* Capt. Hallie, seven weeks out of Lisbon, fell in with the sloop *Fancy,* Samuel Calkins, Master, belonging to New London, but left from this port bound for Little Egg Harbor. He had been blown off course four days before and was very short of necessities, with which Capt. Hallie supplied him and left him steering for land and imagined he might make Virginia.

   By letters from Cape Nichola[7], we learn that it continues to be very sickly there. A letter from that place also advises of the death of Capt. Richard Harris of this town (New London) who died at Turk's Island about the 10th of December.

Susquehanna Purchase notice
   Notice by Samuel Gray, Clerk, to the Proprietors of the Susquehanna Purchase[8] in January 1768, have had two taxes of two dollar each on each share, most of which had been paid in

and improved for the company's use. Those who haven't must pay up or their shares will be forfeited and revert to Company,

meetings of merchants

The merchants of the town of Norwich on Tuesday last made a choice of the committee to attend the proposed meeting of merchants in Middletown on the 20th of February.

We hear that the proposed meeting will be attended by gentlemen from this and every neighboring town, it being very generally approved of, as it is expected many salutary measures may thereby be adopted, which may be of the utmost utility to this colony.

****

From *The New London Gazette*, February 9, 1770

meeting of merchants

At a meeting of the merchants and traders of the towns of New London and Groton, held in New London on the 1st day of February, in consequence of the desires of the Gentlemen Merchants of this Colony "that there being a meeting of the principal merchants and traders of this colony at Middletown to take into consideration the trade and commerce of the colony and conclude on such measures as they judge best for the encouragement of traders and manufactories[9] among us."

Voted that Col. Gurdon Saltonstall, Messrs. James Mumford, Nathaniel Shaw, Jr., Thomas Mumford and Ebenezer Ledyard be made a committee to attend the same.

non importation agreements

The consequences resulting from the general agreement of non importation entered into by the Merchants, is very obvious in the following instance:[10]

The daughter of Mr. F. a wealthy farmer, came into town last week with ten pounds in her pocket in order to purchase a silk gown for herself but on trying all the shops in town was obliged to return home without one to the great grief of her father, no doubt, who was obliged to hoard up the money and the poor girl to sit down and spin herself a gown - a melancholy consequence indeed, that the children are obliged to clothe themselves, while their fathers have money to spare.

died

On the 13th ultimate, departed this life after some months illness, the Rev Elijah Mason, aged 46, formerly pastor of the church in Marlborough, but late pastor of the Church in Chester in Saybrook. He was a gentleman of superior genius, great learning and mighty in the Scriptures. A sermon was preached by Rev. Stephen Holmes .

mad dogs

We hear from Hebron that the inhabitants of that town have been greatly terrified by the prevalence of mad dogs among them[11]. Since the Town act for confining them expired, which was the first of January last, four dogs have been killed raging mad, besides many others which have been destroyed on the first signs of madness. One Daniel Porter of that town was bit by a mad dog about 20 days ago, but as yet the dreadful effects have not appeared. Considerable damage has been done by them biting cattle and hogs. A cow belonging to Mr. John Wright, soon after being bit, discovered the symptoms by bellowing, lolling out of the tongue an overflow of food and water; at length growing raging mad, she was killed and it is remarkable that a dog that was observed to lick the blood only once or twice ran instantly mad.

death at sea

Last Wednesday arrived here, the Schooner *Liberty* of this port (New London), in 33 days from St. Eustatia.[12] On the 26th of last month in a gale of wind, in the evening, Capt. Robert Latimer, late commander of said vessel, fell overboard and was drowned. He left a disconsolate widow and one son.

died

On January 14th died Preston, Mr. Joseph Rose, aged 76 years, nine months and 11 days. On January 30^{th,} died his consort, Mrs. Sarah Rose aged 76 years 10 months and four days. These people had lived together in the married state 45 years, nine months and 11 days. The Rev. Mr. Tyler preached the sermons at each funeral.

pay up
 Hugh Ledlie of Norwich wants everyone to settle his accounts with him.

house to be sold
 by Hez. Leffingwell, a handsome well finished dwelling house, one story high with a shoe maker's shop, situated between Norwich Town and the Landing.[13]

****

From *The New London Gazette*, February 16, 1770

Committee of Inspection
 The Committee of Inspection appointed at Norwich in addition to their Merchants Committee.[14]
 For the First Society: Capt. Samuel Leffingwell and Dr. Theo. Rogers
 For West Farms: Ebenezer Hartshorn and Captain Daniel Hyde
 For Newent: Solomon Safford and Elisha Lathrop
 For Long Society: Elisha Fitch and Elijah Brewster
 For New Concord: Col. William Whiting and Nehemiah Hutchinson
 For Chelsea: Capt. Hugh Ledlie and Capt. Jabez Perkins
 For Hanover: Captain Matthew Perkins and Captain Daniel Bishop
 For the Eighth Society: James Elderkin and Dr. John Barker

meeting of merchants
 The Merchants at their meeting voted that Jabez Huntington, Christopher Leffingwell, Joshua Lathrop, Nathaniel Backus, Jr., Jedidiah Huntington, Hugh Ledlie and Gershom Breed named a committee to attend the general meeting of Merchants be held in Middletown.

river ice
 The breakup of the Shetucket river yesterday has done

considerable damage at the Landing. A sloop belonging to Mr. Guy Brooks was stove to pieces and another belonging to John Tracy has had her timbers on one side stove in and greatly damaged. Some salt has been consumed and some lumber lost. Some of the great bridges on the river came down with the ice and in fact it was a grand, but a dismal, sight to behold.

married
  Capt. Titus Hurlbut to Mrs. Mercy Wheeler, widow of Thomas Wheeler, late of Stonington.

lands to be sold
  by Benjamin Dennis of Chelsea in Norwich at Norwich Landing a good convenient dwelling house, well finished without and within; 35 feet by 24 feet on the floor; well situated for a trader or tradesman; with a garden and good well adjoining the house.
  Also a garden spot, a little distance from the house on the Cove that leads to Mr. Lathrop's, with a garden and barn;
  also 8 acres of good land, under a good fence and under good improvement for plowing, mowing or pasture, adjacent to said cove;
  also three lots of land in the township of New London. One of said lots is adjoining Joseph Coit's on one side and Jeremiah Millers on the other. The other lot lies opposite and adjoins the water and Joseph Coit's on one side and that of Capt. Nathan Douglas on the other;
  also four acres of pasture land on the hill called Town Hill and one seventh's part of one Proprietors right in the common and undivided lands of the township of New London.

administration of estates
  Notice by Hez. Bissle and Eben Grey Jr. that a meeting of creditors will be held at the house of Eleazer Cary of Windham regarding estate of Richard Watt, late of the island of Guadalupe in the West Indies; the administrator is Jeremiah Ross of New London.

      ****

From *The New London Gazette*, February 23, 1770

fire
The 19th of last month, the house belonging to David Robbins in the parish of Westford in Ashford was consumed by fire together with most of the materials within the house to a considerable sum estimated at 30 pounds worth of leather and a sum of money.

agricultural news
On the first of this month, Mr. Ebenezer Gray of the Town of Lebanon killed a sheep, two years old which he had raised and, when dressed the fours quarters of which, plus the rough tallow, weighted 113 pounds. The fat on the rump was three and a half inch thick and one and a half on the ribs.

died
Last Saturday in New Haven, John Miller of this Town (New London)

accident
Tuesday last Mr. Joshua Brooks of this town (New London) fell from an apple tree he was trimming and received a blow in the temple from his axe which was so slight that it did prevent him from the raising of a house that afternoon day, but towards night, he complained of a headache which increasing. He went home and he died the same night.

Town of Flushing on Otter Creek meeting
Notice by James Avery to the proprietors of the town of Flushing under John Henty Lydius at Otter Creek[15] to meet at the house of Nathaniel Williams, inn holder.

to be sold
by Hez.Leffingwell a handsome, well finished one story dwelling house with a shoe maker's shop situated between Norwich town and the Landing.

****

From *The New London Gazette*, March 2, 1770

Connecticut boundaries

John Winthrop of this town (New London) has found among a great number of ancient papers, left by his predecessors, the Earl of Warwick's deed to Lord Say and Seal, Lord Breck etc. and also the deed of the said Lords to the first English settlers in Connecticut. As the lands in these deeds expressly extend to the South Sea and the charter of ths colony is predicated upon this deed, it may now be difficult to assign any solid reason why we should not own, protect and improve such an immensely valuable inheritance, purchased and procured by our ancestors at great expense. [16]

dead man found

Last Sunday one John Dickinson of Marshfield in Massachusetts Province, belonging to Capt.'s Higgins vessel, was found dead on a wharf in Town (New London) near said vessel. The Jury of Inquest was of the opinion that he died in a fit of apoplexy, being subject to that disorder.

burglar gets away

Notice by Nehemiah Tinker, goal keeper, that in the evening following the ninth of February, one Caleb Fitch of Lebanon, who stood committed to Windham goal on a complaint against the said Fitch for theft and burglary, found means to break goal and make his escape. He is a slim, pale, young fellow; wears his own hair which is of a brown color and is about 20 years old.

runaway

from William Dowglass, Jr. in New London, an apprentice boy named Levi Lamphere; near 20 years old; is likely; short of stature and well set; a shoemaker by trade.

administration of estates

Notice to creditors of the estate Benjamin Woodward, late of Windham, deceased, that a meeting will be held to examine claims at the house of Eleazer Cary, inn holder in said

Windham; notice given by Samuel Gray and Samuel Webb, commissioners appointed by the Probate Court.

  Notice to creditors of the estate of Mr. Thomas Burch, late of Stonington, deceased, that a meeting will be held to examine claims at the house of Capt. Giles Russel, inn holder in said Stonington; notice given by John Denison, Edward Hancox and Cyrus Wheeler, Commissioners appointed by the Probate Court.

  Notice to creditors of the estate of Mr Ambrous Hellard, late of Stonington, deceased, that a meeting will be held to examine claims at the house of Capt. Giles Russel, inn holder in said Stonington; notice given by Joseph Dean and John Page, Commissioners appointed by the Probate Court.
      ****
From *The New London Gazette*, March 9, 1770

passage boats
  This is to inform the Public that Clark Truman's Passage Boat, well equipt and accommodated for passengers, will sail from Sag Harbor to New London every Tuesday (wind and weather permitting); from thence, he will proceed to Norwich and return to New London on Thursdays and to Sag Harbor on Fridays. The fare for man and horse to New London is one dollar and for a single passenger three shillings New York currency and to Norwich half a dollar. Attendance will be given at Mr. Fordham's at Sag Harbor, Deacon Waterman's and Mr. Power's in New London.

  This is to inform the Public that James Wiggins has set up a good passage Boat , to ply from Sag Harbor in Long Island to New London and, from thence, to Norwich Landing on Tuesday for New London, on Wednesday for Norwich, on Thursday return to New London and on Friday to Sag Harbor.
  Said Wiggins can be found , when in New London at Mr. Elliot's, the Ferry House and, when in Norwich, at Mr. Fitch's Tavern. Attendance will be given at Mr. Fordham's at Sag Harbor, Deacon Waterman's and Mr. Power's in New London

take notice
The Public are cautioned to be aware of false paper money passing about of several emissions and denominations, which have been altered from a lesser to greater amount, especially 12d. Bills into 10s, 20s, etc. There is a reward of ten pounds offered by the Government for whoever shall make discovery, so that the persons guilty of such practices may be convicted.

shipping news
Capt. M. Cleve who is arrived at New Haven spoke with Capt. Samuel Stillman, in a brig from this port (New London) bound for St. Lucia.

Letters from Barbados inform us that a great number of vessels are arrived there from the Connecticut River and that the markets are very much glutted with horses.[17]

Capt. Melally from this Port (New London), is arrived at St. Lucia. One of the seaman named Asa Comstock of New London was accidently knocked overboard on the passage and was drowned.

sudden death
We hear from Middletown that about ten days ago, Mr. Ebenezer Roberts of that town, a person in a good state of health, about 40 years of age, expired suddenly as he was walking in his field.

letter to the Editor
Mr. Green
At the late meeting of the merchants of this Colony at Middletown, a plan was formed and a foundation laid greatly beneficial to trades, manufactures etc (which gives universal satisfaction to every friend of this Colony as well as American Freedom and Interest) and as sundry important measures were the proposed to be laid before the General Assembly at their sessions in May next, in order for their Approbation and Sanction, I would humbly propose to the Freemen of the several

towns in the Colony that they choose their representatives to serve in the next assembly out of that respectable body which composed the above meting as it may tend to facilitate the attainment of the proposed measure.
I am yours etc.,
NO TORY

administration of estates
To be sold by Andrew Stanton, administrator of the estate of Lieut. Samuel Stanton of Stonington, deceased, all the real estate of said deceased (with the encumbrances of the widow's dower thereon) lying and being in Stonington, near Paucatuck River.

Notice to creditors of the Notice to creditors of the estate of Benjamin Woodward, late of Windham, deceased, that a meeting will be held to examine claims at the house of Eleazer Cary, inn holder in said Windham; notice given by Samuel Gray and Samuel Webb, appointed by the Probate Court.

taken up
by Jeremiah Conkling, a large scow at Montauk, on the East End of Long Island, in the township of East Hampton.

to be sold
a few maps of the Colony remain to be sold by T. Green
****
From *The New London Gazette,* March 16, 1770

Boston Massacre
The town of Boston afford us a recent and melancholy demonstration of the destructive consequences of ordering troops among citizens in time of peace under a pretense of supporting the laws and aiding civil authority. Every considerate and unprejudiced person among us was deeply impressed with the apprehension of these consequences when it was known that a number of regiments were ordered to this town under such a pretext but in reality to enforce oppressive measures, to intimidate and control the legislative as well as executive power

of the province and to quell a spirit of liberty which, however it may have been opposed and even ridiculed by some, would do honor to any age or country.

Our readers will doubtless expect an account of the tragic affair on Monday night last. Several soldiers of the 29th Regiment were seen parading the streets with drawn cutlasses and bayonets abusing and wounding any number of the inhabitants. A few minutes after nine o'clock, four youths named Edward Archibald, William Merchant, Francis Archibald and John Leech, Jr came down Corn Hill together and, separating at Dr. Loring's corner, the two former passed through the narrow alley leading to Murray' barracks in which was a soldier brandishing a broad sword of an uncommon size against the walls, out of which he struck sparks plentifully. A person of mean countenance armed with a cudgel bore him company. Mr. Archibald admonished Mr. Merchant to take care of the sword, at which the soldier turned around and struck Archibald and then pushed at Merchant and pierced through his clothes at the arm and grazed the skin. Merchant that struck the soldier with a short stick he had and the other person ran into the barracks and brought with him two soldiers, one on whom had a pair of tongs, and the other with a shovel. He with the tong pursued Archibald back through the alley, collared him and hit him over the head with it. The noise brought people together and John Hicks, a young lad, coming up, knocked the soldier down, but let him get up again. And more lads gathering, they drove them back into the barracks where the boys stood some time as it were to keep them in.

In less than a minute, ten or twelve came out with drawn cutlasses, clubs and bayonets and set upon the unarmed boys and young folks who withstood them a little while, but finding the inequality of their weapons, dispersed. On hearing the noise, Samuel Atwood came up to see what was a matter and entering the alley from the Dock Square heard the latter part of the combat. When the boys had dispersed, he met the 10 or 12 soldiers and asked them if they intended to murder people. They answered "Yes, by God." With that, one of them struck Mr. Atwood with a club, which was repeated by another. Being unarmed he turned to go off and received a wound on the left shoulder to the bone and gave him much pain.

Thirty or forty persons mostly lads, by this time, had gathered in King Street, Captain Preston, with a party of men with charged bayonets, came in pushing them and, thence crying "Make way"; they continued to push and drive the people off, pricking some in several places. The lads were clamorous and it is said threw snowballs. But on this, the captain commanded them to fire and more snowball balls coming, he again said "Damn you. Fire. Be the consequences, what they well". One soldier then fired and a townsman with a cudgel struck him over the hands with such force that he dropped his musket. However, the soldiers continued the fire successfully, until seven or eight, or as some say, eleven guns, were discharged.

By this fatal maneuver, three men were dead on the spot and two more are struggling for life. Such a degree of cruelty, unknown of British troops at least since the House of Hanover directed their operations, that they fired upon and pushed their bayonets into the persons who undertook to remove the slain and wounded.

The dead are Mr. Samuel Gray, killed on the spot by a ball entering his head; a mulatto named; Crispus Attucks, born in Framingham but lately belonging to New Providence, died instantly; James Caldwell, mate of Captain Morton's vessel in like manner was killed by two balls entering his back; Mr. Samuel Maverick, a promising youth of 17 years of age, son of the widow Maverick and an apprentice to Mr. Greenwood, ivory turner, was mortally wounded and died the next morning.

We hear from Boston that as the Funeral procession was returning from the interment of young Snider, a Son of Tyranny began to hiss the Company. Whereupon a numbers of persons undertook to discipline him which they accordingly did by stripping him naked and plucking all the hair off his head and then would have tarred and feathered him but as the night was extremely old, they ordered him to make his appearance at the garret window of his house where he had taken shelter and there hold a lantern to his face, that he may be plainly seen and known, made him humbly ask the pardon of the public and promise to behave in a decent manner in the future.

to be let

by Duncan Stewart for five year term, a good lot of land within two miles of the Town Wharf in New London, containing about 100 acres, well fenced with a stone wall, a good pasture and well watered, it being the lot lately owned by Matthew Stewart and called by the name of William's Pasture.

To be let on good security by Joshua Hempsted and Joshua Hempsted Jr. of New London, a good farm lying in Stonington, near the Mystic River, adjoining the line between Groton and Stonington, containing by estimation about 300 acres for three, five or seven years, with a dwelling house, good barn, corn house and other conveniences.

help wanted

A most faithful man for a wharfenger and store keeper, and, if he has a wife, capable of the care of a kitchen, they will both be employed for a term. For particulars, enquire of the Printer.

****

From *The New London Gazette,* March 23, 1770

accident

The following melancholy accident happened at Long Island on the 9th instant. As four persons whose names were Richard Brown, Samuel Brown (two brothers), Peter Brown and John King, all belonging to the Oyster Pond and near neighbors, were returning from on board a brigantine that was laying near the Fire Place, so called, off East Hampton where they had been to visit some friends just returned from a voyage, the boat they were in overset at about 40 rods[18] distance from shore and filled. They were heard to call for help but before any assistance could be afforded to them, they were all unfortunately drowned. It is supposed the boat having a mast too heavy for her, and some bad management overset it in a flow of winds. Two of the bodies were found on the boat, one side of which remained above water. Richard Brown has left a widow and five children and Samuel Brown three children.

obituary

On the 5th instant, departed this life at Chelsea[19] in Norwich, Mrs. Zerviah Bushnell, relict of Capt. Benajah Bushnell, deceased, in the 84th year of her life.

cash

to be given for black salts, damaged potash and small furs by John Baker Brimmer at his store in Norwich Landing.

administration of estates

Lydia Latimer has been appointed administratix of the estate of Capt. Robert Latimer, late of New London.

****

From *The New London Gazette*, March 30, 1770

reward

To be paid while you say "Jack Robinson"[20], a reward of 1,000 pounds, Rhode Island currency, by Gregory Cornell of Rhode island to apprehend Shan -ap Morgan, a man of Wales, who eloped from his bed and board on Friday 16th without the least bit of provocation on one part and in direct opposition to his Master's orders on the other. It is apprehended that he will go beyond the sea to prevent his being brought to justice for sundry heinous crimes that will speedily become public. All charitable and well disposed people on this and the other side of the water, should use their utmost endeavor to stop this said Shan-ap Morgan that he may be dealt with according to the atrociousness of his crimes in order in the future to prevent such heinous offenders from breaking the sacred bonds of Society and the orders of their Masters with impunity.

He is about five feet ten inches high; square shouldered and of a sallow complexion; somewhat pox marked; an undetermined, cross, unpromising countenance; very awkward in his walk and address; speaks with a trembling tone and very unconnected in his mode of expression. When he tells a story, he makes it very long and never to the purpose; is very fond of misquoting Acts of Parliament to show his knowledge when they have no connection and always looks very much frightened.

sudden death

This day sudden death happened at the 8th Society in Norwich. Capt. Jonathan Pitcher of this place, fell from a loft over his barn floor, about 14 feet, which proved instantly fatal. He was a professor and friend of religion, a kind husband who left behind a sorrowful widow and his death is greatly lamented.

house and land in Norwich

to be let by Hugh Ledlie, a dwelling house for a term of three years or five. Such house is pleasantly situated in Norwich, between the town and the landing. It is distant from the Town house about three quarters of a mile and from thence to the landing one mile and a quarter. The house is large and commodious and will be completely furnished to the turning of the key; together with a good barn and shed, a good chaise house, wood house etc, with two good wells of water, two gardens, a handsome summer house with about six acres of good land as any in the colony either for mowing, plowing or pasturing. The whole of said lot and gardens is concisely and conveniently interspersed with a variety of excellent fruit trees, such as apples, pears, peaches, plums, cherries (both black and red) etc. and also about 70 cutting or plants of choices English grapevines and will bear clusters from 7 to 13 pounds; the outside gardens etc include a good well and strongly fenced with a good stone wall, posts, rails and a handsome board fence. There is also in said lot a fine spring or run of water, which but seldom fails in the driest of summer, which has been, and may again, be carried or spread over so as to water all of the aforesaid lot.

Also to be let with the above premises, about 6 acres of good plow land in excellent order for present use. Said lot is not more than 50 rods distant the first mentioned lot, on the south and lays east on the great road that leads from Norwich Town to the Landing and adjoins land belonging to Mr. Daniel Tracy, Capt. Samuel Leffingwell and on said Ledlie's own land. Enquire of Hugh Ledlie or in his absence Dr. Daniel Lathrop of Norwich.

N.B. The house is completely finished on the outside and is also well and completely finished; has a good cellar, two stacks of chimneys, with eight excellent fireplaces besides the kitchen and all of them carry smoke very well. The house is two stories high, well and completely glazed with large and commodious windows; on the first floor there are two large front rooms and two large neat bed rooms.

****

From *The New London Gazette,* April 6, 1770

day of fast

    Wednesday the 18th instant is appointed by the Authority for a general fast throughout this Colony

whipping

    Last Wednesday, one John Marshal, a foreigner, who has worked for some time past with a blacksmith near town, received ten lashes at the public post for stealing a man's cloak out of the house of Capt. Titus Hurlbut of this town. He appears to be an old offender.[21]

non importation agreements

    Mr. Green:

    Please to give the following a place in your paper and you will oblige a number of your readers.

    "The seasonable and patriotic resolutions of the citizens of Norwich to support the patriotic Merchants in Boston and elsewhere in carrying into execution their non importation agreements, are not only expressive of their zeal in the cause of Liberty and of the justness of their sentiments in regard to the measures to be pursued in relief in this day of general calamity and distress, but are highly worthy of imitation; it is wished that their laudable example may be followed in every town in the Colony. If the salutary and patriotic measures of the merchants are violated with impunity and those who disregard such economic resolutions are not treated with contemp and exposed to the hatred and resentment of those who wish well to the country, we shall soon become prey to the ravenous jaws of Harpies and those who would eat up people as bread. The innocent blood the has late been spilt in the streets of Boston and the inhumane butcheries committed among those people by the infernal outrage and bloody thirst measures of some of the soldiery, cry aloud for the exertion of every nerve in defense of our just rights and privileges and from the united efforts assistance of the friends of Liberty, to strengthen and confirm the generous measures of the merchant of Non Importation. It is therefore earnestly recommended for the selectmen of the several towns to warn a meeting of their respective citizens in order to adopt measures similar to those of Norwich."

The above was wrote at the desire of a number of the Sons of Liberty.

****

From *The New London Gazette*, April 13, 1770

Mohegan burial

Last Friday died of consumption at Mohegan, Isaiah Uncas, Sachem of th Mohegan Tribe of Indians in the North part of this Town (New London) and on Tuesday the Indians of said tribe dug up the body of his father, Benjamin Uncas (their late Sachem), who was buried at Mohegan the last year, and carried both corpses and interred them in their old Burying Ground at the Little Plain in Norwich. The Indians acted with great decency and seemed pleased at the respect showed to their Sovereign by a numerous concourse of white people who attended the funeral.

babies

Last week a woman in Enfield was delivered of three female children, weighting 18 pounds, at one birth and all likely to do well.

prayer before Freemen's meeting

We hear from Pomfret by a vote of that Town, it has been their practice for several Freemen's meetings to have a short discourse adopted for the occasion, delivered by one of the ministers in the town prior to the votes being given. This laudable practice has also lately been adopted at Woodstock and it would be both doubtless agreeable and proper to have this practice become more general in the colony, it being found by experience that it occasions a more general attendance of the Freemen in the Towns where it is practiced.

General Assembly elections
The following gentlemen are chosen representatives to sit in the next General Assembly for:

New London: Col. Gurdon Saltonstall, William Hillhouse
Norwich: Elisha Fitch, Christopher Leffingwell
Preston: Capt. John Tyler, Robert Crary
Stonington: Charles Phelps, Capt. Phineas Stanton
Groton: Capt. Moses Fish, Capt. Benadam Gallup
Lyme: Capt. Joseph Mather, Joseph Lay 2nd
Saybrook: John Moredock, Hez. Whittlesey
Windham: Nathaniel Wale, Jr., Capt. Jonah Rudd
Lebanon: Capt. William Williams, Joseph Trumbull
Pomfret: Col. Ebenezer Williams, Deacon Samuel Craft
Woodstock: Capt. Elisha Child, Manassah Hosmer
Canterbury: Jabez Fitch, John Curtis
Plainfield: Capt. John Dowglas, John Pierce
Coventry: Phineas Strong, Deacon Richard Hale

whipping
Yesterday one Richard Jordan, an Old Country man received ten stripes at the public post in this town (New London) for stealing from Mr. John Champlin, Goldsmith, sundry articles of wearing apparel.

administration of estates
Notice to the creditors of the estate of Nathaniel Butt, deceased, late of Norwich, that there will be a meeting at the dwelling house of Benjamin Burnam, Inn holder; notice given by Commissioners Elisha Lathrop and Benj. Burnum.

passage boat
This is to inform the Public that Zebulon Elliot has set up a good passage Boat, to ply from New London to Norwich on every Monday, Wednesday and Friday and from Norwich to New London on Tuesday, Thursday and Saturday in the forenoon of the day. Said boat goes light with oars, so there is no fear of being hindered in the passage by failure of wind.
Attendance in New London at Mr. Elliot's, the Ferry

House and, when in Norwich, at Mr. Ebenezer Fitch's Tavern.

****

From *The New London Gazette*, April 20, 1770

prayer for elections
   We hear that the Rev. Mr. Stephen Johnson of Lyme is nominated by his honor the Governor to preach the Anniversary Election Sermon.

new inn in town
   Notice by T. Allen to all Gentleman travelers that the London Coffee House[22] will open in New London on April 25; it is situated on the bank near the Courthouse where may be had genteel entertainment for man and horse.
   There is adjoining a large and commodious wharf for navigation with store, stables and yards for the reception of horses and stock.

hats for sale
   Advertisement by Abiezer Smith, Hatter at Norwich Landing, having served a regular apprenticeship to the felt manufacture, hereby informs the public that he makes and sells all kinds of felt hats at his store, near the Meeting House.

town meeting in Lebanon and Liberty
   At a town meeting at Lebanon, the inhabitants of the town of Lebanon in full town meeting, assembled, now and ever impressed with the deepest and most affectionate loyalty to His Excellent Majesty George, the Third, the rightful King and Sovereign of Great Britain and the English American colonies; and being tenderly attached to and tenacious of the precious Rights and Liberties to which, as English subjects, we are born and instilled by the British Constitution and which have also been dearly earned by the treasures and blood of our forefathers and transmitted as their most valuable legacy to us their Posterity. In those circumstances we view with the most sensible grief, anxiety and concern the sufferings and distress to which this country is subjected and exposed, in consequence of measures planned by a few artful and deceiving men, unhappily

of too much influence, the aim and tendency of which is to deprive these colonies of their free Constitution and reduce them to a state of bondage. Particularly, we deplore the unhappy fate of the Town of Boston being so long subjected to the imposition of a standing army quartered upon them, and lately, of the barbarous murder of a number of their inhabitants.

But in the midst of these calamities, this town has occasion to rejoice in the union and harmony which continues to prevail throughout the American colonies and in their firm and fixed attachment to the Principles of Liberty and Loyalty and do hereby declare their high approbation and grateful acknowledgment of the generous self denying and truly patriotic spirit and conduct of the respectable merchants throughout the colonies in refusing to import British Manufacture into this distressed and impoverished country until it should be relieved of those burdens and grievances of which we do justly complain.

Attest: Wm. Williams, Clerk

****

From The New London Gazette, April 27, 1770

fire

During Divine Service on the late Sabbath, the dwelling house of Mr. Caleb Lyon of Woodstock was consumed by fire.

Last Monday, the dwelling house of the Rev. Mr. Johnson of Groton took fire on the roof by a spark from the chimney, when a hole was burned in it six foot square, but there being assistance near at hand, no further damage accrued.

help wanted

Wanted a Maid who is capable of doing all sorts of house work. Enquire of the Printer

****

From *The New London Gazette,* May 4, 1770

Letters left at Post office in New London

	Butler, Zebulonn - Lyme
Avery, Theph - Groton	Barber, Thomas - Groton
Adams, Michael - Killingly	Billings, Lucretia - New

London
Beebe, Eliphalet - New London
Buell, Abel - Killingworth
Comstock, James - North Parish, New London
Dolbear George - North Parish, New London
Elderkin, John - Groton
Greenleaf, Stephen - Norwich
Howe, George - Groton
Harris, Mary - New London
Leach, Johnson - New London

Maton, William - Lyme
Miner, Nathaniel - Stonington
Pcker, Daniel - Mystic
Penderson, Catherine - Groton
Penderson, Ebenezer- Groton
Perkins, Luke - New London
Parks, James - Groton
Teague, Jesse - New London
Thompson, George - New London

burglary ring broken up
    Last Saturday night, the house of Ebenezer Ledyard in Groton was broke open a quantity of English goods etc. of a value of 30 pounds, were taken. On Monday, John Hanly and John Riney, transient persons, were taken up on suspicion of having committed the theft and examined before Authority, when Hanly was ordered to goal for trial in the June Court and Riney, being admitted King's Evidence, was recognized to appear at said court. On Tuesday, one David Bernard, also a transient person was committed. He had been pursued and taken at Westerly in the Colony of Rhode Island with part of the goods in his possession. The same day, Mrs. Elizabeth Latham of Groton, a widow, was also committed to goal on suspicion of receiving and concealing part of said goods.

administration of estates
    Notice to creditors of the estate of Captain John Miller, late of New London, to bring all claims to the attention of James Rice of New Haven or Russell Hubbard of New London, Executors.

house for sale in Stonington
    To be sold a place called Long Point at Stonington harbor, a large dwelling house, a small barn on a lot of about 35 rods; well fitted for a trader or tradesman; from the Estate of Gilbert Fanning; notice given by Assignees John Williams, Jabez Smith and Pelatiah Fitch.

runaway
    from John Mumford of Lyme, a slave named Sambo; about five feet and a half high.
            ****

From *The New London Gazette*, May 11, 1770

administration of estates
    All persons with claims to the estate of Captain Richard Harris, late of New London or who owe the estate are advised that Mary Harris has been named adminstratrix.

slave for sale
    To be sold a likely Negro boy, ten years old; enquire of Jeremiah Huntington in Norwich.

strayed or stolen
    from Robert Patrick of Lebanon, a sorrel mare; if found, deliver to Robert Patrick or Jabez Dean of Norwich.
            ****

From *The New London Gazette*, May 18, 1770

invention
    We hear from Norwich that on 5th instant, John Bliss of that Town, finished a fire engine, which for workmanship is supposed equal to any made in America. Although the pipe is only five-eights of an inch in diameter, it delivers one hundred and ten gallons in a minute.

sudden death
    We hear from Waterbury that on Monday se'nnight, Mr. Benjamin Wetmore of that place was found dead in the street, supposed to have died from a fit.

Susquehanna Company
　　Notice to the Susquehanna Company of meeting in Hartford "as the affairs then transacted may be of the utmost importance to said company, it is hoped that there will be a universal attendance as possible; notice given by Eliphalet Dyer, Samuel Gray and Gershom Breed.

stocking weaving
　　Christopher Leffingwell carries on that business in a shop adjoining his pot ash works in Norwich. He makes all kinds of fine thread, worsted and cotton stockings, jacket and breeches pieces.
　　He continues purchasing salts of lye, good and bad potash.[23]

hatting business
　　Advertisement by William Capron that he continue to carry on the Hatting Business.
　　N.B. Said Capron wants a quantity of lamb's wool and such as is too short for weaving will answer for his purpose; he will give felt hats of the best sort in exchange for such wool.

food stuff
　　Indian corn, ship bread and flour to be sold by David Gardner, Jr. at his shop near the New Courthouse in New London.

found
　　a copper chafing dish and sauce pan. Enquire of Charles Jeffery.
　　　　　　　　**********
From *The New London Gazette*, May 25, 1770

lost child
　　Last Thursday in the forenoon, a child of Mr. Daniel Tracy (living about a mile from the Court house in Norwich) two years and three months old, was missing from her home when diligent search was made for it at the neighbors and in the neighboring fields and woods, but it not being found, a large

number of people from town gathered together, who made diligent search for the whole night but it was not found until about sunrise the next morning, when in a swampy place about a mile from home, by means of dog which was near it. The child was speechless and near perishing with the cold when found but soon after recovered.

British troops
    Last Tuesday, two sloops with soldiers on board were seen going up our Sound, supposed to be the 29th regiment from Boston, bound to New Jersey.

married
    at Christ Church New London, the Rev. Mr. John Tyler, Episcopal minister of said church to Miss Hannah Tracy, daughter of Isaac Tracy.

ran away
    from Joshua Beckwith of Lyme, an apprentice boy named Ezra Davis, about 17 years old: well set and large for his age; had dark brown hair and light gray eyes.

****

From *The New London Gazette*, June 1, 1770

mad dogs
    We hear that a few days ago Mr. John Avery, Jr. of Groton and a child of his were both bit by a mad dog.

fire
    The house of Mr. Caleb Lyon of Woodstock was entirely consumed by fire this day. Two congregations in the town were alarmed by the raising of the flames and smoke, it being the day set aside by the Authority for public humiliation and prayer, and although there was a large concourse of people soon gathered and every possible method used to extinguish the fire and save what they could from the devouring flames, there were only from the full house a desk, a case of drawers, two feather beds and some meat in the cellar saved. The affected family lost all their wearing apparel except what they had on. The loss, estimated by

disinterested persons, is judged to be 500 pounds lawful money.

for sale
     Samuel Wescote, living near the Long Bridge in New London, has choice French Indigo for sale, either by quantity or retail, cheap for cash.

               ****

From *The New London Gazette*, June 8, 1770

stolen property recovered
     Taken from a transient person on Tuesday last, two large silver spoons. The owner may have them again by inquiring of Elizabeth Melally in New London.

maple sugar
     We are credibly informed that there was made in the Town of Goshen, this Colony, in the months of February and March last, from the sap of maple trees, 40,000 weight of sugar. We hear that last year in the same town was made 37,000 pounds.

wanted
     Cash given for good and bad ash and for salts of lye by Daniel and William Hubbard at their shop in Norwich Landing where there is to be sold rum, sugar and molasses. Said Hubbards wants to purchase four prime saddle horses.

dwelling house in Norwich for rent
     Notice by William Hubbard that a commodious well finished house situated on the west side of the main road in Norwich, leading from the Court house to the Landing, and is the house south of Capt. George Dennis' to be let for one year or more. There is a good barn of the premises, pleasant gardens and lot adjoining; Enquire of Mr. Nathaniel Shipman at Norwich Landing.

schooner for sale
     To be sold a likely, well built schooner about 16 ton burthen, fit for passenger, freighting or cod fishing. Apply to

Charles Jeffery in New London.

ran away
     from David Smith of New London, an apprentice boy named John Cook, about 16 years and 8 month old; a lusty lad for that age; one of his ankles stands pretty much in, occasioned by a cut with an axe.

****

From *The New London Gazette*, June 15, 1770

accident
     Last Friday, the oldest son of Samuel Latimer, Jr. fell from a wharf in this town (New London) and was drowned.

obituary
     Saturday last, after lingering illness, departed this life the Rev. Nathaniel Hooker, pastor of the West Church, Hartford.

mad dogs
     Last Tuesday, a mad dog was killed in this town.

pay up
     Notice by Benjamin Chapin of Bridgehampton that he has given the notes owed him to Marvin Wait of New London for suit.

land for sale
     to be sold by Jonathan Calkins administrator for the estate of Nehemiah Smith, late of New London, deceased, about seven acres of improved lands, lying westward of the dwelling house of the deceased or some much of the real estate as will raise the sum of 22 pounds nine shilling.

violation of non importation agreement
     Windham: The Committee of inspection here receiving information that two of the traders in this town *viz*. James Flint and Shubal Abbe, had purchased in Providence and were bringing into this place sundry items of merchandise, imported in a Snow, Capt. Tristman, master, and, contrary to the agreement

of the principal Merchants of America. Upon this information, the said Flint and Abbe were immediately summoned to appear before the Committee of the town and exhibit the reasons for their conduct. Upon which, the said Flint and Abbe cheerfully and freely delivered up their goods and pledged their honor and faithfully to adhere strictly to the non importation agreement in the future.

runaway
     from Daniel Cook on Long Island, a Negro woman about 20 years of age; speaks good English; born on Long Island; about middling stature; she is a likely wench.

****

From *The New London Gazette*, June 22, 1770

title claims
     Notice of petition of Charle Dewey of Hebron against Benjamin Taylor and others to examine into the claims of the parties to a certain large tract of land in Hebron, anciently granted by John Mason, assignee of Uncas, Owaneco and Joshua, Sachems.[24] All people interested should appear at the house of Joseph Water in said Hebron; notice given by Jabez Hamlin, Zebulon West and Nathaniel Wales, Jr.

rape
     Last Saturday, a transient person about 24 years of age, who says his name is Livingston, was committed to goal in Hartford for perpetrating a rape in the woods between Hartford and Bolton upon a married woman named Lunkhorn, about 20 years old. The villain appeared to be, upon examination, very unconcerned and behaved with the greatest indecency.

administration of estates
     Notice that Eliza Hallam has been appointed Executrix to the creditors of the estate of Nicholas Hallam, late of New London.

runaway
     from Samuel Andrues in Groton, the guardian of

a young man named William Holley, about 20 years of age; has long straight hair with a dark complexion; is large and well made.

taken up
        by John Raymond of New London North Parish, a brown horse.

passage boat
    Notice by Jeremiah Lord of Saybrook that he provides a passage boat, convenient for passengers between Saybrook and Middletown and then to Sag Harbor and back again. The fare for for one man and a horse is one dollar.

              ****

From *The New London Gazette*, June 29, 1770

scissors
    Advertisement by Uriah Hide of Lyme that he makes clothiers shears as good as any imported from Great Britain.

whippings
    Last Friday, one David Bernard being convicted before the county court sitting here, received ten stripes at the public post for breaking open the store of Ebenezer Ledyard in Groton. He appeared by the scars on his back to be an old offender. John Hanly and Elizabeth Latham, who were also charged, one with stealing and the other with concealing part of the goods were both acquitted by said Court.

    Saturday last, one Job Diskel, about 18 years old, convicted before the County Court of stealing a sum of money from the shop of Mr. Gershom Breed in Norwich, was whipped at the pubic post here.

drowning
    On Monday, as Mr. Rufus Welch of Norwich was bathing himself in the river near the iron works of Ebenezer Backus of that town, he was forced by a current over a dam, by which mean he was unfortunately drowned.

for sale
     by Mr. Gershom Breed at Chelsea has a large assortment of English and West Indies goods for sale.

wanted
     a small frame for a shop in New London. Enquire of the printer.

****

From *The New London Gazette*, July 6, 1770

Committee of Inspection
     The Committee of Inspection of the towns of New London and Groton, being informed that a shop keeper in New London had purchased goods in Newport, contrary to the resolutions in this colony; said shopkeeper, being interrogated as to what he had done, acknowledged a purchase of a few goods in Newport without intention to counteract the resolutions and was ready to make all satisfaction in his power. The Committee finding the goods had been purchased before the resolutions were adopted in this colony, demanded that said goods be delivered up to be stored until all the revenue acts are repealed.

land for sale in East Haddam
     To be sold 20 acres of choice land under good improvement on which there is a large barn and dwelling house, formerly the estate of Rev. Hofmer and is situated in East Haddam about one mile north of the Landing. Enquire of Mr. Thomas Fuller, 2d or Mr. Thomas Moseley of East Haddam.

administration of estates
     Notice by James Clark and Zebulon Case, commissioners appointed by Probate Court, that a meeting of creditors of the insolvent estate of Indian man Pyrus Richards, late of Lebanon; will be held at dwelling house of the widow Elizabeth Allen in Lebanon.

stolen
     Notice by John Bannister that a black mare was stolen from his pasture in Middletown, Rhode Island.

From *The New London Gazette*, July 13, 1770

worms
    An uncommon species of worms have appeared in this and neighboring towns. Called the Palmer worm, which have done considerable damage in the fields of grain and mowing grass which they have attacked. The most successful measures that have been heretofore to prevent their attacking of field is the digging trenches about 5 to 6 inches deep, round the infested inclosure. The same destructive vermin made their appearance here about 26 years ago when it is said they destroyed very considerable part of the produce of the earth.

died
    at New Haven, Miss Jane Seymour of Hartford, youngest daughter of Thomas Seymour, deceased.

    at Fairfield, the Rev. Seth Pomeroy of that place.

Delaware Companies
    Notice to the proprietors of the First and Second Delaware Companies to meet at Town House in Norwich to consider and act upon some important matters, relative to the proprietors' land lying on or near the Delaware river; notice given by Jabez Fitch, John Curtiss, Isaac Tracy and Elisha Tracy.

    ****

From *The New London Gazette*, July 20, 1770

new school to open
    Notice by Cornelius Conahan of New London that he has opened a school at the Widow Leete's and proposes to teach writing and arithmetic, bookkeeping according to the Italian method and English language grammar.[25]

escapes
    Notice by Clement Miner, Goaler, that broke out and made their escape from His Majesty's Goal in New London, three notorious villains named David Barnet, John Rine and Richard Jordan who were convicted in June last of theft. They

were each of them about 23 years of age; five and half foot in stature.

      Notice by James Chapman Jr., Sheriff's Deputy, in Lyme that George Algt of Lyme made his escape. He had been taken by writ of attachment in favor of Joshua Starr, Daniel Hurlbut and James Tilly of New London.

strayed or stolen
      from Peter Chandler in Pomfret, a dark brown horse
                           ****

From *The New London Gazette,* July 27, 1770

earthquakes in the Carribean
      By Captain William Packwood, we learn that, since the earthquake at the island of Hispaniola on the third of June, there had been a daily trembling of the earth not only at Port au Prince and in the villages adjacent but at the Cape 150 miles distant. In fact, the destruction occasioned by the first shock at Port au Prince surpasses description and any account of it was forbidden to be published lest it might too much terrify and discourage the inhabitants, most of whom had taken shelter on board the ship for nearly a fortnight after the first shock, but on the seeming possibility that the shocks would subside, a number of them returned to the town with the design to build their habitations. However, on the 20th of the month, they had a number of shock still more violent than the first which brought down the only five houses that had survived the first shock and had so much intimidated the inhabitants that it was thought the town would be entirely abandoned and another built in a new spot. We also learned by Captain Packwood that the town of Port au Prince was computed to contain 2,500 houses.

ordination
      On Wednesday last, at the North Society in Lyme, the Rev. George Beckwich Jr. was invested with ministerial authority for the purpose of dispensing the word of the Gospel at the Susquehanna Settlement. The Rev. Stephen Johnson of Lyme made the introductory prayer. The Rev. George W. Beckwith Sr.

preached a sermon pertinent to the occasion. The Rev. William Hart of Saybrook prayed previous to the Charge and Rev. Beckwith Sr. gave the Charge and the Rev. Benjamin Throp of Norwich gave the Right Hand of Fellowship.

****

From The *New London Gazette,* August 3, 1770

shipping news

Capt. Davis arrived at Philadelphia from Lisbon spoke to Capt. Benjamin Algar in a brig from New London, bound for Barbados.

lightning

One day last week, a flash of lightning struck a well pole nearly adjoining the house of Mr. John McCurdy in Lyme, which with the other appendages of the wall were torn to pieces but no other damage ensued.

whippings for theft

Last Wednesday, a man was whipped at Norwich Landing for theft and yesterday another man was whipped in Canterbury for the same offense. It is supposed to be the same fellows lately broke out of the New Haven goal.

wanted

a sober, discreet man, well versed in making earthenware. None but those who can be recommended need apply.

house to be let on reasonable terms

House lately in Norwich belonged to Ebenezer Backus, deceased; it has two good gardens, a merchant shop. Enquire of Samuel Huntington or Samuel Wheat, living in Norwich.

peace with the Six Nations

By letters from Wyoming, we have advice that two Indian Chiefs of the Six Nations on the 13th last June came to Wyoming to visit the settlers there, sent by the council of said Nation with belts of wampum to confirm friendship. They had been informed that the settlers were worried that the would make war against the

New England people of Wyoming, which was so far from the truth that the aid council had directed them to go to all the smaller tribes and parties of Indian and charged that not by any means whatever were they to be induced to take any part in the quarrel between the New England settlers and the Pennsylvania proprietors.

pay up
    All persons indebted to the late company of Messrs Lord, Durkee and Abel of Norwich are desired to settle their account; notice by Dudley Woodbridge.

runaway
    from Amos Clift of Preston, an apprentice boy, named Rufus Randal; about 17 years old; of light complexion; brown hair curls a little; one of boy's great toes is very crooked occasioned by a cut.
    ****
From *The New London Gazette*, August 10, 1770

accident
    One day last week, the Rev. Mr. Boardman of East Haddam had a child scalded in such a manner that it died soon after.

rum for sale
    Advertisement by Charles Chadwick of West Indian rum, sugar, cotton, wool etc. for sale at his store in New London.

runaway
    from Isaac Coit of Plainfield, a Negro man named Boston, a stout thickset fellow of middling stature; about 30 years old; very black.
    ****
From *The New London Gazette,* August 17, 1770

accident
    Last Saturday, a child five years old, son of Captain Sylvanus Tinker, was drown in East Haddam Landing. The same

gentleman lost a son, 12 years old, about two yeas ago, by a like accident.

shipping news
    Sloop *Dispatch,* Moses Pierce, Master, is at Norwich Landing ready to set sail for Nova Scotia.
    N.B. A good supply of Nova Scotia grind stones for sale at Norwich Landing at a reason rate for cash or produce.

theft
    Notice by Oliver Hazard of the Island of Conanicut of Rhode Island that a small schooner in New London harbor was left in the care of William Stannis who stole a number of items from it; he is five foot eight inches high; between 30 and 40 years old; dark complexion; either pock marked or freckled.

house in Norwich for sale
    Notice by Benjamin Huntington that for sale in Norwich is the dwelling house and lot of land now inhabited by Mr. Joseph Tracy, containing a number of fruit trees, a small barn and a commodious building spot thereon, facing the town street, near the center of the town.
    ****
From *The New London Gazette,* August 24, 1770

whales
    Last Tuesday. a whale about 14 feet in length was discovered by a small fishing schooner off Marshfield, which was then attacked by three large sharks, one of whom the fishermen killed. It measured 16 feet long and, upon opening it, they took out of its paunch as many pieces of the whale as would make a barrel of oil and it was thought the liver of the shark would make two or three barrels more. The whale was so wounded and worried by the sharks that it became an easy prize to the fishermen who carried it to Marshfield.

died
    on Friday the $10^{th,}$ on Long Island, the Rev. Mr. Charles Jeffrey Smith.

non importation agreement
On Monday last there was as full a town meeting that has ever been known, when the town voted, almost unanimously, to adhere to the former non importation agreement.

pay up
Notice by Hugh Ledlie of Hartford to his creditors to settle accounts.

slaves for sale
Just imported, sundry slaves boys and girls, one about 16, the others ten and twelve. Enquire of James Mumford of New London.

strayed or stolen
from the pasture of Capt. Joseph Williams of Norwich, a horse; notice by Zebediah Andrus Jr.

****

From *The New London Gazette,* August 31, 1770

obituary
Last Saturday, died here in New London and was decently interred the next day, John Aitchison, a planter from Grenada who had come to New London to regain his health.

medical mystery
We hear from Waterbury that a woman in that town being is in her fourth or fifth month of pregnancy was taken with a most violent longing to eat the flesh of her husband's arms. He indulged her but her teeth were not sufficient for the purpose and her unaccountable longing went to her delivery, which was about three weeks ago. The infant, refusing the breast or any of the sustenance given to babies, it was offered the raw flesh of a fowl cut fine and dipped in the fowl's blood on which it has fed heartily ever since its birth and is the only food the child has taken till a few days since when it ate a little bread mixed with blood.

runaway
　　from Daniel Tyler of Canterbury, a mulatto servant named Sampson; about 28 years of age; is about 5 foot, eight inches high; had a squaw and a child of three years old with him.

found
　　On the road leading from Norwich landing to Pequotanuck, a woman's red short cloak.

****

From *The New London Gazette,* September 7, 1770

obituary
　　Last Saturday night, died at Stonington, Amos Cheseborough, Lt. Colonel of the Eighth Regiment of militia of this colony.

horse stealing
　　Last week, one Joel Gay at Hebron was committed to goal in Hartford for stealing a horse of Zeb Andrus. It is suspected that Gay was connected to a number of villains in and near Hebron, who improve on every opportunity the practice in the art of horse stealing, but they have the misfortune to be frequently detected.

not responsible
　　Notice by Henry Norris of New London that he will no longer be responsible for the debts of his wife.

runaway
　　from Lemuel Fitch in Colchester, Job Diskel; 18 years of age; five feet, four inches high; slender made; has a large scar on his left hand just above the fore knuckle on his forefinger and a number of warts on each hand; black eyes; dark hair and is freckled.

pay taxes
　　Notice by Aaron Storrs to those in the town of Lebanon who are late paying their taxes, to pay up.

taken up
    by Barney Fink of New London harbor, a long boat.

administration of estates
    Notice to claimants to the estate of Capt. Azel Fitch, late of Lebanon, to come to the house of Elizabeth Alden, inn keeper of that town for a hearing; notice given by Ichabod Robinson, William Williams and Samuel Hide Jr.

****

From *The New London Gazette,* September 14, 1770

letters left at New London Post office

James Avery, New London
Humphrey Avery, Norwich
James Avery, Norwich
Michael Adams, Killingly
Peter Bigarant, New London
Capt. Thomas Barber, Groton
Capt. Belton, Groton
John Brown, Groton
John Bowls, Stonington
Adam Crisp, New London
Mary Chapman, New London
Elizabeth Champlin, New London
Singleton Church, New London
David Carter, Plainfield
John Denison, Stonington
Joseph Denison 2d, Stonington
Charles Elridge, New London
Rev Nathaniel Eells, Stonington
John English, Lebanon
John Friend, New London
Ebenezer Goddard, New London
Joseph Gallup, Groton
Rev. Geo. Gilmore, Voluntown
Abigail Howard, New London
Elizabeth Howard, New London
Thomas Harris, New London
Widow Harris, New London
Rev. Aaron Kine, Groton
Solomon Kellogg, Colchester
Jonathan Leach, New London
Isaac Leach, New London
Tithy Lumis, New London
Joseph Noyes, Stonington
Rev. Samson Occom, Mohegan
Elijah Pitcher, Norwich
Nathan Palmer, Stonington
William Skinner, New London

Capt. John Smith, Groton
Allen Stevenson, Voluntown
Moses Stork, Branford
Pardon Taylor, New London
Capt. William White, New London

Bliss Willoghby, Norwich
Joseph Woodbridge, Groton
Jonathan Williams, Groton
Samuel Williams, Groton

suicides

We hear from Southhold in Long Island that about the 14th ultimo, a young woman of that place, wife of Mr. Gershom Aldridge, having been for some time melancholy and disordered in her mind, put an end to her own life in the following manner. She told a little girl who tended her child to take it out of doors and play with it there. As soon as the girl went out, she observed the woman go into a bedroom, shut the door and soon after heard the snap of a gun. After this she saw the woman come out, take a powder horn, go again into the bedroom, fasten the door and presently after hearing the report of a gun, entered the bedroom where the woman had shot herself in the breast and was now dead.

The same week, at Montauk, an Indian named Cyrus, remarkable for being of a serious religious turn of mind, put an end to his own life by stabbing himself.

accident

About the same time, a Negro man belonging to John Tuthill of that place was found drowned in shallow water thought to be self murder or accident, but a dumb Indian of that neighborhood by signs has the people to understand that he was murdered by two other Negroes one belonging to Joseph Reves, the other to John Wells and thrown into the water, that it might be supposed that he drowned.

obituary

On Tuesday night, departed this life at the age of 64, Mrs. Lucretia Proctor of this town (New London). She was first married to Nathaniel Saltonstall of this town. After his death, she remained a widow for some years and was married to Mr. John

Proctor of Boston, whose widow she died.

General Assembly
The following gentlemen were elected to the General Assembly:
New London: Col. Gurdon Saltonstall, William Hillhouse
Groton: Capt. Bendam Gallup, Capt. Robert Geer
Stonington: Charles Phelps, Benjamin Clark
Norwich: Elisha Fitch, Elijah Backus
Lyme: Samuel Holden Parsons, Dr. Eleazer Mather
Kllingworth: Benjamin Gale, Theophilus Morgan

small pox
Whereas it is enacted as a law of this Colony "that whenever it should happen that any ship or vessel shall come from any place where the small pox or other contagious sickness is present, it shall be the duty of the master of such ship or vessel, and in the case of his disability, it shall be the duty of the next officer successively, upon their arrival in any harbor, road or creek in this colony to forthwith give information to one or more of the selectmen of such town where such vessel should first arrive, the true circumstances of the people and cargo on board;

And, whereas this town (New London) is much exposed to vessels and boats running back and forth to New York, where the small pox is prevalent, makes it necessary that the laws be strictly adhered to; notice given by Selectmen John Hempsted, John Richards and Richard Law.
****
From *The New London Gazette,* September 21, 1770

non importation agreements
At a general meeting of the merchants and landholders of the Colony of Connecticut, held in New Haven, it was Resolved that they would strictly adhere to the non importation agreements and not import any goods or merchandise from Great Britain, directly or indirectly, except those items excepted by the Assembly.

married
Last evening Sunday was married Samuel Wheat of Norwich, Merchant, to Miss Sally Dershon, the only daughter of Capt. John Dershon of this town (New London), a young lady possessed of every valuable that can render the continued connubial state agreeable and happy.

newspaper price hike
It being found that since the enlargement of the *New London Gazette*, the labor and expense of such paper is so greatly augmented that the same cannot be continued without a manifest loss, without an addition of 3d a year to the purchase price.
****
From *The New London Gazette,* September 28, 1770

non importation in Philadelphia
We learn from the Western Post that the Philadelphians have come to a resolution to import from Great Britain as usual except for tea.

strayed or stolen
Notice by Daniel Parsons and Jedidiah Bliss of Springfield as to missing black mare.

stolen from the pasture of Mrs. Elizabeth Alden of Lebanon, a mare.

administration of estates
Notice to the creditors of the estate of Samuel Cotton of Pomfret that there will be a meeting at the dwelling house of Mrs. Mary Cotton of Pomfret; notice by Seth Pine, Jr., Ephraim Tucker Jr. and Stephen Williams.
****
From *The New London Gazette,* October 5, 1770

whaling news
Last Friday, the *Mermaid*, Capt. – arrived here from a whaling voyage with 228 barrels of oil.

accident
We hear from Canaan that as Cynthia Dunham, daughter of James Dunham of that place, was drawing water from a deep well when she got the bucket down to the water the pole broke off, which flew back with such force that it sprang out of its crotch, fell on her head and wounded her to such a degree that she died in seven hours.

Susquehanna Purchase
We have received accounts from our settlers on the Susquehanna Purchase of the most interesting nature, both with respect to said settlers and said company as also accounts from information of importance from Great Britain relative as to said purchase.

This, therefore, is to warn the purchasers of the Susquehanna purchase to meet at the courthouse in Windham on the 17th of October instant to take such matters in consideration; notice by committee of Eliphalet Dyer, Samuel Gray, Jedidiah Elderkin, Gershom Breed and Ebenezer Baldwin.

taken up
by Seth Flitcher, a Negro boy of about 18 years of age; his name is William Woomsley, belonging to Benjamin Smith of Smithfield in Rhode Island; he stammers in his speech and is ragged.

****

From *The New London Gazette,* October 12, 1770

feathers needed
Cash given for good feathers at the London Coffee House in New London by Thomas Allen; also wanted a good able young man who understands taking care of horses.

runaway
from Ebenezer Weeks in Pomfret, an apprentice boy named Stafford Cady, about 18 years of age; of a right complexion, brown hair which he wears tied; has small blue eyes; is about 5 foot eight inches high; round favored and pretty well set.

whaling news
    Since our last the Schooner *Liberty*, Capt. Squire, arrived here (New London) from a whaling voyage with 170 barrels of oil.

died
    Last Saturday died at Lebanon, Mr. Nathan Bushnell of that place in the 85th year of his age. As he was eminent in piety and exemplary in religion, he has left a good hope that through Grace, he is gone to Glory.

deserted from the Brig Royal
    William Rockwell, master, reports the desertion of Noah Scranton, a seaman about five foot high; light complexion; light hair, cohabits in Killingworth and is expected to go there; deliver to William Rockwell of New London or William Coit of Norwich.

strayed
    from John Clark of Lebanon, a mare of sorrel color.

township of Pomfret on Otter Creek, New York
    Notice given to the proprietors of the township of Pomfret on Otter Creek in Col. Lydius' patent near Lake Champlain in the Province of New York to meet at the dwelling house of Mr. Abner Flint of the Third Society of Windham, called Scotland, in Windham county to choose a moderator to preside at such meeting, to consider the expediency of the actual settlement of said lands and to make preparations therefor; notice given by John Howard, John Cary, Jr. Jacob Simons and Gideon Hebard.

              ****

From *The New London Gazette,* October 19, 1770

accident
    We hear from Lyme that a few days since one Tubbs, a young man of about 16 years of age, was driving a team in that town, by some accident the wheel ran over his head and killed him on the spot.

pastures

Good fall pasturing for cattle and horses may be had of Freeman Crocker.

****

From *The New London Gazette,* October 26, 1770

death in a storm

We hear from Southampton on Long Island that in the storm which happened about the 9th instant, one Mr. Elihu Cooper of that place, being on the beach about 8 miles from his house, set off with an intent to go home on foot. Being missed the next day, a number of inhabitants went in search of him and found him dead on his face, near a spring of water at some distance from the road. It is supposed that his strength being exhausted coming against the storm and drinking too freely of cold water, it killed him immediately. He was about 27 years of age, of a reputable family and universally esteemed. He has left a disconsolate widow to mourn the loss of her tender and affectionate husband.

run aground in storm

On Friday night last and part of the next day, we had a very severe storm of wind and rain from the N. E. by which two vessels were drove ashore in this harbor (New London), one of which was the New York Packet, bound from New York to Newport, Rhode Island which had put in there the evening before. It received little or no damage.

humor

A lady being asked "How it could be consistent with a Christian Life and Character for married men and women to assemble together and make sumptuous entertainments and balls" answered "Oh, I do not imagine there is any harm in it, for it is very customary in Boston."

hue and cry

Seize the assassin. Dr. James Thomson, a native of Scotland, for some time past a resident of the town of Hartford, did wound and stab with a sharp iron weapon the body of James Shepard of Northampton, coming behind and attacking him as he was peaceably and innocently walking on the Main Street; said Thomson is about 25 years of age, about five feet six inches high; gray eyes; has something of a Scotch manner of pronunciation.

house for sale in Lyme
    to be sold by Jonathan Bolles, a convenient dwelling house and barn, commodiously situated in the Lyme Old Society, on the Post Road, near Saybrook ferry; said buildings are almost new.

pay up
    notice by Jonathan Kennedy of Windham to all those indebted to Messrs. Kennedy and Badger to settle their accounts immediately.

****

From *The New London Gazette*, November 2, 1770

shipwreck
    We hear that the Sloop *Lily*, Capt. Vredenburg which left Newport a day or two before the late storm is castaway on Fisher' Island. Part of her cargo is lost and it is feared the vessel will suffer the same fate.

fire
    Last Tuesday se'nnight the house of Mr. Thepphilus Merriman, inn holder of Wallingford, was consumed by fire with most of the household furniture.

died
    Last week at Derby, Samuel Riggs of that town.

****

From *The New London Gazette*, November 9, 1770

Boston Massacre trial
    We hear that the trial of the soldiers who were involved in the massacre at Boston the fifth of March last, will commence on the twenty seventh of this month.

death

Last Friday se'nnight, Mr. Joel Dodge of Canterbury, having a tooth drawn, he in a few hours bled to death. He had been taken with a fever a few days before.

runaway

from Aaron Wait in Salem, a Negro servant man named Pomp, a leather dresser by trade; is about five feet seven inches high; speaks good English; has a large scar on one part of his forehead; about 23 years of age; said Negro was seen on board Capt. John Roger's sloop at East Greenwich in the colony of Rhode Island, who was bound to New York and the North River.

combs for sale

Horn combs of all sorts and sizes to be sold by Joseph Knight in Norwich.

****

From *The New London Gazette*, November 16, 1770

escaped

from the goal in South Kingston, Rhode Island four men: William Reynolds, Thomas Clarke, Elisha Reynolds and Samuel Casey, said Casey being under death sentence.

fulling mill

Notice by William Hill of New London North Parish has lately set up a fulling mill[26]. Any person on Long island that is willing to employ him may send their cloth by passage boat, to Mr. Zebulon Eliot's in New London, who will take care of it and, when done, will return it by the said passage boats with all dispatch. Any kind of grain, provision or flax will be taken in payment.

stray or stolen

Notice by John Fox of Coventry in the county of Kent in the colony of Rhode Island of a horse which strayed or was stolen from the pasture of James Downer, in Lebanon.

****

From *The New London Gazette,* November 23, 1770

deaths by small pox
    Last Thursday night died at Lebanon of the small pox, Mr. Daniel Hyde of that town. His death is universally regretted by his acquaintances and friend, who were numerous.
    Last Wednesday, a child of Mr. Hyde's died of the same distemper.

strayed or stolen
    from the pasture of Mr. William Manwarinng, a horse; notice given by Nathan Douglass of New London

land for sale
    lying in New London, bound southerly on land belonging to the heirs Capt. Peter Harris, late of New London, westerly on the Main Street and easterly on the Mill Cove, and is opposite the dwelling house of Capt. Guy Richards; said lot is three rods in front, six rods deep to high water mark and is well situated for a merchant, mechanic or tradesman; enquire of Avery Power in Norwich, First Society.

****

From *The New London Gazette,* November 30, 1770

died
    Last Tuesday, se'nnight died at Guilford, the Rev. Mr. Ruggles of that place.

****

From *The New London Gazette,* December 7, 1770

married
    Last Sunday morning was married here (New London), Mr. John Osgood of Boston to Miss Lucy Torry of this town, an agreeable young lady.

to be sold a farm
    lying in the first Society in Lyme, containing about 50 acres of land, the whole of which is under improvement and well fenced; there is on said land an orchard which will make 30

barrels of cider,[27] a good dwelling house, barn and grist mill; enquire of Elihu Wade and Elisha Wade in Lyme.

died
Sunday night died here (New London), Mrs. Abigail Davis; aged 90.

Last Friday se'nnight, died in New Haven, aged 88, Mr. Stephen Howell of that town.

wanted
a boy, 9 years old or upwards, to tend to a gentleman's family.

****

From *The New London Gazette*, December 14, 1770

champion wool spinner
We hear from Woodstock that on the 29th of last month, Mary Harding, a young woman employed in the family of Abel Leonard, spun up eight pounds of wool in twenty skeins and two knots –i.e., 142 knots which is two skeins over and above three days work of hired spinners. She kept two carders employed with th utmost diligence the whole time and by an exact computation of the steps she took in spinning the above, she went 16 miles and 340 yards.[28]

died
On the 4thh instant died in Tolland, Zebulon West, of His Majesty's Council for the county, probate judge for Tolland and a Judge of the Qurorum of Hartford County.

Yesterday se'nnight died at Kent, where he had gone on a visit, Capt Jonathan Rudd of Windham, from which town he frequently had been a representative to the General Assembly.

A few days since, died at Hartford, Mr. R. Wheelock, son of Rev. Doct. Wheelock.

thefts
    One James Watson, who for some months has worked in this town (New London) in repairing clocks and watches, on Monday night left off privately with between 20 and 30 watches belonging to different persons in the neighboring towns.

    Notice by Duncan Stewart, Collector at Port and Thomas Moffatt, Comptroller, that a report by Thomas Dare, Surveyor, regarding the thefts of sails and riggings from the Custom House Boat.

found
    by Ephraim Barker of Norwich, three sides of leather.[29]

taken up
    by Nathan Rogers of New London, Great Neck, three miles west of New London harbor, a batteau[30] with pine sides and oak bottom.

hats and furs
    Advertisement by Samuel Clay, hatter, in New London that he purchases small furs, suitable for hats, and has for sale good beaver, castor and felt hats.

****

From *The New London Gazette*, December 21, 1770

strayed or stolen
    from Simon Wolcott of New London, a dun colored mare

Keep the Sabbath
    The following act passed at the last session of the General Assembly: "An act, in addition to the law of this colony, for the due observation and keeping the Sabbath Lord's Day and for preventing and punishing disorders and profaneness of the same.

whales
    The following act passed at the last session of the General Assembly: An act of the encouragement of the Whale and Cod fisheries.

died

    Last Monday departed this life, Col. John Whiting, who during the last war had a principal command in the troops raised in Rhode Island. He came to New London for the benefit of his health, having long labored under a very painful disorder of the lungs.

going home

    Duncan Smith, Collector of the Port, has left for Boston, then to London. The good esteem which the citizens of the town entertain for this gentleman is evident in their universally regretting his departure.

drownings at sea

    Wednesday last, Capt. Melally arrived here from the West Indies. Three days before his arrival, three of his hands were by a sea washed off the bowsprit, one of which Joseph Lothrop of this town (New London) was drowned, the other two taken up.

drugs and medicines

    to be sold cheap for cash by Simon Wolcott, near the courthouse in New London.

strayed

    from Jonas Prentice in Groton, a white barrow hog of about 100 pounds weight.

          ****

From *The New London Gazette*, December 28, 1770

fire

    Last Wednesday evening, a very large barn, belonging to Col. Jabez Huntington of Norwich and situated near his dwelling house, was consumed by fire. We hear there were upwards of 30 loads of hay, and near ten head of cattle and horses consumed in it. It was suspected to have been purposely set by some malicious person.

died

    A few days since died in Norwich, Captain Daniel Hide

of that Town in an advanced age.

taken up
a stray by John Adam Park at Bolles Mill in New London, a likely sorrel mare.

****

1771

From *The New London Gazette*, January 4, 1771

trusses
Whereas great inconveniences often attend those bursted people, for want of suitable spring of bandage to keep up the fallen parts, this is to give notice that trusses for the above purposes are made in the neatest manner and sold at reasonable prices by Stephen Johnson in Ashford.

fire
The night following the 15th of last month, the dwelling house of Mr. John Payson of Pomfret was consumed by flames and most of the contents therein, which were very considerable. When the family awoke, the fire had gotten so ahead that they had the opportunity to get out comparatively little of the household furniture and even the lives of some of the family were in imminent danger. It is not known how the house took fire.

****

From *The New London Gazette*, January 4, 1771

list of letters at New London Post Office

Michael Adams of Killingly
Cornelius Annabel of East Haddam
Bryant Brown of Killingly
David Belton of Lyme
David Brooks of Haddam
John Braddick of New London
Stephen Babcock of Stonington
Amos Cheseborough of Stonington
Jared Crandall of Stonington
Elizabeth Cardwell of New

London
Joseph Denison of Stonington
Elizabeth Downer of New London
George Dolbeare of New London
Joseph Gallup of Groton
Elisha Gallup of Stonington
James Greenfield of New London
Stephen Herrold of New London
Charles Jeffars of New London
Aaron Kellogg of Colchester
Jabez Lord of Norwich
Davis Latham of Lyme
Cyrus Lee of Lyme
Miner, Henry of Stonington
Nathaniel Miner Jr. of Stonington
General Morgan of Norwich
Alexander Merils of New London
Clement Miner Jr. of New London
Luke Perkins of Groton
Elijah Palmer of Stonington
David Pool of Norwich
Timothy Rowely of Millington
Alexander Reed of Groton
Philip Rollins of Norwich
James Rogers of New London
Joseph Spencer of East Haddam
Jabez Smith of Groton
Paul Schink of New London
Mary Waterhouse of New London

died

Last Friday departed this life in Stonington, Mrs. Elizabeth Seabury, relict of the late Deacon John Seabury, aged 94.

administration of estates

Notice by Philenach Whiting, administratrix, to creditors of the estate of Col. John Whiting of New London to bring their accounts for settlement.

runaway

from Alexander McNeill, an apprentice boy named Henry Jones, about 13 years of age.

****

From *The New London Gazette,* January 18, 1771

agricultural news
We hear that last week that Isaac Chapman of Groton killed a two year old sheep, which was a twin, that weighted 87 and one quarter pounds and had in it 27 pounds of tallow.

ferry leases
Whereas the ferry leases in the town of New London are about to expire and that is customary for the Selectmen to hold a meeting regarding same, such meeting is to be at Edward Palmes inn holder in New London.

pay up
Request by Walter Hyde of Lebanon that those who owe him settle their accounts.

thief
Notice by John Harrison of Norwich Landing that James Perkins, seaman, is suspected of stealing; he is 22 years of age, five foot nine, full faced; well set and round shouldered.

farm for sale in New London Great Neck
Notice by Dennis and James Denison, living on the premises, that they have a farm to sell in Great Neck, New London, about 50 acres of choice land, well fenced and with two orchards of choice fruit; dwelling house, barn, corn house; likewise to be sold a choice tract of 30 acres on the opposite side on the highway to the farm, chiefly woodland with a small dwelling house.

****

From *The New London Gazette,* January 25, 1771

died
On the 4th instant died in Wethersfield of small pox[31], aged 50, Mr. William Woodhouse of that town.

Last Sunday se'nnight, died in New Haven, Roger

Newton of Milford.

Last night died here (New London) after a lingering disease, Basil Winthrop.

a productive lad
The following instance of industry is doubtless worth knowing. There is a boy, about a nine year old, living in the North Parish of New London whose parents are rather needy who cards and spins 25 lots of yarn a day and has continued to spin about the same quantity a day for the last two years.

runaway
from Samuel Swaddel of North Parish of New London, an apprentice boy, Eliphalet Button, cooper by trade; about 20 years of age; pretty slender made; something round shouldered.

from James Street in Groton, an apprentice boy Robert Bronnuck, 18 years old and small for his age.

farm in Lebanon for sale
To be sold by Jacob Eliot, a farm in Lebanon about a mile from the Meeting house in the Society of Goshen in Lebanon; about 48 acres of choice land; consists of mowing, plowing pasturing and orcharding lands, well watered; a house, good barn, shed etc; inquire of Jacob Eliot living near the meeting house in said society or Capt. Joseph Trumbull or Jonathan Trumbull Jr,. or James Thomas at Lebanon or Lt. James Bill in said Goshen.

for sale
choice writing paper to be sold by Printer.
****

From *The New London Gazette,* February 1, 1771

died
Late last Tuesday, died at Norwich at an advanced age, Daniel Tracy of that town.

mild winter in Quebec
We learn from Quebec that the winter hereto has been very moderate, that about the first of January there was not the least appearance of ice in the St. Lawrence and but little ice in any of the waters.

wanted
a Negro woman that understands all kinds of household work and to be well recommended.

good encouragement will be given to a plaid weaver and dyer by Elisha Leffingwell in Norwich.

runaways
from Alexander Bushnel of Hartlad, an apprentice boy named Roswel Waid; about 17 years of age; of dark complexion, brown hair; pretty full face and well made.

from Martin Kellogg of Colchester, an apprentice named Ezra Tubbs; about 19 years old; five feet nine or ten inches high; light brown hair, cut square behind.

strayed
from John Munsell, Jr living in Lyme, a brown mare
****

From *The New London Gazette,* February 8, 1771

mail robbery
Wednesday night, the Newport Post rider had his saddle bags robbed of 120 dollars value in silver and gold.
****

From *The New London Gazette,* February 15, 1771

storms
last Saturday, we had a most violent storm of wind and rain from the Southward. There was a fuller tide in the harbor than has been known for a number of years and which has done considerable damage to the wharves and some old buildings near the water as also to the roads. It is feared that a considerable

damage has been done by this storm at sea.

accident
    We hear from Long Island that on Monday the 12th, four men on riding on Hempstead Plain, near Mr. Waters Tavern, in order to try the speed of their horses in a frolic set out to race, when one of them, whose parents live a mile from that place at the village of Bethpage and are named Whiston, in attempting to stop his horse suddenly, it fell on the young man whose skull was fractured in the fall and he immediately died.

mail robbers captured
    Mention was made in our last paper that the Newport post had been robbed of a sum of money. We since learn that the theft was committed by two Indians in Stonington and that all the money, except $20, was found on one of them.
                                ****

From *The New London Gazette,* February 22, 1771

Susquehanna Company
    Notice from the Susquehanna Company "whereas our settlers at Wyoming are unjustly and by force drove off from their settlements and it is judged necessary that some effectual measures be done soon to put an end to this dispute, there will be a meeting at the court house at Windam; notice given by Eliphalet Dyer, Samuel Gray, Jedidiah Elderkin, Ebenezer Baldwin and Gershom Breed.

to be sold
    at the dwelling house of Captain Edward Palmes inn holder in New London, a commodious dwelling house situated on the bank in said New London with three rods of land adjoining and bounded on the water; anyone who wants to know the conditions should apply to Joseph Coit or Pygan Adams of New London.

    Land to be sold containing about 40 acres, lying 4 miles from the New London's Ferry on the upper road to Lyme. It is known to be some of the best land in these parts and has on it a good house, barn and an excellent well of water convenient to the house; also a choice orchard which, in bearing years, produces apples sufficient for 100 barrels of cider; the soil is good for grass, corn or wheat. It has a fair prospect to the sea and not one mile from the Niantic River; also for sale a tract of land about a quarter of a mile south of the land above adjoining to a road which leads to the Great Neck containing about 58 acres, joining on the West to Stewart's farm and about 200 rods from a cove called Kenny's Cove; such land is good for corn and the grain; it has a good quantity of walnut timber of young growth; inquire of William Morgan.

To be sold by James Lamb of Groton a farm lying on the Mystic River containing about 120 acres of land.
****

From *The New London Gazette*, March 1, 1771

for sale
By John Martin, assorted goods including pipes, cloths, gloves, buttons at his store at Norwich Landing.

by hook or crook
Origin of the proverbial expression by hook or by crook: "Hook and Crook were two of our judges at the beginning of the last century. They were both men of eminence in their profession but not more remarkable for anything than for the perpetual diversity of opinion that prevailed upon them on the seat of justice. Be the case what it was, every suitor was assured to get either a hook or crook on his side.
****

From *The New London Gazette*, March 8, 1771

mad dogs
By a gentleman who from Danbury, we are informed that the inhabitants there had lately been under not a little consternation from mad dogs. About five weeks since, a dog in the nighttime ran around into several enclosures in that town and bit a number of cattle, swine and nine and dogs. Ten or twelve days after this that, the cattle which were bit were infected with

the disorder and ran mad. None of them could be made to eat or drink anything. They discovered a wildness and fierceness in their looks and some of them are of the disposition to run at everything which came in the way. They continued and incessant howling (the most dolorous ever heard) till they died. eight cattle and some hogs died in this manner, all of them, it is thought, by the bite of this dog, although upon some there did not appear any external wounds.

A few nights ago, another dog mad as was supposed went through the town and bit a number of hogs, poultry etc. He was pursued but made his escape. In Bethel, the next parish he bit nearly 20 cattle hogs, and dogs and finally went off without being captured.

shipwrecks

A vessel belonging to Rhode Island ran ashore on East Hampton on Long island a few nights past. It is said the cargo may be saved and the vessel got off.

Lemuel Moore, master on his passage from Rhode Island, ran ashore on Gardiners Island but it said he may get off.

We hear that Capt. Brown arrived at New Haven a few days ago, who brought with him Capt. Ward, the master of one of the vessels wrecked in the recent gale. Capt. Ward's vessel was owned by Theophilus Morgan of Killingsworth.

ferry stolen

On Monday night, a large ferry boat rigged sloop *Fashion,* belonging to Mr..Zebulon Eliot, was stolen from the town wharf and carried off.

taken up

by Josephus Fitch in the Sound between Fisher's Island and the mainland and towed into the mouth of the Mystic River, in Groton and secured, a large scow.

runaway

from Nathaniel Comstock, Jr. of New London North

Parish, an apprentice boy, Amos Butler; about 14 year old, large and well set.

not responsible
Notice by Zebadiah Scott that he was no longer responsible for Hannah who has left and departed his house and family and neglects to return thereto.

****

From *The New London Gazette*, March 15, 1771

storm at sea
Captain Stillman from New London in the sloop *Collin* lost all his stock off the deck but six horses and arrived at Antigua.

ordination
On the 21st of February the Rev. Joel Benedict was ordained to the pastoral office in Newent. The prayer before the sermon was made by the Reverend Mr. Kine of Groton. The sermon was preached by the Reverend Mr. Hart of Preston and the Reverend Mr. Rossiter of Preston made the prayer after the sermon. The Reverend Mr. Fuller made the prayer after the Charge and the Reverend Borroughs gave the Right Hand of Fellowship[32]. The whole was performed in a manner, suitable to the importance and solemnity of the occasion.

infanticide
Last Monday, a mulatto girl about 17 years old, owned by Mr. Daniel Judd of Colchester was delivered of a child, unknown to any of the family, a few rods from the house. Upon suspicion she was examined and confessed the fact that she struck it on head with a stone and concealed it in a hog sky where it was soon after found dead.

whaling
The Brig *Mermaid* of this port on a whaling voyage was at Dominica and she had got 20 barrels of oil.[33]

shipping news
    Captain Champlin in a brig belonging to this port set out from Cape Nichola.

****

From *The New London Gazette*, March 22, 1771

died
    Saturday se'nnight instant, died here in New London, Doctor Thomas Walker of Middletown of a paralysis, with which he was seized about three months ago; a gentleman of reputation and his death is universally lamented by his acquaintances.

storm at sea
    A letter from St. Eustatia, dated January 20 instant, says "we have daily accounts of Northern vessels being lost and dismasted: Captain Ward from Guilford lost a vessel and cargo and all the people, except himself and two hands, who were taken up in his boat. Captain Wickham from Middletown lost his vessel and cargo and all perished except an Indian man who was taken from the wreck there after five days. He says that, about at sunset, a Gale came on at North East and blew very fresh and about 12 at night, she overset the vessel. The Captain and one Royce were at the helm and went into the sea first. Mr. Samuel Drake of Hartford, who the Indians says was mate of the vessel, went after them in about ten minutes and the rest shared the same fate. Soon after, Captain Allen Stillman of Wethersfield was dismasted and lost his horses on deck; his brother Samuel Stillman shared the same fate.

smallpox
    We are informed that there is upwards of 20 persons at Lebanon are sick of the smallpox.

Irish linens for sale
    Zephaniah Jennings at his shop next door to Backus Tavern at Norwich Landing has for Sale Irish linens either by the piece or retail and a number of other European articles.

wanted to go whaling
        immediately a number of raw hands for whaling the ensuing season. Whoever inclines to go may have a voyage upon wages or other terms by applying to Caleb Trapp, who also wants a quantity of barrel hoops poles by the first of next month.[34]

****

From *The New London Gazette*, March 29, 1771

for sale
        Rule book containing all the laws which are in force in the Colony of Connecticut with a new and accurate table is to be sold at the printing office in New London and at the shop of Christopher Leffingwell in Norwich.

        Made and sold by Jabez Avery, near the courthouse in Norwich coaches, chariots, facetons, sulkies and chairs[35]. Note well said Avery employs two excellent workman from London who served a regular apprenticeship to coach and harness making.

pay up
        All persons indebted to *The New London Gazette*, whose accounts are one year standing, are requested to make immediate payment.

waterfront home to be let
        by Joseph Hurlbut, a large and commodious dwelling house with four rooms on a floor pleasantly situated at the mouth of New London harbor with 30 acres of land in contiguous; a good orchard and a number of fruit trees.

shipping news
        Last Wednesday, Captain Robinson in a brig belonging to Stonington, arrived here in 32 days from Cape Nichola Mole.

        Captain Dudley Saltonstall was arrived at Guadalupe in 30 days from this port (New London). Captain William Billings, also from this port, arrived at Guadalupe on the 16th of February.

whaling ships seized by Spanish
　　　　Captain Atwell from Turk's Island about a fortnight ago spoke with Captain Smith in a sloop bound to Boston from a whaling voyage and had 170 barrels of oil. Captain Smith had two men on board who belonged to a whale man that with three others was taken by twos Spanish coastal ships on the south side of Hispaniola and carried to Santo Domingo where it was expected that they would be condemned.

drowning at sea
　　　　Captain Daley arrived here since our last from St. Eustasia. In his passage, one of his hands named John Ward, a young man about 22 years of age, son of Mr. John Ward of this town (New London), accidentally fell overboard and was drowned.

day of fasting
　　　　His Honor, the Governor, has issued a proclamation appointing Thursday, the 18th of April next for a general fast in this colony.[36]

fire
　　　　Last Wednesday night, the house of Mr. Robert Cleland of the North Parish in this town (New London) took fire on the inside which consumed part of the bed and some other wearing apparel belonging to a young woman in the house but the fire, being discovered by a neighbor, the house was happily saved.
　　　　　　　　**********
From *The New London Gazette,* April 5, 1771

drowning
　　　　Last Friday, se'nnight, James Forster of Sag Harbor fell out of the schooner in which he was bound to New York and was unfortunately drowned.

died
　　　　Last week died at Southhold, William Hubbard, Collector of his Majesty's Customs at that place.

fire
     Besides's the loss we mentioned in our last which accrued to a young woman by means of Mr. Cleland's house taking fire last week, we since learn that Mr. Cleland's loss, considering his circumstances, is considerable, namely a bed with its furniture, a quantity of cotton, cotton yard, flax and linen yarn and some cloth belonging to in his wife.

Lackwack Township
     Notice hat a meeting of the signors of the Lackwack Township will meet at the house of Mr. Absalom Pride, inn holder in Norwich in the East Society on the 17th of April to agree upon such measures relating to said township as shall be thought proper.[37]

*passage boa*t
     Webb's passage boat will ply between Sterling and New London as usual during the summer season twice a week, *viz.*, the boat will sail from Sterling for New London on Mondays and Thursdays and return from New London on Tuesdays and Fridays, weather permitting.
               ****
From *The New London Gazette,* April 12, 1771

shipping news
     On the 26th of last is arrived at Newport, Captain Sison who spoke with Captain Perkins from this port (New London) bound for Antigua. All is well.

     Last month the sloop *Swallow*, Captain Davison, belonging to Norwich was cast away at Cape Hatteras in a passage from this port, New London, to Virginia. The vessel was lost but the people and cargo saved.

Pomfret Otter Creek
     Notice given by Jacob Simons, Clerk of the Proprietors of the Township called Pomfret in Colonel John Henry Laddies' patent on Otter Creek[38] that a meeting will be held to at the dwelling house of Mr. Abner Flint, Inn holder, in Scotland

Society in the town of Windham.

****

From *The New London Gazette,* April 19, 1771

election sermon
We hear the Governor has nominated the Reverend Mr. Cogswell of Canterbury to preach the anniversary elections sermon on the ninth day of May next.

died
Last week, a young man named Judson, belonging to East Hartford was drowned in the Connecticut River near Wethersfield.

Last Tuesday se'nnight, died in New Haven, Colonel Nathan Whiting of that place.

trouble in North Carolina
We learn from North Carolina that the regulators had begun new insurrections and that Governor Tryon with a considerable body of the militia was preparing to march against them.[39]

cure for dropsy
Whereas many persons at Hispaniola, New Orleans etc. have been effectively cured of dropsy[40], even after they had been tapped and given over by the physicians: Take an ounce and a half of gum of Guiacum (gum of Lignum Vitae). Dissolve it in a quart of rum or brandy, or, if the patient dislikes spirits, in Madeira or any other white wine. After the gum is dissolved, take every morning fasting small glass full. Those may be repeated two times or three times a day as the patient can merit, that is - before dinner and going to bed. It will purge gently but if it works too powerful, the quantity may be lessened. Continue this medicine until the disorder is removed, generally on taking two or three bottles. The patient in two or three days will find sensible relief.

runaway husband

Notice by Sarah Kelley that runaway with her husband, Benjamin Kelly, of New London, Great Neck, a short thick girl, with a short black nose, like that of a skunk and with a scolded head; very much given to lying and whoring; now gone away with my husband Benjamin Kelley and deprive me of my dear loving husband. Whoever will take up the above detailed whore shall have thirteen pence.

****

From *The New London Gazette,* April 26, 1771

pay up

Notice by Nathaniel Wales, Jr. of Windhm, that whereas the trade and business carried on by my brother, Seth Wales, for several years passed, has been much in the credit way, by means whereof there are many outstanding debts and accounts open as also sundry sums due by note of hand, in which debts the subscriber has some interest in their being collected, and as my said brother, by reason of his business, cannot without great damage attend the collecting of these deaths, this is to give notice to all whom it may concern that I have taken all his notes and shall be obliged to put them and his book into suit at next June's court in New London County, unless settled before.

new Episcopal office

We hear from Stratford that the Reverend Dr. Johnson has taken a house in that town for the Dean of Limerick whom he expects daily being appointed to inspect into the state of the Episcopal Church on the continent and make return annually from this colony. He is to continue in office for four years. Whether this office is to be established or whether it is only to prepare the way for an American bishop, we do not yet learn but this is evident that the present method of information by the missionaries in their letters to the home society rendered as it highly necessary that there should be some other way than what has been usually practiced for the right information of the Episcopal churches in these colonies and the conduct of their missionaries and the great need they stand in.

twins
     We hear from Saybrook that on the 16th instant, the wife of Mr. Handley Bushnell of that place was delivered of twins, a son and a daughter. The last children she had had before these two were twin daughters who are now in nearing their 11th year. The twins were christened last Sunday and were carried by their twin sisters which is esteemed a singular instance.

          ****

The *New London Gazette,* May 3, 1771

shipping news
     Last Tuesday arrived here in 20 days from St. Kitts. Captain Samuel Chew in a brig belonging to New Haven. He set out from Cape François on the sixth of January lastand ,after being beaten on the coast several weeks and being within a few leagues of Block Island, had the misfortune to carry away the head of his Main mast which together with a very bad leak, occasioned by a violent gale he had in February, obliged him to bear away for the West Indies and he was so fortunate as to get to St. Kitts the last of March after being 83 days at sea, where he stopped the leaks and it is now so as well as he could.

     Captain William Packwood from this port of New London is arrived at St. Lucia.

fire
     East Haddam: Last night happened the most surprising accident here. The dwelling house of Mr. Nathan Fisher was discovered to be on fire about 11 o'clock. He had gone from home earlier that evening and the others in the family, not knowing he had returned. His two sons, asleep in the upper chamber, were suddenly awakened by hearing, somebody calling from below, upon which they immediately jumped out of the chamber window and found the lower part of the house in flames which was soon consumed. Some persons in the morning going to view the rooms found to their great surprise some part of the body of Mr. Fisher that had fallen into the cellar. The remainder had been consumed in the flames. It is generally thought that upon Mr. Fisher's return that evening, he left the fire carelessly or

did not put out the candle which was the occasion of a house taking fire.

theft
   Notice by Adam Shapely that, on the night of the first of May, his shop was broke open and sundry articles stolen.

passage boat
   Notice by James Wiggins, who occupied a passage boat the last year, has since built a large new boat for the same purpose which is well equipped with good sails and rigging and has exceptional accommodations for gentlemen and ladies, having a good fireplace and conveniences for lodging. The passengers may depend on being very comfortable on board; said boat will sail from Sag Harbor to New London every Monday and Friday and return the day following to Sag Harbor, wind and weather permitting. The fare is one dollar for man and horse and three shillings New York currency for a single passenger.
   As the subscriber's circumstances are needy and he having been at great expense to furnish himself to serve the public in this manner, he requests a custom of gentlemen and ladies and passages general who, in return, may depend on the most civil and kind treatment from their obedient humble servant James Wiggins.

   The *Robin* passage boat. Henry Booth, Master, will ply between Long Island and New London weekly; she will sail from Long Island on Thursdays and return from New London on Fridays. The fare is three shillings New York currency for a passenger and one dollar for man and horse.
   Note well: she has good accommodations for gentlemen and ladies.

strayed or stolen
   from Matthew Bircharde living in Norwich a black mare.
         ****

The *New London Gazette,* May 10, 1771

child's death from alcohol
     We hear from Killingly that on Sunday morning last, a child about seven years of age drank freely of a quantity of rum that had been left open and died in the evening.

to be sold
     Two pair of French Burr millstones imported from London in the brig *Four Sisters.* Inquire of Russel Hubbard at his store in New London.

stocking weaving
     These may inform the public that Martin Bauman and Frederick Raughmanen from Germany are carrying on the stocking weaving business in all of its branches at the house of Mr. Aaron Kellog Jr. in Colchester where are all woven breeches and where Westcoats, coarse and fine, fine worsted yarn and linen stockings are for sale.

lost or stolen
     the pocket book of James Angell of New London, containing eight 40 shillings notes of Connecticut currency.

runaway
     from Oliver Walton of Preston, an Indian servant man named Isaac Kaye, also known as Quacheets; 25 years old; 5 feet nine inches high; a stout, well set fellow.
                    ****
The *New London Gazette,* May 17, 1771

theft
     On Monday night the sixth instant, the shop of Daniel Hall was broken into and sundry articles stolen out of the same, including linen and other cloths.

administration of estates
     Any persons who have any just demands on the estate of Colonel Amos Chesebrough, late of Stonington, deceased, are

desired to exhibit their accounts to the undersigned by the 10th day of July next in order for a settlement. All persons indebted to said estate are desired to make payments to me, Samuel Chesebrough, Executor.

All persons having any demand against the estate of Captain John Morgan, late of Groton, deceased, are desired to bring in their accounts for settlement and those indebted to said estate of desired to making me payment to Shapely Morgan, Executor.

All persons indebted to, or that have any demand on, the estate of Mr. Robert Stoddard, late of Groton, deceased, are desired to settle their accounts immediately with Ichabod Stoddard and Mark Stoddard, Executors.

shipping news
For Nova Scotia, a sloop, Moses Pierce, Master, will sail in a few days. For freight or passage agree with the Master at Norwich Landing.

runaway
From Ebenezer Holt of New London, an apprentice boy named Daniel Butler; about 16 years old; large and well set.
****

The *New London Gazette,* May 24, 1771

for sale
The store of Hubbard and Greene at Norwich Landing has for sale cod and mackerel lines and hooks, hemp, seaming twine, powder and shot etc.

strayed
from James Sparrow of East Haddam, a black mare
****

The *New London Gazette,* May 31, 1771

captured
Last Wednesday se'nnight, the thief who broke open Mr.

Daniel Hall's shop, as lately advertised in newspapers, was committed to jail at Norwich. He was taken in Litchfield County and most of the goods with him.

drownings
On Friday the 17th instant, as three men named Elihu Brockway, Mr. Lewis and Mr. Banning were coming down the Connecticut River in a scow deeply loaded with stone, the scow sunk about 3 rods from shore when Brock way and Lewis were drowned, but Banning swam to land.

lightning
Wednesday se'nnight, in a thunderstorm, a horse and seven sheep were killed by lightning at Stonington and the lightning also struck a stack of straw and about 20 trees in different places in that town.

smallpox inoculation
Dr. John Eli of Saybrook has erected a hospital on an island against the west parish of Saybrook, commonly known by the name of Duck Island, in order to carry on inoculation against smallpox and adds that said island is very agreeably situated with a delight some Grove. The doctor being in partnership with Dr. William Colome of New York, a gentleman whose reputation is fully established by his long practice and universal success, is to reside with him at said hospital where there will be every necessary provision to render the operation; said hospital being so contrived as to accommodate both gentlemen and ladies in a very decent manner to the number of 30 or 40 patients at one time; the terms will be so reasonable that the poor as well, as the rich, may be freed from the term up so fatal a disorder.

strayed or stolen
from Titus Hurlbut in New London, a mare.
****

The *New London Gazette*, June 7, 1771

worms
From several parts of the country, we learn about the

considerable damage that has been done to the grass and fruit trees by destructive kind of worms against which the industrial husband and cannot secure his lands. The discovery of an antidote against these devouring insects which frequently do incredible damage is certainly worthy of the attention of every ingenious person.

for sale
      The very best of a New England rum at the Distill House in New London at the moderate price of two shillings per single gallon and cheaper by the quantity.

taken up
      in the enclosure of Jeremiah Ross in New London, North Parish, a bright sorrel mare.

to be sold
      At public venue by Nathan Fordham Jr. two necks of land situated in the manor of St. George's in the Township of Brookhaven on the south side of Long Island in the County of Suffolk containing by estimation 1000 acres with a good dwelling house and barn thereon; between the two necks runs a fine stream on which stands a good gristmill and saw mill; about half a mile below the mills on the stream is a most extraordinary place for fishing where a few months passed upwards of 2000 pounds worth of fish can be taken with seines; and the same being well wooded with an orchard and otherwise under good improvement; also for sale one Negro woman, three Negro boys and a girl; 20 head of cattle. To learn further apply to Mr. Henry Havens. living near the premises.

Susquehanna purchase
      Meeting called by Samuel Gray to the Proprietors of the Susquehanna Purchase that a meeting will be held at Windham.

runaway
      from Thomas Gould of Killingly, one Joseph Thompson; about 20 years old.

****

The *New London Gazette,* June 14, 1771

promotion

We learn that Duncan Stewart, Collector of His Majesty's Customs for the port of New London, is appointed to the honorable Board of Commissioners of His Majesty's Customs in America in the room of John Robinson, who is appointed judge of the court of the Admiralty at Halifax.

died

On Monday last, departed this life, after a distressing illness, the Reverend Joseph Fowler, Pastor of the First Church of Christ in the East Haddam; a person of exemplary piety and disinterested benevolence who live beloved and died lamented. His funeral was attended by a numerous assembly and a sermon was preached by the Reverend Mr. Little of Colchester.

Last Wednesday died at Norwich, Captain John Bowles of Charlestown, Boston.

administration of estates

Notice by the Honorable Judge of Probate for the District of New London the below named individuals appointed Commissioners of the estate of Mr. Demmen Latimer, formerly of Lyme and late of Nova Scotia, deceased and represented to be insolvent, that a meeting will be held at the house of Captain Edward Palmes in New London. Notice given by Jeremiah Chapman, Titus Hurlbut and Nathan Dowglas, Commissioners.

Notice by the Honorable Judge of Probate for the District of New London that the below named individuals appointed Commissioners of the estate of Mr. Reuben Latimer, formerly of Lyme and late of Nova Scotia, deceased and represented to be insolvent, that a meeting will be held at the house of Captain Edward Palmes in New London. Notice given by Jeremiah Chapman Titus Hurlbut and Nathan Douglas, Commissioners.

for sale

at public venue, a good dwelling house and land

adjoining on what is now in the possession of Captain Joseph Ellis. Said house is well situated for tradesman. Any person inclining to purchase may know the terms by applying to us at Sag Harbor: John Foster, David Corwither and Robert Hudson.

do not extend credit
These are to give public notice that I, Nathaniel Woodsworth, do hereby forewarn and forbid all persons from trusting my wife Priscilla Woodworth with any money, goods or chattel. I am be determined not to pay or discharge any debts of her contracting after the date hereof for I have reason from her own mouth and ill conduct to believe she is soon to elope from me and cohabit with another man which she likes better, notwithstanding I have provided the necessaries of life suitable for her and conducted myself agreeable to my duty towards her.

runaway
from Peirpont Bacon of Colchester, a Negro servant man named Archie; about 30 years old; of middling stature and very well set; was born in Africa and is marked with small group of several strokes on one or both cheeks.

****

The *New London Gazette,* June 21, 1771

new laws
Passed at the last General Assembly: an act for the prevention of frauds and perjurers; an act relating to quartering of his Majesty's regular forces in this colony; and an act to prevent the selling or transporting of untanned hides or skins out of this colony.

died
On the fourth instant died at the Windsor, Captain John Talcott.

body found
A few days ago the body of a drowned man was taken up at Rocky Hill in Wethersfield. He had on a pair of double soled shoes, tied with string, a second woolen shirt and had his cap in

his hand.

storm
      A farmer in this town, New London, in a storm of rain on Tuesday night last, lost upwards of 60 sheep that were lately sheared.

bankruptcy notice
      This is to give notice to all creditors to Amasae Jones of Colchester in the County of Hartford, an insolvent debtor, that there will be a meeting of creditors at Captain Dudley Wright's, inn holder in said Colchester. Notice given by Henry Champion and Elias Worthington, Trustees to said estate.

runaway
      From Peter Latimer of New London, an apprentice boy named James Maynard; 19 years old; of dark complexion; has light brown hair and square shoulders.

****

The *New London Gazette,* June 28, 1771

lightning hit at sea
      On the 11th instant, the schooner *Pompey*, Capt. Leeds, sailed from this port (New London) for the West Indies, three days after which the vessel was rocked by lightning which, entering the topmast, ran down and shivered the mast stunned and knocked down every person on board but they happily will recover; it killed seven horses and wounded several others.

died
      at New Haven Mrs. Mary Trowbridge, aged 61, relict of the late Captain Joseph Trowbridge of that town.

runaway
      Notice by Levi Lee regarding runaway from Elisha Lee of Lyme, a boy named Joseph Miner, about 18 years old; short and well set; full faced; something freckled and works at the shoemaker trade.

bankruptcy notice
Notice by Oliver Woolcott, Joseph Trumbull, and Thomas Darling on the petition of William Jepson of Hartford praying to be discharged, shall meet to hear said petition at the house of Captain Hugh Ledley in Hartford.

strayed or stolen
from William Steward in Groton, a brown mare

not responsible
Notice by Jonathan Curtice of Mansfield that his wife Elizabeth has for some time past refused his bed and board and still continues in neglect of her duty. This is to warn all persons from trusting her on my account and hereby declare that I will pay a not one farthing of anything she may contract.

pay up
All persons indebted to the estate of David Hosmer, late of Norwich, deceased, are desired to make speedy payment. Notice by executors Benjamin Huntington of Norwich and Benjamin Converse of Killingly.

shipping news
The ship *London Packet*, now lying at Norwich Landing is bound for London; for freight or passage apply to the master on board.

for sale
Nails just imported and to be sold for cash by Jedediah Huntington; also a variety of other articles.
****
From *The New London Gazette*, July 5, 1771

agricultural news
Ephraim Miner of Stonington had 20 sheep sheared this season; the weight of the wool taken as a whole and weighted in the presence of several gentlemen was 103 pounds, 30 ounces; the lightest fleece weighted 4 pounds 20 ounces, the heaviest 7 pounds.

died
    Yesterday se'nnight, son of William Hillhouse of this town, aged six, died suddenly in a fit.

wanted
    A quantity of bark for which cash will be given by John Baker Brimmer.

farms for sale
    To be sold a farm lying in Lyme containing about 140 acres with a good house, barn and orchard thereon; well wooded; all under improvement and well divided for mowing, pasture and plowing. For further particulars, inquire of Curtis Comstock on said premises.

    A small farm to be sold in East Haddam near the landing containing about 13 acres, well divided for mowing, plowing and pasture land with a good orchard, dwelling house and barn; they are within three quarters of a mile of the Meeting House; for further particulars, inquire of Joseph Gilbartt living on the premises.

runaway
    from Ignatius Barker of Lebanon, an apprentice boy named David Johnson; about 20 years of age; slim make; with dark complexion and black hair.

    from Thomas Np. Niles of Groton, an apprentice boy named Bilade Edwards; about 19 years of age; large and well set; light colored hair and eyes; has a sly; down look; one of his feet scarred occasioned by the cut of an ax.

             ****

From *The New London Gazette,* July 12, 1771

list of letters in the post office at New London

Samuel Avery, Norwich	London
Ebenezer Blaksley, New	Zacceus Beebee, New London

Ichabod Bartlet, Lebanon
Thomas Barber, Groton
Amos Belton, Groton
John Barney, Norwich
Elihu Cheeseborough, Stonington
Asa Champlin, Stonington
Marcy Chapman, New London
Elizabeth Cardwell, New London
Henry Champion, Colchester
Edward Chapel, Groton
David Dougal, Stonington
Nathaniel Deen, Plainfield
Eward Eels, Stonington
John Friend, New London
Joseph Fish, Stonington
Nathaniel Fish, Norwich
Ebenezer Goddard, New London
Joseph Gallup, Groton
Samuel Gilbert, Hebron
William Harris, New London
Joseph Harris, New London
Joseph Harris Jr., New London
Benj. Hodgehden, New London
Doctor Homes, New London
Stephen Jeron, Lyme
Aaron Keane, Groton
John Lord, New London
Freelove Lewis, New London
James Lyons, Norwich
Abner Lee, Lyme
Nathaniel Lane, Jr., Long Island
Nathaniel Miner, Stonington
Nathaniel Matson, Lyme
Amos Parker, Stonington
Cyrus Punderson, Groton
William Stark, New London
Joseph Spencer, East Haddam
David Sprague, New London
Andrew Waterman, New London
Daniel Whitemore, New London
Abner Waters, Norwich
Amos Welles, Colchester
Ann William, Lebanon

whooping cough cure

A recipe to cure the whooping cough. Take Spikenard roots[41]; wipe clean and separated from its woody or inner a part, a small hat crown fall. Add Spring water 1 gallon. Put the roots in the water and boil it away to 3 pints, then strain off the Liquid and press the root dry. To the strained liquid, add of the best sugar and a sufficiently quantity to make a syrup. A dose is two of three spoonfuls, to be taken after the fits of coughing. One quart will cure one person.

runaway
from Alexander McNeill, an apprentice boy named Henry Jones; about 14 years old; of middling size for that age; had sandy hair and light eyes.

****

From *The New London Gazette*, July 19, 1771

wrecked at sea
Last Friday night came to town from Philadelphia, Mr. John Chester of Groton, late mate of the sloop *Fancy*, Captain Richard Hubbard, owned by Mr. Richard Alsop of Middletown, which vessels sailed from this port of New London on the 19th of December last down to the West Indies with with a cargo of horses. On the 25th of the month in a most violent gale of wind, the vessel overset. While they were cutting away the mast, a sea struck the vessel which swept the deck of everything thereon, filled her with water and washed every person overboard, at which time, the Captain and supercargo Mr. Samuel Farnsworth of Hartford and five of the people were all drowned but the mate and two of the hands named - Gilbert and Justus Taylor, both of East Haddam - got on board again and secured themselves on the bowsprit. Three days after this, a schooner hove into sight and beat the whole day to get to them but the wind being small, they at night stood within a mile of each other On the first day of January they were all washed off the bowsprit, when Gilbert was drowned, the other two again secured themselves to the bowsprit and, on the second day of January, Taylor through hunger, fatigue and despair grew delirious. Chester at night secured with a rope but at the next morning, he untied himself while Chester was asleep, falling into the water when the where he was drowned.. About six hours after this, a snow from Philadelphia, Captain Dean, bound to Lisbon was discovered by Chester in a direct course to him, but when he was about a league distance, she tacked and stood from him and after an hour, she tacked and came within a mile. When the snow was again putting about to leave, providentially one of the hands at that instant discovered him. A boat was sent to take him on board. Chester the was so weak that he could not stand for a month and it was owing to kind usage and prudence of Captain Dean, under God, that he

recovered. A great part of his clothes all washed of his back and his flesh much chafed and worn off the day after the vessel foundered. They got a cask of water out of one of the holes which two days after was carried off by a sea. They also got some pieces of pork which floated out of the fore peak.

mad dog

Tuesday last week, a mad dog bit a cow and two hogs in the North parish of this town, but was afterwards killed in attempting to bite a man.

whipping

Last Saturday, one John Harris was convicted of theft by people of the civil authority of Coventry in taking sundry bonds of steel from the shop of Elijah Ripley. He was sentenced to receive 10 stripes. When the sentence was read to him, he made a pained appearance of fainting and fell on the floor, entirely helpless, but being carried out and made fast to the post and finding that his strategy would not prove sufficient to avoid the execution of said sentence, his senses were apparently very quick and lively and his body very active, while the constable was levying his execution.

cure for distemper

A recipe to cure horn distemper in cattle of which many have lately died: Cut the horn off near the head, then take urine and salt it to almost brine and dissolve it in a small piece of blubber and pour it into the horn every day. Keep the horn open that it may discharge a putrid matter. I lately cured an ox in a short time whose head was so rotten that, when I began, the liquor would run directly out of his nostrils.

cash given

for a good live feathers at the London Coffee House in New London.

lost

from Enoch Bolless Jr.'s library, a book entitled the *British Apollo* with the name Edward Robinson written inside.

strayed
    from the pasture of the Mather Peck of Lyme, a dark brown mare,

found
    in the pasture of Amos Latimer in Lyme, three ewes and a ram lamb, all of which are white.

****

From *The New London Gazette*, July 26, 1771

died
    Departed this life on Tuesday the 16th instant, the Reverend Ebenezer Devotion, the first pastor of the Third church in Windham in the 58th year of his age and 36th of his ministry. He lived in good harmony and peace with the church and society; highly esteemed by his acquaintances and his death is greatly lamented.

to be sold
    by Simeon Avery, executor of the estate of Mr. Samuel Chapel late of Groton, deceased, about 3 ½ acres of good mowing land with an orchard thereon, lying about a mile from the London Ferry and near the Meeting House in said Groton.

to be sold
    a strong likely Negro woman, about 36 years old who is acquainted with all kinds of housework. Inquire of the printer.

****

From *The New London Gazette,* August 2, 1771

administration of estates
    Notice by Commissioners Benedam Gallup, Stephen Billing and John Morgan, appointed by Charles Phelps, Judge of the Probate Court of the District of Stonington, to the creditors of the estate of Gideon Avery, late of Groton, deceased and represented insolvent, that a hearing will be held at the house of Captain John Morgan, inn holder in Groton.

farm to be sold

a farm containing a 100 acres of good land with a choice orchard, lying 4 miles and a half from the court house in New London. There is a dwelling house, good barn with a choice well of water on the premises; for further particulars inquire of James Douglas, living on the premises.

shipping news

Last Monday, arrived here Captain William Packwood in 16 days from Trinity in Martinico, which place was very sickly with the diseases of measles and yellow fever; he lost three of his people with the fever, viz, his cooper, Benjamin Philllimore, of Norwich, William Young of this town, New London, and a Frenchman.

****

From *The New London Gazette,* August 9, 1771

died

Last Saturday, died at the parish of Scotland in Windham, Elisha Hurlbut of that parish, Merchant, aged 45 years.

This morning died here, Pomfret with a seorbutic ulcer and leaving his acquaintances to bewail his loss, that excellent man in every social relation, Captain Zechariah Spalding. He was for a number of years one of the select men. He was born in Chelmsford in the Province Massachusetts in October, 1704 and he left that town in the early part of life and came with his father into this place, where he has lived ever since, an honor to his country.

lightning

We hear from Stratford that on Sunday the 16th at the time of divine service, the steeple of the Meeting House in Stratford was struck and much shattered with lightning which at the same time gave a great shock to most of the congregation and struck many of them down, but they all recovered, except John Burr and Mr. David Sherman, who were instantly killed.

The same day, about the same time, at the Meeting House

in New Haven, four horses were struck dead with a flash of lightning, which also knocked down three men, two women and a child but they all happily recovered.

for sale
  Winthrop Saltonstall begs leave to acquaint his customers and others that he has just opened for sale a general assortment of dry goods and ship chandlery at his shot opposite the Ferry Wharf in New London.

  This is to give notice to the public that Moses Yeomans of Colchester and Thomas Smith Sterne, lately of Europe (who lately worked for Mr. Durham in Lebanon) now carry on the clothier business in all branches.
****

From *The New London Gazette,* August 16, 1771

died
  Last Saturday died here in Windham of a nervous fever in the 46th year of his age, Mr. Elisha Hurlbut of this town, merchant. He was for many years been largely industrious and prosperous in business.

stolen or strayed
  from the pasture of Gershom Breed, of Norwich, a mare.

run away
  from Caleb Humaston of Lyme, a Negro man named Boston, formally owned by Mr. Ezra Selden of Lyme; about 25 years of age. He is a short, well built fellow and has had smallpox and has lost one of his fore teeth.
****

From *The New London Gazette,* August 23, 1771

church dedicated
  Trinity Church in Pomfret was dedicated on Friday by the Reverend Mr. Tyler of Norwich. Mr. Peters of Hebron read the prayer and assisted in the solemnity.

christening
last Sunday se'nnight was baptized by the Reverend Mr. Tyler, Polly Walton, daughter of Dr. William Walton. Colonel Godfrey Maibone, his lady and Mrs. Aplin stood sponsors.

smallpox
We hear a number of people in Middletown are now sick of the small pox.

violence in Wyoming
We hear from Wyoming that one John Dick, an Irish fellow, with a party of about 30 ruffians in the night time of the 30th of July last, surprised the Connecticut people at Wyoming by firing on the sentry, one Richard Cook, whom they killed outright, but the Connecticut people rallied and soon dispersed those militants. This is the same John Dick that has been has been a pretended constable this two or three years to worry the Connecticut people with his colleague, or brother constable, one James Logan, a mulatto fellow. Those two have been principally improved under the famous, or rather infamous, Captain Ogden as civil officers. They are perhaps two of the most daring, infamous radicals that the two nations of Ireland and Negro race can afford and it is the same John Dick and James Logan that sometime past broke into the house of one Brink of lower Smithfield on the Delaware River, ravaged his daughter and snapped a pistol at his wife with such surprise, she miscarried. Brink pressed to have justice against them and have them bound over, but they were so useful in murdering and robbing the Connecticut people at Wyoming, they were released and no justice could not be had against them. And they likewise were the same villains that last winter perpetrated the cruelty on the wife of one Partial Tracy. A great evidence of the badness of the Cause is when the vilest of men and measures are made use of to support it, when ,at the same time, the Connecticut people are ready and desire to have settled it in a legal way without difficulty or bloodshed.

died
We hear from Branford that about 10 days ago, as Deacon

Foot of that town was walking from his house to his pasture to catch a horse, finding himself suddenly taken ill, he returned home and just entering the door, told one of his family he felt strangely, when he fell down and expired in an instant.

found
    on the road from New London to Norwich, a gold button; the owner may have it by applying to the printer and paying charges.

shipping news
    The sloop *Dispatch,* lying at Norwich Landing, is bound for Nova Scotia and will sail in about 10 days. For freight or passage, inquire of Moses Pierce at Norwich Landing.

for sale
    Just imported from London via Boston and to be sold in Pomfret, a general assortment of drugs, among which are Hill's Pectora, balsam of honey, Godfrey's Cordial, Dr. Bateman's Pectoral drops, Hooper's Female pills, Anderson's true Scotch Pills and Dr. James's Fever Powders.
    N. B: Practitioners of physic and surgery or private families may be furnished here with the most genuine medicines, cheap for cash or short credit.

    Abiezer Smith, Hatter at his shop opposite Gershom Breed's at Norwich Landing, has for sale for cash or country produce at wholesale or retail, this country manufactured felt hats of all sorts.

****

From *The New London Gazette,* August 31, 1771

strayed or stolen
    from Silas Stark out of a barn in Norwich, a chestnut brown mare; two dollar reward if returned to the subscriber in Colchester or to Mr. Jedidiah Hide in Norwich.

taken up
    by Jonathan Hill of New London as a stray in the North

Parish of New London, a bright bay mare.

died
On the 18th died here and on the same day was respectfully interred, Mrs. Mary Way, wife of Mr. Ebenezer Way of this town (New London), shopkeeper.

administration of estates
Notice by Commissioners Elisha Marvin and Ezra Selden, to the creditors of the estate of Elihu Brock way, late of Lyme deceased and represented insolvent, that a meeting will be held at the house of Captain William Bockway, inn holder in said Lyme.

civic improvements
The Gentlemen Proprietors of the new school house in New London are desired to meet at the London Coffee House on Monday next.

The inhabitants of New Haven are about erecting a market house in that town.

Mt. Vesuvius
From Naples, the volcano at Mt. Vesuvius, having made a new opening, has destroyed many hundreds of acres of land and doom to several individuals.

****

From *The New London Gazette,* September 6, 1771

died
Last Saturday died at Windham, in Scotland parish, minister Jacob Burnet, a person of note in that parish.

Ling fever
We learn that 20 persons are at this time sick of Ling fever in the Scotland Parish in Windham within the compass of three fourths of a mile.

for sale
    Imported in the last ship from London, a great assortment of English and European goods to be sold by Nathaniel Backus Jr.

farm for sale in Groton
    To be sold, a farm, barn, containing about 200 acres of good land lying in Groton about 6 miles from New London ferry and two miles north of the Post road; it has a good dwelling house, 40 x 28 feet, a barn 50 x 30 feet, a wash house and other conveniences; also a good orchard and cider mill thereon; for further particulars inquire of Daniel Lamb living on the premises.

    To be sold about six square rods of land with a dwelling house and cooper's shop thereon situated opposite the dwelling house of Col. Gurdon Saltonstall in New London; for particulars inquire of Colonel Saltonstall in New London or Clement Bishop in Hartford.

strayed or stolen
    from the Jonathan Forsyth of New London North Parish, a large chestnut mare.

taken up
    by David Brown in Groton in a suffering condition, a large horse which is low in the flesh and appears to have been over ridden.

              ****

From *The New London Gazette,* September 13, 1771

shipping news
    Last Friday, Captain George Champlin arrived here in 21 days from Cape Nicola. He left Captains Crocker and Daley of this port (New London) who are to sail in six days. He also left at the Cape, Captains Chew and Welles of New Haven and Jacob Goodwin of Middletown. Benjamin Dennis Jr. of Norwich, who was with Captain Crocker, died a few days before Captain Hamblin left the Cape where it was very sickly.

died
On last Tuesday se'nnight died at Hartford, John Ledyard of that town in the 71st year of his life.

A sloop of which Israel Abbot of the Connecticut River was master, arrived at Cape Nichola from North Carolina. Captain Abbott died on the passage four days before his vessel reached at Cape.

General Assembly
The following gentlemen were chosen representatives for this and the neighboring towns for the next General Assembly:

for New London: Col. Gurdon Saltonstall and William Hillhouse
for Norwich: Benjamin Huntington and Samuel Tracy
for Groton: Nathan Gallup and John Fish
for Preston: John Avery Jr. and Timothy Lester
for Windham: Nathaniel Wales Jr. and Capt. Jabez Huntington
for Lebanon: Major William Williams and Captain Joseph Trumbull
for Canterbury: Col. Jabez Fitch and John Felch
for Pomfret: Ebenezer Williams and Thomas Williams
for Woodstock: Capt Elisha Child and Deacon Jedidiah Morse
for Plainfield: John Dowglass and John Pierce.

river properties for sale
At public auction at the London Coffee House in New London, a very commodious house situated on the river bank in New London, near the Courthouse, now in the occupation of Mr. David Manawaring with a good barn and lot adjoining. Likewise, a shop, wharf, warehouse and bake house all well situated for a gentleman in trade. Inquire of Russell Hubbard at New London or William Hubbard at Norwich.

for sale
To be sold at his store in New London by J. Mumford ozenbriggs and check linen by piece or yard.

land in Lebanon for sale
Two tracts of land lying in Lebanon in the parish of Goshen, the one containing about 48 acres, the other about twelve acres. For particulars inquire of Joseph Green in Boston, Merchant, Mr. William Hubbard of Norwich or and Mr. Russell Hubbard of New London.

sloop for sale
on easy terms, a small sloop burthen about 20 tons. For particulars, apply to Marvin Wait in New London.

Lyme farm for sale
To be sold a farm lying in the East Society of Lyme containing about 40 acres of good land with a dwelling house, barn and orchard thereon. For further particulars, inquire of Elisha Bogue, living on the premises.
****

From *The New London Gazette,* September 20, 1771

died
We hear from Weathersfield that last Wednesday the honorable John Chester of that place died very suddenly with a bit of apolexy.

mackerel
About three or four years ago, a few mackerel was discovered to be in New London harbor and River. They were very small but had every years since been increasing both in size and in quantity. There has been such a plenty of these valuable fish the present year that from 40 to 70 boats had been daily employed below the town catching them. By the best computation that can be made, about 300 barrels have already been counted this season from the first of August to the present time nearly equal in size to those taken in Boston. Last Tuesday, six barrels of these fish were taken in a seine at Norwich Landing.

thunder and lightning storm
By gentlemen from Fairfield, we learn they had the most

severe storm of thunder, lightning and rain have been known in the memory of the oldest inhabitant. The whole atmosphere seemed to be charged with electric fire which continued for almost 4 hours and did considerable damage. The concussion was so great that the houses shook and rocked. So great the tremor that the pewter was thrown off the shelves.

administration of estates
    John Bradford is appointed administrator of the estate of Joseph Willoughby late of New London North parish. All creditors are to attend a hearing at the house of Dr. Seth Holmes in said Parish.

taken up
    by Thomas Morgan in Groton, a dark bay mare
****

From *The New London Gazette,* September 27, 1771

fire
    Sunday the 15th, the dwelling house of Mr. Caleb Stone of Guilford took fire while the family was attending divine service and was entirely consumed with the chief of the furniture and the loss is very considerable.

hailstorms
    Zerubabel Slater returned from a fishing voyage informs us that, while at Gaspe in July, they had a most extraordinary storm of hail, attended with thunder and lightning, which continued about three fourths of an hour. One of the hailstorms stones he measured was 5 inches and a quarter one way around and 6 inches the other. Great numbers of them were of equal size and came with such force as to put the people in the most consternation whether their shelter would be beat down. One man in the boat was knocked down by the hail and stunned before he could get shelter.

Susquehanna Company
    Notice from Eliphalet Dyer and Jedidiah Elderkin to shareholders of the Susquehanna company that matters of

consequence strongly urge their attendance at a scheduled meeting.

passage boat
    This is to inform the public that Clark Truman's passage boat, well equipped and accommodated for passengers, will sail from Sag Harbor to New London every Wednesday, wind and weather permitting and return to Sag Harbor on Thursday.

made and for sale
    by Noah Hidden, all sorts of horn combs. His store is near Jabez Huntington in Norwich. Said Hidden will give pay nine shillings per hundred for good ox bones delivered at his shop.

****

From *The New London Gazette*, October 4, 1771

whipping
    Last week, one John Johnson, alias John Richardson, a transient person, was convicted of burglary before the Superior Court sitting here in breaking into the shop of Mr. Daniel Mall of Norwich and stealing a number of articles and, on Tuesday last, he was publicly whipped fifteen stripes, had one ear cut off and branded on the forehead with the letter "B".

drowning
    Last Wednesday evening, a man fell out of a canoe near Gale's Ferry and was drowned.

Indian talks
    With Captain Winn, who is arrived in New York from London, came a passenger Dr. William Samuel Johnson, late special agent from this colony. We hear the cause between the Mohegan Indians and this colony was not settled when the doctor embarked.

died
    At Millington, Mrs. Arnold, wife of Mr. Enoch Arnold.

    Last Wednesday in Coventry, Mrs. Hannah Huntington,

wife of the Reverend Joseph Huntington of this place. The funeral was attended by a vast concourse of people augmented by many mourning friends from the neighboring towns. A discourse was delivered on the melancholy occasion by the Reverend Samuel Lockwood. She was 28 years old and the second daughter to the late Reverend Mr. Devotion of Windham.

shipping news
These sloop *Delight* is now lying at Norwich Landing and will sail for Annapolis in Nova Scotia on the 20th instant. For freight or passage, inquire of Captain Samuel Doggett on board or of John Cady of Norwich Landing.

please return books
Notice by Ebenezer Devotion, Executor, to all persons having book from the library of the late Reverend Devotion are asked to be kind enough to return them.

taken up
by Ichabod Fitch in Lebanon, a 10-year-old mare
****
From *The New London Gazette*, October 11, 1771

ordination
Yesterday se'nnight, the Reverend Ephraim Judson was ordained pastor of the Church of Christ at Chelsea in Norwich. The Reverend Jabez Wright made the introductory prayer; the Reverend Noah Benedict of Woodberry preached. The Reverend Aaron Kinne read the votes of the church and society respecting the call. The Reverend Benjamin Law prayed and gave the charge; Reverend Abner Rossiter prayed after the charge and the Reverend Levi Hart gave the Right Hand of Fellowship.

whaling
Monday arrived here, (New London) a whaling schooner, Captain Pease of Providence, with 180 barrels of oil.

We hear a whaling sloop is arrived at Stonington dismasted.

wanted
At the distillery in New London, 150 cord of straight saddle oak wood for which cash shall be given upon delivery.

administration of estates
Notice by Commissioners John Lyman and Jonathan Trumbull Jun., appointed by Probate Court in Windham, to the creditors of the estate of Moses Waters, late of Lebanon, deceased and represented insolvent, that a hearing to examine claims will be held at the dwelling of Mrs. Alden, inn holder in said Lebanon.

lost
in New London, near Hogs Neck, a pillow bier containing in it one pound of tea, tied in a checked homespun handkerchief, half a yard of black Persian and a small quantity of black thread. The person who lost the same is a poor widow living in Lyme who has five children and an aged mother to provide for. Whoever has found such is requested to leave them with the printer here.

strayed
from Benjamin Malleson in New London, a bluish colored pig, half guinea breed.
****
From *The New London Gazette*, October 18, 1771

man missing
A young man named Hitchcock, an apprentice to Dr. Benjamin Chapin of Southampton on Long Island, being on his return from a journey to the North part of this colony, he on last Tuesday put up that Captain Leffingwell's Tavern in Norwich and Thursday, after he walked into the fields and across some woods to the house of Mr. Gifford about 2 miles West of the said Leffingwell's. It being rainy, dark weather and the young man unwell and the as the sun was about to set, he asked for entertainment till the next day but Mrs. Gifford being sick, he was told they could not entertain him. Whereupon he set out with the intention to return to Captain Leffingwell's but has never

been seen or heard from since though the woods and fields for several miles round have been diligently searched by hundreds of people.

shipping news
Last Monday of the Spanish ship an anchor off Block Island came up to our harbor (New London) in order to refit. She is not a galleon as mentioned but a merchant man burthened about 400 tons and laden with sugar. She was in route from Havana to Cadiz in Spain but met with a violent storm the 22nd of September when she lost her mast and suffered considerable damage to her hull.

Since our last Captain Joseph Powell is arrived here from the West Indies. On the 22nd of September in a gale of wind they shipped a sea, which washed the Captain and Mr. Zaccheus Wheeler Jr. of this town (New London) overboard. The Captain would difficulty regained the vessel but Wheeler was unfortunately drowned.

Last Wednesday, a Negro man longing to Mr. Nathaniel Shaw Jr. of this town (New London) fell out of Captain Chappel's vessel in a passage from New York and was drowned.

Since our last, Captain Cotton, bound to this port from the West Indies in a brig belonging to Middletown, was cast away on Narragansett beach. Vessel and cargo lost.

for sale
Notice that Caleb Allen, brazier, of Boston has lately opening his shop in Norwich landing near the meeting house. Any gentlemen pleased to favor him may depend on their orders being duly and carefully executed with alacrity and fidelity.

administration of estates
Notice by Commissioners Joshua West and Simeon Gray to the creditors of the estate of John Baldwin, late of Lebanon, deceased and represented to be insolvent, that a hearing will be held at the house of Mrs. Elizabeth Alden in said Lebanon.

****

From *The New London Gazette,* October 25, 1771.

shipping news

On August 20 last, Captain David Packwood sailed from this port (New London) bound to Martinico and, on the 9th of September at five p.m., he met with a violent hurricane, when the vessel was overset and lay on her beam ends for fifteen minutes in which time the on deck cargo of 46 horses and oxen and almost every item was washed off the deck and the main mast carried away below the deck. At eight p.m., the vessel was overset again and the foremast carried off ten feet above the deck. At 10 p.m. they shipped a sea which drove in 17 of the top timbers and the next day a sea stove in the Dead Lights and filled the steerage with water. On the $12^{th,}$ they spoke to a ship bound for the Isle of Mann, Captain John George, which gave them sundry articles they were in need of. The same day they spoke with a Spanish Man of War, which had lost its main mast mizzen sail and rudder. On the 23rd of September, they had another gale and on the same day met with Captain McAlpine in the ship *St. George* bound from Bristol to South Carolina, who took the crew on board. They left the brig with seven feet of water in her hull.

Capt. Kellogg, who arrived here last week from the Turks Island, spoke with Captain Friend who told him that, after the hurricane, he spoke with Captain Richards in a sloop from Norwich who was under jury masts and bound for New Providence to refit.

elections

The following gentleman we learn are nominated for election next May

Johnathan Trumbull	William Fitkin
Matthew Griswold	Roger Sherman
Hezekiah Huntington	Robert Walker
Shubel Coneant	Abraham Davenport
Elisha Sheldon	William Samuel Johnson
Jabez Huntington	Joseph Spencer

Oliver Wolcott
Hon Thomas Fitch
Ebenezer Silliman
Gurdon Saltonstall
Jabez Hamlin

James Abraham Hillhouse
Daniel Sherman
Eliphalet Dyer

for sale
    A small assortment of ship chandlery; also rum, sugar and molasses to be sold by David Gardiner Jun. at his shop near the Courthouse in New London; he gives cash for beeswax, small furs and ox horns.

strayed or stolen
    from the pasture of Jeremiah Ross, four heifers
                  ****

From *The New London Gazette*, November 1, 1771

day of thanksgiving
    The 15th instant is appointed to be observed as a general day of thanksgiving through the colony.

accident
    One day last week, a boy named Miner, about 11 years old in attempting to lift the water gate at Mr. Treadway's grist mill at Colchester fell into the trough and went under the water wheel, which put an end to his life.

shipping news
    A sloop from the West Indies, belonging to New Haven, spoke with Capt. William Powers in a sloop from this port, New London, bound for North Carolina, who had been in a gale of wind and lost most of his sails, both cables, boat, etc and was very leaky.

whaling
    Wednesday arrived Captain Pease from whaling with 90 barrels of oil.

for sale
    to be sold in New London, 900 Spanish hides to be put up 100 in a lot; enquire of Nathaniel Shaw Jr.

    Samuel Belden just received a load of European goods, suitable for the season, to be sold at his shop next door to the Courthouse.

    John MClarren Breed at his store at Chelsea in Norwich has sundry articles for sale upon the most reasonable terms for cash or country produce.

help wanted
    at the stocking manufactory in Norwich, two or three likely boys from 12 to fourteen years of age as apprentices to that business. Inquire of Christopher Leffingwell.

stolen
    out of the shop of Walter Hyde of Lebanon, sundry pieces of cloth.

run away
    from Zechariah Becknell of Ashford, an apprenticed lad named Daniel Ruste. He is short and thickset.

died
    Saturday se'nnight, departed this life, Madame Sara Raymond, relict of Joshua Raymond, in the 71st year of her age. She had been in a declining state of health for some time, yet was able on the Sabbath before her death, to attend public worship, both parts of the day. She retained the reason to the end and enjoyed tranquility under the apprehension of the last.
                    ****

From *The New London Gazette*, November 8, 1771

for sale
    John B. Brimmer informs his customers he just received a further supply of fall goods all of which will be sold extremely cheap, for cash or country produce such as beef, pork, wheat, rye,

corn and oats; also rock salt to be exchanged for flax seed; cash given for bees wax, old pewter and brass.

dissolution
Notice that the co partnership of Ripley and Carey of Norwich is dissolved.

anniversary
Eight years have expired since the publication of *The New London Gazette*

child identified
The child who was left at a tavern in Farmington, as mentioned in our last, we hear belongs to New Haven and the unnatural mother is the wife of one Benjamin Osborn.

health of Danbury
We are credibly informed in the parish of Danbury in this colony, where there are 1200 souls, it has been so remarkably health, that only one person has died in the parish in the last 13 months and that an old Negro.

accident
One evening last week, a man who was going with a team from Mansfield to Norwich, improvidently rode on the tongue of the cart where he soon fell asleep and dropped to the ground, but providentially the wheels passed on each side of him and he was unhurt, although in eminent danger as the cart had near a ton of weight in it. It is strange that the frequent instances of people being killed by carts running over them should not make others more cautious.

married
Christopher Christophers of this town, New London, Mrs. Elizabeth Andrew, widow of Samuel Andrew of Milford.

house for sale
to be sold house where Joseph Chew now lives, about two acres of land, the great part of which is improved with very

good gardens containing a variety of the best English and American fruit. The house is very well finished; there is a good warehouse, barn, stable, smokehouse and other outbuildings very convenient. The situation is on the water and as pleasant as any in New London. For terms apply to Charles Ward Apthorp in New York or Joseph Chew in New London.

administration of estates
Notice by Phineas Stanton, Samuel Mason the 2d and Alexander Bradford, Commissioners appointed by Probate Court to the creditors of the estate of Amos Cheesebrough of Stonington, deceased and represented to insolvent, that a hearing will be held at John Denison, innholder at Stonington Harbor.

****

From *The New London Gazette*, November 15, 1771

for sale
Sundry items to be sold by Joseph Gale at his shop near the Rev. Mr. Lord's Meeting House in Norwich.

turned up
in Samuel Leffingwell's pasture in Norwich, North Plain, one red steer.

list of letters in New London Post office

Martin Boughman, Colchester
Enoch Bolles, Sen., New London
Asa Bullan, Groton
John McCundy, New London
John Carsey, Colchester
Nathan Dean, Plainfield
John Dart, New London
Goerge Dolbeare, New London
Samuel Denimore, Lebanon
Leonard Dussel, Norwich
Samuel Dawson, Lebanon
Nathaniel Fish, Norwich
Joseph Feribaul, New London
Ebenezer Goddard, New London
Richard Groves, New London
Sarah Gould, New London
Aaron Keane, Groton
Nathaniel Miner, Stonington
Josiah Morris, New London

Rev. Samson Occom, Mohegan
William Potter, New London
Jabish Palmer, New London
Cyrus Punderson, Groton
Eliakim Raymond, Norwich
Cornelius Read, Saybrook
Nathaniel Stone, Stonington
William Williams, Stonington

shipping
    Last Tuesday arrived here, Capt. Daniel Starr in 28 days from Guadalupe. He had sundry hard gales and much bad weather in his passage.

hay harvest
    We are credibly informed that William Johnson of Canterbury in the County of Windham, during the last season, cut 19 tons of hay off three acres and a100 rods of ground.

whaling
    By a whaleman from Davis Straits, we learn that, about the first of June last, a Dutch whaling ship of about 500 tons was destroyed there by means of a mountain of ice, which she was near, breaking from the top and falling upon her, but the people were taken up and saved by a fleet in company.
    ****
From *The New London Gazette*, November 22, 1771

found
    On the North Shore of Long Island at Oyster Pond, an old long boat. Owner may have it back by applying to Eleaser Truman of Oyster Pond or Clark Truman.

houses in New London for sale
    To be sold by Mary Harris, Executrix of the estate of Richard Harris, a dwelling house or store and several rods of land near the beach in New London and next door to Mr. Nathan Baley; also a dwelling house and wharf opposite the house of Samuel Latimer.

for sale
 Lucy Gaylord, widow, has for sale at a store next to the printing Office, the best white chappel needles, pins, thread, tape, boltea tea, snuff, tobacco, pipes, candles, Penny Royal Waters, the best New York butter biscuits, bread etc.
Note Well. She also keeps a school for reading and sewing.[42]

stolen
 from Richard Skinner of Glassenbury, a light mare.

 from the pasture of Greene Hungerford of East Haddam, a brown mare.

notice f bankruptcy
 Notice by Trustees Richard Law and Theophilus Morgan to the creditors of the estate of Joseph Chew of New London, insolvent debtor, that a meeting will be held at the house of Edwards Palmes, inn holder in New London.

clothes cleaning
 William Hill, clothier in the North Parish of New London, advises his patrons that he has lately employed a workman from London who revives scarlet and other colors when defaced; removes spots for silks of all sorts and presses silk gowns.

administration of estates
 Notice by Commissioners Abraham Fitch, Samuel Williams, Silas Phelps, appointed by the Probate Court of Windham, to the creditors of the estate of Abel Buel Jr. of Lebanon, deceased and represented to be insolvent, that a meeting will be held at the house of Mrs. Elizabeth Alden, inn holder in Lebanon.

to be sold
 the hull of a likely new sloop, just off the stocks, burthen about 24 tons, well calculated for freighting, fishing or trading; now lying at the head of the Niantic River; for further particulars, apply to Eliphalet Beebe at the head of said river.

died
 Last Friday se'nnight, died at Guilford, Nathaniel Hill, a representative of said town and a justice of the Quorum[43] of the County of New Haven.

****

From *The New London Gazette*, November 29, 1771

accident
 Pomfret: Last Monday, the following event happened here as one Daniel Cloud, who had been involved in building the new Meeting House in town, was ascending the tower of the steeple within side (which is quite open to the bottom, being near the top) he slipped on a round piece of timber on which he stood as he was endeavoring to reach another stick above him and fell about some 50 feet with his side against some joyce which were fixed to lay the lower floor on. He was taken up immediately and brought to a house nearby where the best means were used for his recovery but without success. He continued in great pain until about 2 o'clock in the morning and then expired, having the employment of his reason the whole time. He left a widow and four young children to lament his death.

theft
 Last Saturday the shop of Wintrop Saltonstall was broken into and robbed of a considerable amount of European goods. The person who committed the robbery early next morning procured a boat and went off with the goods to Long Island where it is hoped he will be taken.

taken up
 by James Chapman of New London, a heifer.

****

From *The New London Gazette*, December 6, 1771

thief caught
 Last Friday, the thief who had broken into Winthrop Saltonstall's store was brought to town from Long Island where he had disposed of all the goods. He appears to be an old offender by having both of his ears cropped.

runaways
     from William Stewart of New London, an Indian servant about 19 years of age, named Warren Tatson, a lusty, well built fellow.

     from Eleazer Huntington of Mansfield an apprentice boy named Benjamin Bugbee, aged about 18; a short, thick set fellow; has light brown hair cut shorts; has holes bored in his ears.

chocolate for sale
     at Christopher Leffingwell makes and sells chocolate by the quantity at his shop in Norwich.
              ****
From *The New London Gazette*, December 13, 1771

alcohol
     Perhaps nothing is stronger proof of the general infelicity of life and the propensity of mankind in all countries and situations to drunkenness. Drunkenness does nothing more than to suspend the sense of our real condition for a short interval, yet this delusion is so sweet that it is indulged in at the risk of Fortune, Health, Life and Reputation. We have therefore contrived a great variety of names and short phrases, most of them whimsical and ludicrous, to battle a turpitude, pleasing in itself. I believe few people are aware how far this has been carried or have any notion that the simple high gear of having drank too much like is expressed to in more than four score different ways.
     I send you a list of them for the amusement to of the readers of your magazine.
              I am your humble servant
                   T. Norworth

	5 rocky
1.drunk	6.tipsy
2 intoxicated.	7.merry
3.fuddled	8. half seas over
4.flustered	9. as great as a lord

10. in for it
11. happy
12. boozy
13. top-heavy
14. chuck full
15. hockey
16. hiccins, probably from hiccuping
17. crop sick
18. cup stricken
19. cup sprung. This is said to be the favorite state and expression of a great genius who is at present Porter to University College, Oxford
20. hot headed
21. switchery
22. pot valiant
23. swipey
24. Maudlin, from Magdalen the Penitent who is always remembered as weeping in which she is resembled by those "who drink till the liquor flows out of their eyes."
24. a little "how came ye so."
25. groggy. This is a West Indies expression, rum and water without sugar being called Grog.

27. in drink
28. in his cups
29. in his beer
30. crank. This is a sea phrase. A ship is said to be crank when by excess of lading or some other cause she is liable to be overset.
31. cut
32. cheery
33. cherry maker
34. overtaken
35. elevated
36. forward
37. crooked
38. castaway, a sea phrase for being dead drunk
39. concerned
40. bosky
41. in his altitudes
42. Tipperary, probably from being likely to tip or fall down.
43. topsy frizzy
44. exhilarated
45. on a merry pin
46. half cocked
47. a little in the suds
48. as wise as Solomon
49. over the bay
50. jolly

It is often said that he:

51. has business on both sides of the way
52. got his hat on

53. bunged his eye
54. get a drop in his eye
55. been in the sun

56. soaked his face
57. come home by the villages. This is provincial. When a man comes home by the fields, he meets nobody; consequently he is sober; when he comes home by the villages, he calls first at one house, then another and drinks at all.
58. got a spur in his head. This is said by brother Jackies of each other.
59. Got a crumb in his beard
60. had a little
61. had enough
62. got more than he can carry
63. got his beer on board
64. got glass eyes
65. Been among the Philistines, a pun upon the word "fill".
66. lost his legs
67. been in a storm, a sea phrase for being less than dead drunk.
68 been in the Crown Office, a pun upon the word crown being used for the head.
69. got his nightcap on
70. got his skin full
71. got his dose
72. had a cup too much

Besides these modes of expressing drunkenness, the following express it by what he does:

73. clips the King's English, i.e. does not speak plain
74. heels and sets, a sea phrase used of a boat in a rough sea.
75. heels a bit
76. shows his hob nails. This is a provincial phrase for being so drunk as to be unable to stand so that the nails at the bottom of his shoes are seen.
77. looks as if he could not help
78. crooks his elbow
79. goes over th tops of trees. This is provincial and alludes to the unequal pace of a drunken man, like that of stepping from a high tree to a low one and from a low one to a high one.
80. makes a Virginia fence

To these mut be added phrases that expresses drunkenness by what a man cannot do; it is said by the sons of science at Oxford that a man in ebrious circumstance was :

81. as drunk as the Devil
82. as drunk as a piper
83. as drunk as an owl
84. as drunk as David's sow
85. as drunk as a lord

86. as fuddled as an ape
87. as merry as a Gregg
88. as happy as a king

married
    at Norwich, Mr. Joshua Huntington, son of Col. Jabez Huntington to Miss Hannah Huntington, daughter of Col. Hezekiah Huntington.

lost
    by Zedediah Bolles of New London, lost out of his pocket between Norwich West Farms and Stoddard Ferry, near Massapeauge, eight 40 shilling bills.
    ****

From *The New London Gazette*, December 20, 1771

shipwreck
    In the snow storm the 5th instant, a small vessel, Captain Hatchet from Lyme, bound to New York, was drove on the north shore of Long Island; the vessel and cargo lost but the people (who were three miles from a house), with great difficulty, saved their lives.

    We also learn that a brig and sloop were cast away on Long Island in the same storm. The brig was from Liverpool bound for Guilford, where she was owned. The sloop we hear was from Rhode Island, bound for this port, Capt. Gibbets Perkins, Master.

election
    At a town meeting held in New London Monday last, the following gentlemen were chosen selectmen for the ensuing year: John Richards; William Coit, Capt. John Deshon, John Brown and Capt. Jeremiah Tabor.

married
Mr. Silas Church Jr. to Miss Rebecca Palmes, daughter of Captain Edward Palmes.

died
Mrs. Sarah Rogers wife of William Rogers.

for sale
by Joseph Howland at Hubbard & Greene at Norwich Landing, an assortment of English and hardware goods; also an assortment of very genteel looking glasses.

runaway
from Daniel Diggs of East Haddam, an apprentice boy, 19 years of age; a short thick fellow, named Joel Beebee.

****

From *The New London Gazette*, December 27, 1771

shipwrecks
In the snow storm the fifth instant, Capt. Chappel in a schooner from this port (New London), bound to New York, was cast away on Long Island. The vessel is lost, but the people and cargo are saved.

In our last, we mentioned the loss of Captain Perkin's sloop on Long Island. We have since learned that after the captain and people got on shore (it being extremely dark and stormy) they could not find a house and were obliged to shelter themselves under rocks etc. as best they could. But notwithstanding all the pains they took, a lad about 17 years of age, named Michael Carey was frozen to death in the peoples' arms; the captain and another man were also much frozen.

It is learned that several other vessels were cast ashore on Long Island in the same storm but we have not learned who they were.

watch out
Sundry counterfeit New Jersey and New York bills have

been put off in this town which should make people cautious how they receive such bills; the print on the counterfeit bills is badly done; as well as the signers names; the paper is soft and flimsy.

married
    Mr. Daniel Richards to Miss Mary Palmes, daughter of Captain Edward Palmes.

pay up
    All persons who are debtors or creditors to the estate of Elijah and Peter Peck, both of Lyme, deceased, should bring in their accounts to Jediiah Peck, Administrator, in Lyme.

strayed or stolen
    from the pasture of Gillam Philips of Pomfret, a brown colt.

runaway
    from Amos Robinson of Lebanon, an apprentice boy named Nathan Gambell; about 19 years old; has short black curled hair; it is believed he took certain items of value from Robinson's shop as they were missed soon after.

found
    on the road from Norwich to New London by Jonathan Smith, some money, a pair of mens' mittens and a handkerchief.

to be sold
    by Samuel Tiley on board the Sloop *Clarissa*, lying at Higgin's at Lyme, good West Indies and New England rum by the hogshead or barrel for cash only.
N. B. Said rum may be had of Noah Miller Jr. on said sloop.
****

1772

From *The New London Gazette,* January 3, 1772

shipping news

Last Wednesday arrived here (New London), the ship *London Packet,* Captain Chester, from London which he left on the 27th of September and that has had 11 weeks passage.

Wednesday night, Captain Chester's ship took fire by means of a candle being left and in a few minutes, was past recovery, had not some people from shore along with the hands on board who happily extinguished it.

sudden deaths

Last Friday Captain Throop of Lebanon, having been out, as usual upon returning home, he sat down in a chair, soon after complained of being unwell, and immediately thereon expired.

About a month before the above, Mr. Comfort Brewster died in the same town as sudden. Having gone outside his door to bring in some wood, he returned to his house and fell down on the floor and died instantly.

pay up

Notice by Joseph Ayer that all persons indebted to the estate of Timothy Ayer, late of Norwich, deceased, are desired to makes the payment owed and to submit old demands against the estate.

****

From *The New London Gazette,* January 10, 1772

shipwreck

Last Tuesday came in to Stonington harbor, a sloop, Captain Lilley, owned by Mr. Jasper Griffing of Guilford. The Sunday before, the sloop was anchored at Block Island and was drove on shore on that island, suffered considerable damage, lost both anchors and had to cargo taken on shore. After getting the vessel off again, the Mate brought her into Stonington as above without anchor or any ballast on board.

died
at Hartford, Mrs. Susanna Jepson, wife of Dr. William Jepson.

list of letters at New London
Oliver Budington, Stonington
Stephen Chalker, Saybrook
Jared Crandal, Stonington
Elisha Edgerton, Norwich, West Farms
Christopher Ellis, Groton
Eleanor Henry, Lebanon
Robert Hall, New London
Nathan Kempels, Pomfret
Samuel Lord, Lyme
Joseph Noyes, Stonington
Samson Occum, Mohegan
James Peters, Goshen
Jeremiah Philips, New London
Eliakim Raymond, Norwich
Timothy Tiffany, Lyme
Amos Weeks, New London
Henry Wall, Stonington

****

From *The New London Gazette,* January 17, 1772

died
Last Tuesday sen night, died at Stratford in the 76th year of his life, the Reverend Samuel Johnson, missionary from the Society for Propagating the Gospel in Foreign Parts and late President of New York College.

Last Tuesday, died here very suddenly aged 36 years, Mr. Daniel Whittenmore, for many years a noted tailor in this town.

In Preston this day died, the widow Ruth Forbes. She was in the 72nd year of her life and was a person of unblemished character. Her husband, John Forbes, died in the year 1739 from which times since she lived a widow.

accident
Last Wednesday evening, Uriah Chester of Groton fell through the ice in the shipyard in this town (New London) and was drowned. His body was found and conveyed to Groton.

to be sold
   at public venue by the order are of the Court of Probate for the District of Windham, all the real and personal estate of Captain Azel Fitch, late of Lebanon deceased. Said sale is to be at the house of Mr. Steve in Rogers in Lebanon; notice given by Eleazer Fitch, Administrator.

   Samuel Noyes, jeweler, at his shop near the Meeting House in Norwich Landing has for sale, on the lowest terms for cash, gold shoe and knee buckles.

wanted
   a likely boy as an apprentice to the goldsmith's business, about 12 years old
   ****
From *The New London Gazette,* January 24, 1772

found
   on board the ship *London Packet*, lying at New London, a silver spoon. Inquire of printer.

to be sold
   Just published and to be sold by T. Green Ames Almanac for 1772.

taken up
   a small longboat, with two oars. Apply to Paul Burrows of Groton.
   ****
From *The New London Gazette,* January 31, 1772

administration of estates
   All persons having demands on the estate of Mr. John Stodder, late of Groton, deceased, are desired to bring their accounts to M. Stodder for payment.

died
   Last Friday morning, died at Middletown very suddenly, Mrs. Lydia Bull, wife of Mr. Samuel Bull of that place and

daughter of Capt. Gleason, late deceased.

Tuesday died Mrs. Saufley, widow of Captain Nathaniel Saufley, aged 93 years.

agricultural news
We hear from Plum Island that horticulture is carried out there with good success by Dr. Abner Barber.

just imported
by Jedidiah Huntingon and to be sold at his shop in Norwich, clothes and hats, school books and a variety of paper hangings.

stolen
from John Fox's store in Groton, assorted clothing.

for sale
All sorts of bone and other combs, made and sold by Noah Hidden at his shop in Norwich Landing, near Jabez Huntington's store.
****
From *The New London Gazette,* February 7, 1772

died
Last Saturday died here in New London, Mrs. Mary Drew and, on Wednesday, died John Drew, husband and wife.

for sale
Advertisement for the shop of John Champlin, Goldsmith in New London. Business carried on in its several branches, clock and watch making, mending and cleaning in the very best manner.

From Jabez Avery, chair maker, in Norwich, an apprentice boy named Peter Latham; about 5 feet and 9 inches high.

To be sold at public venue by the order of the Court of

Probate district of Windham, the personal estate of Moses Waters late of Lebanon at the dwelling house of Captain Ephraim Carpenter in Lebanon. Notice given by Jacob Waters, Administrator, in Mansfield.

strayed
  from Jonathan Nobles, a one-year old steer in Norwich Great Plain.

lottery
  Notice is hereby given that a lottery for the roofing of the church steeple in Providence town and of the purchase of a clock of the church in Providence town, is to be drawn during the middle of March. Tickets at two dollars a piece are with the Reverend Mr. Graves in New London.

      ****

From *The New London Gazette,* February 14, 1772

accident
  On Wednesday se'nnight, a Mr. Moses of Groton died in going out of a swamp in town with a burden of wood upon his back, he fell upon some thing and drowned, leaving a widow and five children.

crime
  The adjourned County Court for the County of New London concluded its business at Norwich on Wednesday last without the trial of so much as one jury trial, a circumstance that seldom happens.

fire
  Last Friday, the dwelling house of Mr. William Huntly of Lyme took fire and was entirely consumed, together with almost all of the furniture. Mr. Huntley was so terribly burned that his recovery is doubtful.

died
  in New London, Mr. William Hill, clothier.

to be sold
at public vendue, the Old Court House in the town of New London. Said sale is to be at the house of Captain Edward Palmes in said New London by the order of Daniel Coit, Clerk of the Court.

****

From *The New London Gazette,* February 21, 1772

fire
Last Saturday about one o'clock in the morning, the dwelling house of Mr. Edward Rockwell of Middletown took fire and was entirely consumed, together with all the household furniture, clothes etc. which was very valuable. The family narrowly escaped by jumping out of the windows. Mr. Rockwell was considerably burned in getting out of the house.

Susquehanna Company
Notice of a meeting in Wyndham of the Proprietors of the Susquehanna Company, given by Eliphalet Dyer, Jed. Elderkin, Samuel Gray, Ebenezert Baldwin and Gershom Breed.

stolen
from John Tainter of Colchester at the house of Mr. David Bull, of Inn holder in Hartford, a bright sorrel horse.

****

From *The New London Gazette,* February 28, 1772

shipping
Yesterday se'nnight Captain Buckland of Hartford arrived here in a sloop from the West Indies and on Tuesday last the sloop was left to the care of the mate and a pilot to be carried into the Connecticut River. She arrived at Saybrook the same evening when the pilot and hands went on shore leaving the mate and a boy on board. The vessel, an hour or two after, drove out of the river, it is supposed, by means of the ice and was forced to sea. She has not since been heard of.

flooding
Last Friday morning, the greatest freshet at Norwich

Landing that has been known for 30 years past occasioned by sudden thaw and the breaking up of Shetucket River. The rise of the water was so sudden that there was not time to secure but a small part of the goods which were exposed. Upwards of 5000 bushels of salt, a large quantity of sugars and other West Indies goods; also European goods to considerable amount lost. The town has sustained damages in its bridges this season and it is said that town has set up 3000 pounds in damages.

ship seizure

We hear about 10 days ago, a schooner from this place, New London, Crowell, Master, was seized at Boston under the pretense of having eight hogshead of sugar on board which had not cleared at the Custom House in this port.

married

John Stille, miller, to Miss Henrietta Saltonstall.

died

Mr. Samuel Turner of the North parish.

for sale

By Jedidiah Huntington, large English clover seed and many sorts of garden seed.

runaway

from William Jacks of Voluntown last Monday night, a Negro man servant named Abraham; about 16 or 17 years old; is tall and large for his age; was lately the property of Joseph Hurlbut Jr. of New London; straight limbed and well built.

theft

Notice by Joseph Peck of Norwich that a small Negro man stole out of his house a beaver hat and a black Barcelona handkerchief.

farm for sale in Norwich

To be sold or let on reasonable terms, about 35 acres of land lying in Norwich in the parish of Newent, together with a good house and barn, lying on a public road and convenient to carrying on the clothing is business; also a shop and utensils all in good order, having a stream of water near the same. For further particulars, inquire of Benjamin Kennedy living on the premises

****

From *The New London Gazette*, March 6, 1772

tax foreclosure
    To be sold by agents for the town of Stonington, Thomas Prentice and Benjamin Clark, for back taxes a farm lying in the center of said town, 170 acres of good meadows and pasture and' well wooded and watered with a dwelling house, barn and corn house thereon, with a good orchard that made 80 barrels of cider last year.

taken up
    Notice by David Gardiner, Jr. two anchors were taken up by John Smith on the west side of Gardiner's Point.

theft
    Last Friday night, the cabin of the Brig *Nancy*, Captain Champlin, was broken into at Shaw's Wharf and some wearing apparel belonging to the Captain taken.
    On the same night, Harris' sloop, lying at the same wharf, was broken open; also one of the New York Packet boats.

for sale
    Choice brick, made and sold by Rufus Tuthill on Plum Island for 3 dollars per thousand.

    About 10,000 pound of perch, drawn this day by Norwich Landing, are to be sold by Jonathan Story, near said landing and by William Wheeler, near Stoddard's ferry.

small pox inoculation
    John Ely and Elisha Ely have built an addition at the hospital on Duck Island for those who wish to be inoculated with the small pox.

for sale
A large new dwelling house, neatly finished, and a new barn with a large garden and excellent well of water with a pump very convenient to the house and garden; another lot with a blacksmith and gunsmith shop thereon and a set of blacksmith's tools, all on Ferry Road north of the Courthouse and church; for further particulars, inquire of Nathan Bailey

****

From *The New London Gazette*, March 13, 1772

rescue
Last Thursday evening, as a man named Gidron Jones of Hebron was passing a river that was full of ice and dangerous, he fell from his horse into the river and drifted about ten rods down stream where he caught hold of a tree, but the water rising faster, climbed up and was obliged to remain in the tree a quarter mile from his house through the whole night, although very stormy. A number of persons came to the river but could offer him no assistance until the next day when by means of ropes they got him ashore.

pay up
All those indebted to Jonathan Fitch of New Haven are requested to settle accounts.

All those indebted to the estate of Jonathan Lambert of Canterbury, deceased, should pay administrator Thomas Adams.

land for sale
A piece of land with house in Plainfield, lying on the road by the North Meeting House; by Timothy Pierce.

died
At Canterbury, after about 24 hours of a throat disorder called "the rattler" George Foster, son of Mr. Daniel Foster, a very promising child of four years old who exceeded most. The Rev John Fuller of Plainfield preached the sermon.

wanted
David Manwaring of New London wants to buy two and half and two inch white oak plank.

newspaper renewals
Notice by Bushnell and Amos to those subscribers to *The New London Gazette* at Preston that their year subscription is completed and they should settle accounts and give notice of their plans for the coming year.

reading and needle point teacher
Elizabeth Hern hereby informs the public that she is to teach reading and all sorts of needle work - i.e working of pocketbooks and samplers; also wax work and how to paint on glass.

runaway
from Thomas Strong of Lebanon, an apprentice John Calkins, 16 years of age; small for his age; clear, light complexion; light blue eyes and light brown hair.
****
From *The New London Gazette*, March 20, 1772

pay up
Notice by Silas Church of New London that he wants to withdraw from trade and want all to settle up.

Delaware Companies
Notice by Jabez Fitch, Isaac Tracy and Elisha Tracy to shareholders of the First and Second Delaware Companies to meet at house of Azariah Lathrop in Norwich to discuss sundry important matters about their land.

ordination
The Rev. James Cogswell was installed in the parish of Scotland in Windham; the Rev. Mr. Huntington opened the business of the day; the Rev. Mr. Throop preached the sermon; the Rev. Mr. Ripley made the prayer before the charge; the Rev. Mr. White gave the Charge; The Rev. Mr. Devotion made the

last prayer; and the Rev. Mr. Whitney gave the Right Hand of Fellowship.

died
at Norwich, Elizabeth Rogers, wife of Zabadiah Rogers and daughter of Isaac Tracy.

****

From *The New London Gazette*, March 27, 1772

jail break
We hear that John Brown who is under a sentence of death for burglary about 3 weeks ago, broke out of Lichfield goal and made his escape.

burglary
Last Wednesday, a villain broke into the store of Nathan Dowglass of this town (New London) and stole 40 shillings in money.

pay up
J. Mumford of New London asks that those indebted to him settle accounts.

help wanted
Notice by Lemuel Pattengall of Newent that he wants two active lads, about 16 or 17 years of age, to become apprentices to learn the mason trade or to hire two men artists in all branches of that trade.

socks for sale
Advertisement by William Russel of Norwich of his stocking manufactory.

farms and land for sale
Notice by Jabez Dean of Norwich Landing of farm for sale in Old Parish, Lebanon about 2 miles from the Meeting House, adjoining half a mile on the road that leads from Lebanon to Windham court house; 160 acres well watered and wooded; a good house and barn thereon and well fenced mostly with stone

wall and a good orchard; now under improvement by Messrs. Gambell and Liman.

To be sold, a small dwelling house in the possession of John Warner, lying in the center of the parish of Scotland.

Four hundred acres of land in Killingly, Thompson Parish; improved by Joseph Town and William Richards; a short distance from the County road and Meeting House; also two lots of land in Voluntown; apply to Joshua Henshaw of Boston.

To be sold at public auction in the town of Lebanon, Goshen Parish, at the house of Jacob Huell of Goshen, one tract of land of 14 acres in Goshen, a mile away from the Meeting House, now in the occupation of Seth Bartlet; another 90 acres with dwelling house in westerly Goshen, now in the possession of James Wite.

Susquehanna Company meeting
Notice by Eliphale Dyer, Jed Elderkin, Samuel Gray; Ebenezer Baldwin and Gershom Breed of a meeting of the Proprietors of the Susquehanna Company.

for stud
Flying Buck, owned by Benjamin Morgan of Preston; horse had been owned formerly by John Hulksey of Colchester.

died
In the North Parish of New London, George Dobeare, 57 years of age, after a long illness; his sermon preached by the Rev. Mr. Jewett; he left a widow and six children.

In Southold, Long Island, Rev. Nemihia Barker, pastor of one of the churches of that town; his death preceded by a few days that of his amiable daughter of the same distemper.

punishment for burglary
Last Wednesday, one Campbell, having been convicted by the Superior Court sitting in Norwich of breaking open and

robbing the store of Winthrop Saltonstall of this town (New London) was publicly whipped, cropped and branded in Norwich. By the marks on him, he is an old offender.

river ice
Last Sunday, the ice in the Connecticut River broke up.

agricultural news
We are told that on Tuesday last a ewe, belonging to Mr. Stephen Hall of Chatham, brought forth four lambs in a litter.

shipping news
New London and Norwich passage boat continues to ply between the two, wind and weather permitting; notice by Samuel Stockwell and John Springer.

administration of estates
Notice by Commissioners, appointed by Probate court John Stocker and Nathaniel Brown, to the creditors of the estate of Capt. Israel Abbot, late of Middletown, that a meeting will be held at the house of Capt. Comfort Sage of Middletown, Administrator.

****

From *The New London Gazette,* April 3, 1772

farms for sale
by Zebediah Andrus of Norwich a farm containing 213 acres lying in Norwich East Society. There is on said farm two dwelling houses, each two stories high, two barns, a wash house, corn house and three excellent wells of water convenient to the house. There is also a good orchard of about 160 apple trees, now in their prime for bearing, besides a variety of excellent fruit trees of various kinds such as pears, peaches quinces and cherries. No land has any stronger fertile soil, well wooded. It is known to be some of the best land in the parts, for plowing, mowing or pasture. Inquire of William Andrus living on the premises.

To be sold by Samuel Huntington a farm lying in the First Society in Norwich, about 3 miles from the Meeting House situated on a public road, a convenient dwelling house and other buildings.

administration of estates
Notice by John Stocker, Nathaniel Brown and Elihu Starr, Commissioners appointed by Court of Probate to the creditors of the estate of Captain Israel Abbot, late of Middletown, that a meeting will be held at the store of Comfort Sage.

debts owed to be paid
All persons to have any demands on David Gardiner of New London should apply to William Adams Jun. of said New London for settlement.

****

From *The New London Gazette,* April 10, 1772

shipping news
Wednesday evening, Captain Braddick arrived at the mouth of New London harbor in 36 days from Guadalupe. His mate and three of his hands were sick of smallpox. Captain Dudley Saltonstall of this port was to set out from there in a few days after Captain Braddick.

bad weather, no news
The late severe weather has so interrupted our intelligence that we have received no papers from Boston or New York later than March 23.

died
In Ashford on March 4, died William Watkins in the 75th year of his life. He was well all the day, rode out from home for several miles upon business, and, returning, he ate hearty, then rode to his barn to take care of his horses and cattle. There he was taken with a heart beat and lay down up upon the hay. But finding it grew no better, he got up upon his horse and rode back to his house and was immediately led to bed and told his wife he never felt so before and believed he was dying and in a few minutes he expired. He was a man well loved and died much lamented, having faithfully served his generation. He was one of

the first inhabitants of the town having almost 55 years lived in the same place without leaving his first farm. He was buried upon the same by his first wife.

barley wanted
 Cash for good clean barley. Inquire of Captain Nathaniel Coit of New London, Inn keeper.

to be sold
 a likely, healthy, a female Negro child about two years old. Inquire of the Printer.

 by Alexander Fostick, card maker, all sorts of cards such as cotton and woolen, wholesale or retail.

land for sale
 Two square blocks of good land, both fenced with stone walls, one of 18 acres has a considerable stand of wood on it. The other, about four acres, with a good orchard upon. Both lying about a mile from the town of New London on the road leading to the Great Neck. For more particulars, inquire of Enoch Bolles.
****

From *The New London Gazette,* April 17, 1772

escapee recaptured
 John Brown, on sentence of death, who lately escaped from Lichfield goal, we hear, is taken up and returned to said goal.

fish catch
 Last Friday morning, Mr. John Hall of this town (New London) caught 120 pounds of fish and two seals in a common fishnet.

died
 Last Friday died here (New London), Captain David Crocker in an advanced age.

elected to General Assembly
for New London: Gurdon Saltonstall and William Hillhouse
for Norwich: Rufus Lathrop and Benjamin Huntington
for East Haddam: Daniel Brainerd and Capt. Dyar Throop
for Lyme, Major Samuel H. Parsons and Samuel Seldin
for Groton: Captain Ebenezer Ledyard and Nathan Gallup.

accident
On the second instant, a little before nightfall, a melancholy accident at the house of Mr. Howard of Pomfret occurred. Three neighboring young women and two of Mr. Howard's children, sitting by the fire, were all, especially three of them, terribly scalded by a kettle of boiling beer (the leg pole burning off, then falling). The youngest of the two children, 15 months old that very day, was so terribly scalded that it died in about three hours.

died
On Sabbath morning in Windham at half an hour after two o'clock, departed this life in the 48th year of her age, Mrs. Alice Cogswell, the late amiable and prudent consort of the Reverend James Cogswell. A funeral sermon was preached by the Reverend Mr. Whitney.
****

From *The New London Gazette,* April 24, 1772

shipping news
A schooner, William Krupa, Master, bound for Egg Harbor from Taunton River, was lately lost on the South side of Long Island. The people and the vessels rigging were saved. On the 10th, the sloop *Ruby* William Howell, Master, bound to Newport, was cast away on Fisher's Island and a great part of her cargo lost. It is thought the vessel cannot be saved.

Captain Andrew Palmes of this place (New London) in a schooner from Jamaica, bound for South Carolina, was lately cast away at the latter place. The vessel is lost but the people are saved.

The sloop *Dispatch*, Moses Pierce, Master, will sail in a few days for Nova Scotia. Apply to the master at Norwich Landing.

ordination
On Thursday the 16th instant, the Reverend Solomon Morgan was ordained in his pastoral office over the church in Nazareth in the south part of Voluntown. The Reverend Ephraim Judson made the introductory prayer and the Reverend Aaron Kinne preached a sermon and the Reverend Jacob Johnson made the ordination prayer and gave the Challenge. The Reverend John Fuller of made the prayer after the Challenge and the Reverend Levi Hirtt gave the Right-Hand of Fellowship.

died
Last Sunday died in Scotland in Windham, of a mortification of legs, Mrs. Abigail Palmer, wife of Amas Palmer.

for sale
A quantity of Indian corn tar and white Oak hogshead heading to be sold at the Distill House in New London.

Daniel and Joshua Lathrop of Norwich do hereby inform their customers that they have just received a fine assortment of European and India goods.

John B. Brimmer has a quantity of choice deer skins, fish oil and tar and turpentine for sale.

dissolution
The partnership between Jonathan Starr and Elisha Leffingwell in the clothier's business in Norwich is dissolved.

runaway
from James Perkins in Groton, an apprentice boy named Ichabod Darrow; about 20 years old and of middling stature.

from Lemeul Moor of New London, a servant man named Peter Crocker; about 30 years of age.

From *The New London Gazette,* May 1, 1772

fires
Last Sunday the house of Mr. Samuel Instead of East Hartford took fire in the time of the divine service and was entirely consumed together with the greatest part of its contents.

Last Wednesday evening, two barns, one belonging to Reverend Lockwood and the other to a Mr. Bridges of Wethersfield, by some unknown accident took fire and were entirely consumed

stud
Notice by John McCurdy his horse young *Wildair* will stand stud this season. This subscriber also wants immediately a cargo of Jamaica horses for which he will make good pay.

****

From *The New London Gazette,* May 8, 1772

runaways
from Nathaniel Wales Jr. of Windham, one Daniel Farnham an apprentice; 20 year of age; is straight built; has a black curly head; a clothier by trade.

from Ebenezer Walker of Ashford, an Indian servant boy about 16 years of age; named George; a well set fellow.

****

From *The New London Gazette,* May 15, 1772

shipwreck
About three weeks ago, a small fishing boat bound from Westerly to Newport was drove on shore on Point Judith and three man were in her drowned. Their names were Joshua Brown, who was for several years a Captain in the Rhode Island service during the late war, John Bent and Mr. Hawk, all of Westerly. Brown and Bent left families.

died
    Wednesday died here in New London, William Hancock for many years a noted coaster Boston and New York.

    At Colchester, Mr. Aaron Kellogg, aged 60.

    On Saturday last in Windham, departed this life in the 23rd year of her age, Miss Alex Cogswell, the very dear and only daughter of the Reverend James Cogswell. The Reverend Mr. Lost of Preston preached the sermon at the funeral.

wanted
    by James Thompson, by May 22, a number of likely shipping horses.

sloop to be sold or let
    on reasonable terms by Comfort Sage of Middletown, a sloop 84 tons burthen and 14 months old.

to be sold
    by Cyrus Punderson of Groton, a small lot containing 16 acres of good land with a handsome, convenient dwelling house, barn and orchard. It is well watered with two living streams crossing it. It is pleasantly situated on a road that leads from the Meeting House in North Groton to Stoddard' Ferry and from Preston to New London. It is very convenient for a trader or tradesman.

escaped
    from Braddock Cory, Constable of South Hampton in Suffolk County in Long Island, a Robert Craig of Norwich in the colony of Connecticut, who was taken into custody and convicted for passing counterfeit bills. He appears to be between 30 and 40 years of age and six foot high.

stage wagon
    Notice that the stage wagon is established from Sag Harbor Long Island to New York, leaving Monday morning and another wagon will set out from Sag Harbor every Monday

morning and exchanging passengers with the other wagon, return again to New York on Wednesday. These carriages it is expected will greatly facilitate traveling between the New England and southern provinces as a passage boat by James Wiggins, having excellent accommodations for passengers, sails from Sag Harbor for New London every Thursday morning and returns again to Sag Harbor on Saturdays.

Each fare for passengers from Sag Harbor to New York in the wagon is 18 shillings New York currency, and in the boat from Sag Harbor to New London, three shillings like money.

for sale
All sorts of horn combs made and sold by Noah Hidden, near Colonel Jabez Huntington's store in Norwich.

****

From *The New London Gazette,* May 22, 1772

runaway
from on board the sloop *Esther,* John Bradick, Master, lying at New London, Elisha Johnson, just came with the smallpox and much pitted with the same; a square well set fellow, about 5 feet 6inches high. Notice given by John Herttell.

married
Last Wednesday was married at Colchester, the Reverend Edward Eells of Middletown to Mrs. Patience Lord, the widow of Mr. Ichabod Lord.

christening of four cousins
Marlborough in Colchester: This day he being the Lord's day, the Reverend Mr. Benjamin Dunning baptized four children namely Abel, Andrew, Chloe and Eliphas Loveland, who were children of four brothers, all the sons of Mr. Robert Loveland of this Society and all of these infants were born in the space of the eleven days time.

administration of estates
Notice by William Avery and John Dolbeare, the administrators of the estate of George Dolbeare, to all those who

have demands on the estate to file claims.

commercial notice
    by Rufus Perkins that he is carrying on the clothier business in Colchester.

lost
    Notice by Rufus Perkins that a red narrower of his has puréed
****

From *The New London Gazette,* May 29, 1772

lost
    in these streets of New London or between this place and Jordan Brook, a small seal set in the gold.

administration of estates
    Notice by Titus Hurlbut and Nathaniel Douglass, Commissioners appointed by the Probate Court for the District of New London that a meeting will be held at the house of Mrs. Lady Whittemore regarding the estate of Mr. Daniel Whittemore, late of New London, deceased and represented insolvent.

land to be sold
    Nine rods of choice land, fenced with stone wall, with a house 28 ½ feet one way and 25 feet the other, with a fine baker's oven. The house is well finished situated in Norwich in the Chelsea Society, fronting the road that leads to the Ford Way board that crosses the Shetucker River. Inquire of Eliha Lathrop of Newent, Joseph Wright of Norwich East Society or to Jabez Perkins of said Chelsea.

    Notice from I. Robbinson, Walter Hyde and Ichabod Fitch, Commissioners appointed by the Probate Court of the District of Windham, to the creditors of estate of Mr. Dan Hyde of Lebanon that a meeting will be held at the house of Mr. Simeon Gray, inn keeper in said Lebanon.
****

From *The New London Gazette,* June 5, 1772

fire

Last Tuesday night, a ship owned by Mr. Ralph Isaacs and lying in New Haven Harbor (about 260 tons and almost new) took fire but, by what means we did not learn and was burnt down to the water.

lightning strike

Last Thursday night, the house of Mr. Joseph Way of Chesterfield Society in this town (New London) was struck by lightning which came down the chimney first, opened all the doors and windows in the house, ripped off the window caps, raised the chamber floor and roof; moved one of the main posts of the house several inches from its place; burst down the partitions and entered a bedroom where a child lay in bed and destroyed a case therein and killed a dog. Though a number of persons were in the house providentially none of them received any hurt.

shipping

The brig *Victory* James Rogers, Master, will sail for Liverpool in about 15 days. For freight or passage, apply to David Manwaring.

administration of estates

Notice by Dyah Fowler and Elijah Lamphere, Executors of the estate of Mr. George Lamphere of Colchester, that debtors and creditors are advised to settle their accounts.

strayed or stolen

from Ephraim Cushman in Coventry, a horse.

Township of Fairfield, Province of New Hampshire

Notice that a meeting of the proprietors of the Township of Fairfield in the province of New Hampshire[44] is to be called in order to choose proper offices to agreed-upon methods of laying out the settlement of such town and to lay a tax upon the proprietors to defray the charges of the survey. Meeting to be held at the house of Mr. Jedidiah Strong in holder at Lebanon. Notice given by William Metcalfe, Justice of the Peace.

****

From *The New London Gazette,* June 12, 1772

new trial ordered
We have the General Assembly new trial has been granted to John Brown, now in Litchfield goal, under the sentence of death for burglary.

died
Last Tuesday died suddenly at Ashford, Lieutenant John Avery of that town. He was at a tavern and, complaining of being faint, called for some drink, but before it was given to him he expired.

Thursday evening last died at Windham, Captain Abial Merott, a gentleman truly worthy and useful in his day.

to be sold
By Abraham Gardiner, the sloop *Phoenix*, 80 tons burthen, lying at Sag Harbor on Long Island.

stolen out
of the pasture of Charles Williams of Colchester, a black cow.

out of the stable of Moses Butler of Hartford, a handsome black mare; notice given by Amos Mead.

administration of estates
Notice by Lemeul Barrows and Ephraim Hall, Commissioners appointed by the Probate Court for the District of Windham to examine the claims of the creditors to the estate of Eleazer Stoddard, late of Mansfield, that a meeting will be held at the dwelling house of Lieutenant Lemeul Barrows.

Notice by Samuel Storrs, Jabez Barrows Jr. and Ephraim Whole, Commissioners appointed by the Probate Court for the

District of Windham to examine the claims of the creditors to the estate of Thomas Barneby of Mansfield, that a meeting will be held at the dwelling house of Lieutenant Lemeul Barrows.

****

From *The New London Gazette,* June 19, 1772

the burning of the Gaspee

Monday, a sloop from New York arrived at Newport and, after reporting her cargo at the customhouse, was preceding up the River on Tuesday. The *Gaspee*, an armed schooner then lying near Newport, immediately gave chase to the sloop crowding all the sail she could make. But the people on board, not acquainted with the River, at three o'clock in the afternoon, she ran aground at Namquit, near Pawtuxet. About 12 at night, a great number of people and boats boarded the schooner, bound the crew and set them ashore after which they set fire to the vessel and destroyed her. A pistol was discharged by the Captain of the schooner and a musket or pistol from one of the boats by which to Captain was wounded the ball passing through one of his arms and lodging in the lower part of his belly.[45]

lost

in these streets of New London or between this place and Jordan Brook, a small seal set in the gold.

administration of estates

Notice by Titus Hurlbut and Nathaniel Douglass, Commissioners appointed by the Probate Court for the District of New London that a meeting will be held at the house of Mrs. Lady Whittemore regarding the estate of Mr. Daniel Whittemore, late of New London, deceased and represented insolvent.

Notice from I. Robinson, Walter Hyde and Ichabod Fitch, Commissioners appointed by the Probate Court of the District of Windham that a meeting will be held at the house of Mr. Simeon Gray, inn keeper in said Lebanon regarding the estate of Mr. Dan Hyde of Lebanon.

for sale
　　Silas Church Jr. and Edward Hallam have just opened a shop which was occupied by Mr. Nicholas Hallam, where they have for sale a large assortment of European and West Indian goods.

taken up
　　by John Ripley, a stray in Windham.

pay up
　　All persons indebted to the estate of Mr. Nicholas Hallam late of New London, are asked to settle accounts; notice by Elizabeth Hallam, executrix.

stolen
　　Notice by Daniel Burnam and Joseph Perkins Jr. that various clothes and other items were stolen from them in Norwich.

runaways
　　from Jonathan Forsyth of New London, a boy named Tomas Larabe; between 11 and 12 years old; is much freckled and has brown hair. He is badly burnt in the legs by falling down a chimney into the fire.

　　from Nathaniel West of Tolland, an Irish servant man named Robert Chambers; aged about 22; five feet eight inches high; wears his own hair and goes about stooping.

　　from Samuel Gilbert of Hebron, Olive, a Negro fellow; about 25 years old; five feet ten inches high; well proportioned; very black and of a sprightly countenance. He rolls very much as he walks.

****

From *The New London Gazette,* June 26, 1772

starvation in Europe
　　From Captain Parker, we have an accounts of the scarcity of provisions in most part of Europe, the poor being in great

distress for the means of sustenance. It is said that even the game which used to be brought from France and Flanders is entirely stopped as the inhabitants of those countries are also in great want. In a small town within 10 miles of London all the sheep flocks being bought up by a gentleman for his cats and a lady for her dogs. So the poor of that place cannot get so much as a bit of sheep liver.

died
Last Saturday departed this life in Killingly, Captain Silas Hutchins in the 55th year of his age. He has left a sorrowful widow and eight children. In the beginning of his last illness, he complained of clouds and darkness upon his mind with respect to the sensible enjoyment of God and yet appeared to have an unshaken belief in the Deity. Some days before his death, those clouds dispersed to a divine light breaking upon his mind.

letters at New London
Enoch Bolles, New London
Francis Beatty, New London
Jonas Belton, Groton
Jonas Brown, Stonington
Mary Chapman, New London
Jacob Chency, New London
Samuel Cheseborough, Norwich
John Corkeran, Norwich Landing
Thomas Deiveson, New London
Samuel Dein, New London
David Dougal, Stonington
Richard English, New London
Elijah Edgerton, Norwich
Aaron Eaton, Norwich
Noble Hinman, New London
Joseph Hewit, Stonington
Dennis Kenedy, New London
Harr Leach, New London
Ruth Lathen, Groton
James Loper, East Hampton, Long Island
Samuel Lord Jr., Saybrook
Daniel Makcow, New London
Samson Occum, Mohegan
Joseph Pris, New London
William Rathbon, New London
Caleb Seabury, New London
Elisha Seabury, Lebanon
Robert Swan, Stonington
Samue Toles, Stonington
Elisha Whitsea, New London
John Williams, Stonington

just imported
> in the brig *Hero* from South Carolina and to be sold by Charles Chadwick at his store in New London, choice rum, Muscovado sugar, rice, pork, pitch, indigo and tanned leather.
>
> **********

From *The New London Gazette,* July 3, 1772

murder
> We learn from South Haven on Long Island that last Monday se'nnight, Samuel Brewster of that place, being in words with one of his Negroes and attempting to correct him for some misdemeanor which the Negro resented. He wounded his master by giving him several such violent blows on his head with a piece of wood that he expired the next morning. The Negro was tried the next day, found guilty of the murder and was hanged and drawn in quarters.

embargo
> The embargo on grain which by act of the Assembly was to continue to the first day of July is, by proclamation from his honor the Governor, continued to the 15th of July.[46]

lottery
> for raising 600 pounds to repair and add to the great bridge over the cove at Chelsea in Norwich. Daniel Lathrop, William Hubbard and Jedidiah Huntington the managers. There are 2000 tickets at 15 shillings each. There off 586 prizes, the largest $700.

for sale
> Abijah Jones, clothier, hereby informs the public that he carries upon this business in Salem parish in Colchester.
>
> To be sold by Phineas Pratt, Goldsmith, at his shop situated near the house of John McCurdy in Lyme.
>
> **********

From *The New London Gazette,* July 10, 1772

false rumor of small pox

As it is said in several newspapers that the smallpox is very rife in New London, it may be proper to inform the public that at this time not one person has that distemper or symptoms of it in the town.

storm

Last Saturday at about four o'clock in the afternoon, there was a violent gust of wind over this town from west northwest attended with rain, thunder and lightning. A great number of trees were blow up by the roots. Others broke off in the middle and a large barn belonging to Elijah Bal, two miles from town, was blown down. A large grove of chestnut trees, belonging to the estate of Mr. George Dobeare, was entirely blown down.

lottery

We hear about most of the tickets in the Chelsea Bridge lottery being sold, it is expected that the drawing will commence in three weeks.

imported from London

and to be sold by John B. Brimmer at his store at Norwich Landing jewelry, a great variety of English hardware, also rum, sugar, molasses, tea, coffee, chocolate and spices.

farm for sale

To be sold in good farm in Norwich East Society at the distance of about a mile from the Landing place and on the Stonington and Groton road. Said Farm contains 60 acres of land with a good new dwelling house and barn thereon. The house contains four rooms on a floor and a buttery; also a blacksmith shop on the premises; a good young orchard; a garden and well of water near the door of the house. The farm is well proportioned for pasture, mowing and woodland. For particulars, apply to Daniel Spicer or Benjamin Huntington in Norwich.

runaway
     from Job Winslow of East Haddam, Steven De Woolf, a light complexioned young man of about 20 years of age.

strayed or stolen
     from John Richards of New London, a black mare.

     from the enclosure of the Daniel Bulkley of Colchester, a small black mare.

for sale
     Linseed oil, sold at the printing office.

****

From *The New London Gazette,* July 17, 1772

for sale
     Stephen Johnson still continues the business of making trusses or bandages to keep up falling parts of those who are troubled with the burst.

embargo lifted
     Of the eighth instant, the Governor and Council of this colony met in Hartford to consider whether to continue the embargo on grain after the 15th of this month, when it appeared to them that there was a sufficient supply in the colony for the support of its inhabitants. Therefore they thought it proper not to continue the embargo any longer.

died
     At Killingly, Mary Parker, wife of Lt. Nicholas Parker.

     at Sussfield, died Mrs. Dorothy Austin, relict of Captain Richard Austin, age 99. She was of the mother of nine children, 73 grandchildren, 118 great grandchildren and five of the fourth generation –in all 205.

runaway
     from Thomas Abell, an apprentice boy named William Lothrop Jr. in the 19th year of his age; 5 feet 5inches high; dark

complexion with black hair; a down look and reserved in his talk.

taken up
      adrift in the sound off Southhold Point an old longboat, pretty deep and tight; about 12 feet long. Apply to David Rogers in New London, Great Neck

      by Samuel Lathrop at Newent in Norwich, a light brown mare.

****

From *The New London Gazette,* July 24, 1772

hail storm
      We have accounts from several parts of the colony of considerable damage being done to the fruits of the earth by extraordinary shower of hail attended with high winds, particularly at Simsbury in this colony. There fell a most terrible shower of hail on the seventh instant, some of it nearly the size of hens eggs which destroyed whole fields of wheat, rye, Indian corn and grass. Many wealthy farmers, who had fair prospects of a plentiful crop, in that place will have no harvest this year. Mr. Holcomb, who had near 40 acres of English grain on the ground, had but one single blade left standing and that was under a tree.

died
      Last Tuesday, died very suddenly of apolexy, Mr. Samuel Stocking.

      Last Monday died at Wethersfield, the Reverend James Lockwood, Pastor of the Church of Christ there.

caught
      John Brown is taken and recommitted to his old lodgings in Litchfield goal.

sailing
      for London, the brig *Hero,* William Lovering, master, now lying in the Norwich River. For freight or passage, apply to the master on board or to Joseph Howland at the store of Messrs

Hubbard and the Greene, Norwich Landing

Mohegan road
It is proposed to work on the road at Mohegan on Monday the 10th of August next. Those who are disposed to forward so good a design are desired to meet at said time and place with suitable tools, *viz* spades, shovels and crows. As no provision will be made for eating, it is expected that each man bring his own provisions.

notice
Notice by Joseph Brown of New London that he is no longer responsible for the debts of his wife, Eunice Brown.

strayed or stolen
Notice by Joshua Hall that his horse strayed or was stolen from the stable of John Cartey in Colchester
****
From *The New London Gazette,* July 31, 1772

theft
Last Saturday, two men were committed to goal in this town New London on suspicion of stealing out of the shop of Mr. Douglas Jr. of this town. They say they came from Smith's Manor and their names are Thomas Wilkinson and John Vinderburg. The former is about 23 years old about 5 feet 7 inches high; has light brown hair and pitted with the smallpox. The latter, 22 years about the same stature; has brown hair well set and a large scar from his forehead to under his chin. There is reason to suspect they have been concerned in breaking open and robbing a sloop in the North River.

died
Wednesday died at Norwich Mr. Olive Pettis of that town.

Yesterday died very suddenly in this town (New London) Mrs. Lydia Whittemore, widow of Mr. Daniel Whittemore, tailor.

Lieutenant Eli Stetson of Mansfield, age 54 years, having been at work a small distance from his house, came in about nine o'clock in the fore noon with a number of hands that were at work with him for some refreshment. As soon as he entered his door, he sat down in a chair but immediately fell on the floor and instantly expired. In walking to the house several times it seemed as if he was going to sit down; but never complained of any disorder nor was heard to speak after he left the field where he had been at work.

stolen
Notice by Robert Douglas Jr. of New London that a silver watch was stolen from his store.

lost
Notice by Jesse Edgecombe of New London that he lost a pocket book with a number of account notes in hand and about 30 shillings.

taken up
by Joseph Wight, a stray black mare in the East Society in Norwich.

****

From *The New London Gazette,* August 7, 1772

whipping
Yesterday, Thomas Wilkinson received 10 lashes at the whipping post in this town for stealing a watch from Robert Douglas Jr. John Vinderburg, who was supposed to be an accomplice, was set at liberty.

lottery
The manager of the Chelsea Bridge lottery acquaints the public that they are preparing for the drawing on the 20th of this month at Norwich. A few tickets in the above lottery are in the hands of David Gardner Jr. and of the Printer here for sale.

lost or stolen
Notice by Ebenezer Whiting that, either lost or stolen

from Abraham Delafert of Norwich, was a gold watch.

from Joseph Waterman, four silver tea spoons, slightly worn.

****

From *The New London Gazette,* August 14, 1772

died
in the 92nd year of her Age, Mrs Eleanor Manwaring, widow of the late Richard Manwaring of this town. She was a dutiful wife and affectionate parent, a friendly neighbor and much given to hospitality.

Last Wednesday died here in New London, Mrs. Elizabeth Packwood, wife of Captain Joseph Packwood.

taken up
found adrift by Daniel Truman in the harbor's mouth, a canoe.

Found adrift in Fishers Island Sound an older scow, about 15 feet long. Notice given by John Ward of New London.

run away
from Amos Avery of New London, Great Neck, an apprentice boy named William Otis; 16 years of age; by trade a shoemaker; he is short of stature and small for his age.

farm and stock to be sold
by John Stevens in Ashford, a farm of 500 acres of choice land with a house and barn capable of keeping 60 head of horned cattle besides horses; also to be sold all sorts of farming utensils and five yoke of working cattle, three mares, two draft horses and four colts.

****

From *The New London Gazette,* August 21, 1772

suicide
Last Tuesday se'nnight, a young woman named Dibble,

being in a melancholy frame, hung herself in her father's house in Saybrook.

rattle snakes
    Last Sunday se'nnight, one man killed 46 rattle snakes in the North parish of New London. Four of them were old, the others were young snakes. One of the old had twenty rattles.

calf
    Mr. Elijah Kellogg in Hebron lately killed a calf which had come from a two year old heifer. It was four weeks and one day old. Once killed, the quarters weighted 103 pounds.

fire
    On Tuesday night the sixth instant, a very large and commodious dwelling house belonging to Mr. Joel Thrall of Torrington was consumed by fire, which was accidentally communicated from a candle to some flax in the house by a young man who came home at about 11 o'clock at night. The fire was so sudden that part of the family were obliged to jump out of the chamber windows in shirts. Nothing else was got out of the house but a desk a bed and two coats. The house had been finished but about one month. The loss is computed at upwards of 1000 pounds.

accident
    The proceeding day a boy fell from a mower in Torrington in when a pitch fork that was below ran into his body. He died of the wound the same day.

died
    in Norwich, Mrs. Bushnell, wife of Mr. Benajah Bushnell and sister to His Honor the Deputy Governor.

ran away
    from Philip Turner of Norwich, an apprentice boy named Jonathan Loomis; aged 20 years; 5 foot, 10 inches high; fair complexion; short hair; of a sprightly genius; professor of physic and surgery; genteelly clothed.

administration of estates
   Notice of the discharge of the estate of Dr. Elisha Lord who died in insolvent; notice given by a Elizabeth Lord

   To be sold at Windham courthouse all the real and personal estate of John Backus, late of Windam, deceased; notice by Ebenezer Backus, Administrator.

   Notice by Esther Hill, Administratrix, that all persons having demands on the estate of William Hill, late of New London, should come forward. The fulling mill, tools etc. belonging to the deceased are to be let.

   Notice by William Buel, Administrator, that a sale of the personal of the estate of Abel Buel, late of Lebanon in Windham County, deceased.

land for sale
   To be sold by Ezra May, two tracts of land with the buildings thereon, lying in the Lebanon Second Society commonly called the Crank. One of them contains 62 acres, the other 26 acres. Both are in the occupation of Mrs. Buell and for particulars inquire of him
   ****
From *The New London Gazette,* August 28, 1772

sets sail
   Last Monday set out for London the brig *Hero*, William Lovering, Master, in which vessel was transported back to his own country, one Thomas Wilkinson who was convicted of stealing a watch in this town.

pay up
   All persons indebted to Silas Church of New London are requested to settle their accounts.

strayed
   from Amos Clark of Lebanon, a one year old heifer.
   ****

From *The New London Gazette,* September 4, 1772

lottery
　　Notice for the second and last lottery for raising 600 pounds to repair and add to the Great Bridge over the Cove at Chelsea in Norwich. The Managers is of the lottery are Daniel Lathrop, William Hubbard and Jedidiah Huntington. Tickets to be had from James Flint and John Ripley of Windham, Samuel Mott of Preston; Colonel Ebenezer and Williams of Pomfret, Jonathan Trumbull Jr. of Lebanon; Thomas Terell of Coventry, Russel Hubbard and Timothy Green, Printer, of New London.
　　　　　　**********
From *The New London Gazette,* September 11, 1772

sickness at sea
　　Last Sunday, Captain George Champlin arrived here from Cape Nichola Mole. While there, he lost four of his people by sickness: Clark Corning, George Gardner and a Mr. Cushman of smallpox and Daniel McCoy of fever.

storm at sea
　　Since our last, Captain Latham returned to port having met with a gale of wind in which he lost the greatest part of his stock off the deck.

clothier
　　Notice by John Cary, lately from Europe, that he has set up clothier business at the fulling and mill, lately belonging to Mr. William Hill, deceased .

taken up
　　in his enclosure in Groton by Samuel Andrews, a two year old mare.
　　　　　　**********
From *The New London Gazette,* September 18, 1772

whaling
　　Since our last, arrived here, the snow *Beggars Bennison*,

David Dunn, Master, from South Carolina who said that he spoke to a sloop belonging to Rhode Island, Masters name Atten (or Allen) which had a whale alongside her. Captain informed them that he and his consort, another sloop, had taken five fish.

stolen out
of the pasture of Zachariah Chapman of East Haddam, a four-year-old horse.

wanted
a Negro woman, about 20 years of age, that can be well recommended. Enquire of the Printer.

****

From *The New London Gazette,* September 25, 1772

measles in South Carolina
By gentlemen from South Carolina, we learn that the measles were very rife, most especially among children. He informed that 8 or 9 had died of that order disorder in a very short time.

lightning strike
Last Thursday morning, a barn belonging to Mr. Marsh of New Hartford was set on fire by lightning and burnt to the ground with about 12 loads of hay which it contained.

early frost
We have heard from several towns in this colony that lately there has been a considerable frost which has done damage to the Indian corn.

administration of estates
Any person having demands on the estate of Mr. Aaron Kellogg is desired to bring in his accounts for settlement. Notice given by Mary Kellogg, Executrix.

pay up
Notice by John Bulkey of Colchester to those who owe for the use of his horse this season, that they must make speedy

payment or they will be faced with suit without further notice.

From *The New London Gazette*, October 2, 1772

new pastor
    The Congregation in the Fourth Society in Hartford has made choice of Mr. Nathan Perkins of Norwich to succeed the late Reverend Mr. Hooker in the pastoral office.

for Nova Scotia
    the Schooner *Indian King*, Thomas Ratchford, Master. For passage, apply to the Master on board at Norwich Landing.

runaway
    from Martin Kellogg, an apprentice boy named Enos Blacksee; aged about 19 years old.

stolen
    from the pasture of Thomas Prentice Galllup of New London, several horses by William Billings and confederates.
****

From *The New London Gazette*, October 9, 1772

punishment for burglary
    Last week, John Johnson, alias John Richardson, being convicted before the Superior Court then sitting in New London of burglary, it being the second offense, he was on Friday cropped and branded and received 25 stripes at the public post.

drowning
    Last night, an Indian belonging to Daniel Cooper was drowned at Waterman's Point near Norwich Landing. He was said to be in liquor.

sloop lost
    Lost at St. kits, the 28th of August, a sloop, Brintnell of New London listed as the master. She was in ballast. Its owner is unknown; nothing saved.

died

In Barbados Mr. William Johnson, portrait painter who formally carried out his business in New London.

****

From *The New London Gazette*, October 16, 1772

new pastor

We hear that the church and the congregation of the First Ecclesiastical Society in East Haddam has made choice of Mr. Elijah Parsons for their minister.

deaths in Boston

There was buried in the town of Boston in the month of September, 62 whites and six blacks, most of whom were young children.[47]

whipping

Last Wednesday, a transient follow, who calls himself William Hill, was publicly whipped at Norwich for stealing seven dollars out of vessel at Norwich Landing.

died

Last Tuesday, Elizabeth Gardiner, wife of Mr. David Gardiner.

to be sold

The noted farm belonging to Colonel Whiting, deceased called Massapeague, containing 230 acres, with a large dwelling house and barn thereon, surrounded by a stone wall and consisting of woods, grassland and orchards; well watered and very pleasantly situated lying halfway between New London and Norwich adjoining the West side of the River. Any person inclining may apply to James Haughton or the subscriber Pillenah Whiting, Administratrix.

****

From *The New London Gazette*, October 23, 1772

murder

On the 16th instant, the body of James Johnson, a young

man who had lately worked at the chaise make trade at Norwich and had served an apprenticeship in London, was found dead in Saybrook, near the ferry, a few rods from the road among some bushes, with a three or four wounds in his left breast. One through his right palm seemed as though he were stabbed with a round instrument or shot with a large shot. Several other marks of violence were upon him. It was the opinion of many of the spectators that he had been dead near a week. He was stripped entirely naked and a green coat which he wore was spread over the body.

On Thursday a week before the discovery, said Johnson was at Lyme, having procured a bottle of rum, some bread and cheese for his stores. He had drank so much as to be something intoxicated and he met with a transient person who called himself James Shield or Shells who had lately runaway from a man of war.

stricken with a paralysis

Last Tuesday, a young man named Clark, these son of Mr. Amos Clark of Westerly, had been at a husking in that town and, returning late in the evening, was suddenly, while standing, taken with a numbness in one of his hands and which soon spread over his body and put an end in his life in less than two hours after he was first seized with the disorder. He was a person of good character and well esteemed.

thanksgiving

The fifth of November next is appointed to be observed as a day of general Thanksgiving throughout the colony.

suicide

Mr. Isaac Lockwood of Norwalk was so far prevailed upon by the great enemy of mankind as to hang himself not far from his own house on Monday evening at the 12th instant. He was in the 46th year of his age; was a member of Mr. Dickinson's church in said town and left behind a disconsolate widow and eight children.

administration of estates
    Notice by Mary Baldwin, Administratrix of the estate of Mr. John Baldwin, late of Lebanon, that there will be a sale of his personal estate.

found
    Notice by Edward Hallam of New London that a chest of cloves was left in his store, which came from Nova Scotia. Anyone paying charges and proving it to be their property may have it. Otherwise, it shall be sold.

stolen
    from the pasture of Charles Phelps of Stonington, a brown mare.

****

From *The New London Gazette*, October 30, 1772

murderer caught
    Last Friday, one Thomas Atsatt was apprehended in Newport and committed to goal there on suspicion of having murdered a man near the Saybrook ferry Connecticut.

ordination
    On Thursday the 22nd instant, the Reverend George Beckwith Jr. was ordained as pastor of the Second Church and Congregation of Litchfield. The Reverend Mr. Jonathan Marsh of New Hartford performed the solemnity and was assisted by Mr. Reverend George Beckwith, Sr. of Lyme who preached a sermon suitable to the occasion and gave the charge. The Reverend Joseph Perry of East Windsor prayed after the charge and the Reverend Eliphalet Williams of East Hartford gave the Right Hand of Fellowship.

died
    On the 19th instant, died Mrs. Abigail Park, consort of the Reverend Joseph Park of Charleston in the colony of Rhode Island.

to be sold or let

a good dwelling house with six acres of choice land adjoining and a good barn on the same; pleasantly situated in Groton about 1 mile north of the New London ferry and adjoining to the Norwich River. For further particulars, inquire of Simeon Lester living at the premises.

hats

Notice by John Smith, Hatter, that at his shop near Captain William Packwood's on the street leading to Mr. Shaw's store, he carries on the hat business in all that branches. He also makes beaver hats for the ladies.

strayed

from the Nathaniel Shaw Jr. of New London, a strawberry roan horse.

****

From *The New London Gazette,* November 6, 1772

ordination

Last Wednesday, se'nnight, the Reverend Mr. Elijah Parsons was ordained to the pastoral care of the First Church and Congregation in the East Haddam. The Reverend Mr. Robert Robins of West Chester began the solemnity with a prayer. A sermon, adapted to the location, was preached by the Reverend Enoch Huntington of Middletown. The Reverend Mr. Grindal Rawson of Lyme prayed before the Charge. The Reverend Mr. Ephraim Little of Colchester gave the Charge, the Reverend Mr. Benjamin Pomeroy of Hebron did the Right Hand of Fellowship.

shipwreck

On the 27th of last month, Capt Cornelius Annable in a fishing schooner from Cape Sable bound for this port (New London) was drove ashore in a gale of wind on Martha's Vineyard.

ewe suckled by cow

The last Monday, a twin lamb, only six months old, was killed by David Day of Colchester. The four quarters weighted 62 pounds and a half and the rough tallow 10 pounds. The lamb was suckled by a cow.

murderer still sought
The three men who went in pursuit of the person who committed the late murder at Saybrook, after traveling as far as Poughkeepsie, have returned with out being able to find that the murder.

lightning
We hear from Plainfield that the wife of one Mr. Clift of that town was last Friday killed by a flash of lightning.

church bell
Last Saturday, an excellent bell cast by Mr. John Whitear of Fairfield, weighing 920 pounds; was erected on the Reverend Mr. Little's Meeting House in Colchester.

sermon to be published
In a few days will be published, a sermon preached at the execution of Moses Paul, who was executed at New Haven in September last for the murder of Mr. Moses Barry. It was preached by Sampson Occom, minister of the Gospel and missionary to the Indians.

strayed
out of the pasture of Captain Gershom Bulkey in Colchester, a red roan horse, about five or six years old. Notice given by Comfort Sage.

runaway
from Samuel Willis in Middletown, a Negro boy named Quaco. He is lively and of about 19 years of age.
****
From *The New London Gazette,* November 13, 1772

strayed or stolen
from Timothy Elmor of East Windsor, a large horse, about 14 hands high.

from the pasture of Pierpont Bacon of Colchester, two heifers.

runaway
from Nathaniel Aspenwall of Canterbury, an apprentice boy named Timothy Winter. He is of a middling stature, has dark skin, light colored hair. He shows his teeth much when he the laughs and carries his head low.

to be sold
by John Champlin, Goldsmith, at his shop near the courthouse in New London, several earrings, rings and other jewelry.

schooner saved
The fishing schooner, mentioned in our last to be on shore at Martha's Vineyard, Annable, Master, was got off with but little damage and arrived here since our last.

body found
Last Monday se'nnight, the body of a man greatly emaciated was taken up in the Connecticut River near Springfield. It is unknown who he was but must have been drowned a considerable time.

died
Last Monday died here (New London), Peter Latimer, aged 72 years.

storm
At Plainfield yesterday afternoon came on a most violent storm attended with thunder and lightning, when one of those shafts against which there is no resistance, entered the house of Mr. Samuel Cless, surprisingly shattered it and instantly dried up the source of life in this amiable partner of his domestic felicity. Mrs. Cless was the daughter of Captain Isaac Shepard and had been in the married state but about 12 months.

notice
Notice by Thomas Hartshorn of New London that all persons owing him should pay the same to Mr. Marvin Wait.
****
From *The New London Gazette,* November 20, 1772

school teacher wanted
Notice that a person who is well qualified and understands teaching a school would willingly undertake take care of one for a few months this winter upon suitable and courage mean. For particulars, inquire of the printer.

for sale
Advertisement that Roger Gibson at his shop near the Custom House in New London has for sale European and West India goods.

to be sold
at the house of Mr. Ebenezer Grosvenor, inn holder in Pomfret containing about 16 acres with a large and convenient dwelling house thereon. Said farm lies about half a mile north of said Grosvenor's on Woodstock Road; it is well watered and has on it a good orchard.

Notice that a commodious new dwelling house in Norwich will be sold by Ezra Huntington. It is two stories high, fronting on the town street, and 34 feet by 26; about 70 rods north of the house of John Lathrop, standing on a lot of 40 rods of choice land with a small barn on the same. Said house is but in part finished within and has an excellent cellar under the whole.
****
From *The New London Gazette,* November 27, 1772

whipping
We hear from East Haddam that one John Nicholas, a transient person, who said he belonged to Hartford, is to receive knowledge and stripes at the public post for theft.

We hear from New Haven that Mr. Joseph Howe has

resigned his tutorship at Yale college and Mr. Nathan Strong is chosen in his place.

died
   at New Haven, Mr. Thomas Harrison, in the 23rd year of his life, the only son of Peter Harrison, Collector of His Majesty's Customs at that place.

taken up and put in the goal in New London
   a Negro man; about 6 feet high; well built; has a large scar from his chin inclining to his throat and another scar on his left cheek and very much scarifying on the back from whipping. He pretends to be a good butcher, coach man and table tender. He claims he came from Bucks County and Pennsylvania and that there he waited on Governor Penn, Duchess of Gordon, William Bayard, and John Watts and many gentlemen, both in New York and Philadelphia.

runaway
   from James Braman, one Ebenezer Moses; about 20 years of age; his stature about 5 feet 3 inches; well set with brown hair.

taken up
   by Robert Carr of Lyme, two steers.

strayed or stolen
   from William Hedeson in Middletown, a bay horse; notice to be given to him or to Roger Bulkley in Colchester.
             ****
From *The New London Gazette,* December 4, 1772

for sale
   by Ebenezer Backus Jr. at his store in Norwich, different clothes, linens etc.

watches fixed
   Notice by Thomas Hilldrup that he repairs watches and can be found at the shop of Mr. S. Austin between the North Meeting House and the Courthouse in Hartford.

agricultural

　　　Mr. Solomon one of the East Haddam last month killed a lamb that had sucked only one ewe. It was no more than 54 days old and the four quarters weighted 33 pounds.

to be sold

　　　at public vendue at the house of Captain Edward Palmes, inn keeper in New London, the dwelling house situated near Mr. Samuel Latimer's, lately belonging to Captain Benjamin Appleton; notice by Mary Harris, Administratrix to the estate of Richard Harris of New London

for sale

　　　house and shop, conveniently situated in New London near the Church, by Mary Harris Administatrix to the estate of Daniel Whittemore, deceased.

　　　　　　**********

From *The New London Gazette,* December 11, 1772

accident

　　　We hear from East Hampton on Long Island that last Monday se'nnight, it being training day there, Jedediah Osborn, a young man in the 21st year of his age, was about to spit in the muzzle of his gun that it might give a loud report, but it accidentally discharged and so terribly fractured his head as to lay his brains open to view. In about an hour and a half he expired.

death from apoplexy.

　　　Last Lord's Day se'nnight, about sunset, Timothy Baldwin of Canterbury was seized with a fit of apoplexy. He had just been to supper and ate as heartily as usual, and observed to his wife that he hoped his victuals would do him good. But just as he was about to rise from the table, he sneezed twice and reached his hand to his wife, not saying anything or making much noise. It was perceived that something was the matter with him. He was taken out of his chair and laid in his bed where he lay speechless and senseless. A physician was had as soon as possible who bled him but to no effect. He continued in the same situation until about three o'clock the same night and then expired to the great grief and surprise of his family in the 64th year of his age.

married
    in Sligo in Ireland, William Mooney, tobacco spinner, aged 18 to Widow Vincent, aged 105

runaway
    from John Foster of Southampton Long Island, a Negro man named Cush, this country born; 5 feet 8 inches high. He is supposed to have carried off with him a mulatto squaw named Sybil.

found
    by Thomas Chester in his enclosure in Groton, a deer with one of his ears cropped.

medicines to be sold
    by Simon Wolcott, near the Courthouse in New London, a general assortment of drugs and medicines among which are the following articles: Hoopers and Lockyer's pills; Hill's Balsm of Honey; Batemans Drops, Stoughton's Elixir, Glaubers and Epsom Salt; Jesuit Bark in powder and in quills.

boats for cod fishing
    Any person that wants Clinch work boats proper for cod fishing may be supplied with such made in the best manner by William Giffin at his shed the near Samuel Latimer's shop in New London.

administration of estates
    Notice by James Pettice, Executor and Administrator of the estates of Samuel Pettice, Peter Pettice and Oliver Pettice, all of Norwich, to all debtors and creditors to settle their accounts.

strayed or stolen
    out of the stable of Jonathan Chapin in Palmer, a black mare, about eight years old.

out of the pasture of Pierpoint Bacon in Colchester, two likely heifers.

taken up
    by Robert Carr in Lyme, two steers.

****

From *The New London Gazette*, December 18, 1772

died
    We hear from Stonington that, on the ninth instant, departed this life Mr. Jonathan Copp of that town in the 79th year of his age to the unexpressible grief of all who knew him.

stolen
    out of the stable the Jedediah Smith near the Rope Ferry in New London, a dark gray horse which was the property of Solomon Dart of the said New London. Please return to said Dart or to Captain John Douglass of that town.

to be sold cheap
    by Marvin Wait of New London, a schooner of about 30 tons.

****

From *The New London Gazette*, December 25, 1772

bankruptcy notice
    The commissioners of the insolvent estate of Dan Hyde, late of Lebanon, deceased, hereby give notice to creditors that a hearing will be had at the house of Mr. Simon Gray of New London.

to be sold
    by the order are of the Court of Probate of the District of Windam, all the real and personal estate of John Baldwin, late of Lebanon, deceased, at the house of John Huntington in said Lebanon; notice given by Mary Baldwin, Administratrix.

strayed or stolen
    from Eleazer Lord in Norwich, a light sorrel two year old

mare.

    from Joseph Jewett in the North Societey of Lyme, a yearling heifer.

    strayed from Othniel Brainerd of Chatham, a year old steer.

drowning
    Last Thursday, James Picket, a laborer belonging to Middletown, was drowned in the river in the that place.

selectmen elected
    Last Monday, being the annual meeting of the Freeholders of the Town of New London the following men were chosen selectmen for the year coming: John Hempsted; James Mumford; Silas Church; William Hillhouse and Jeremiah Labor.

taken up
    in Lebanon by Silas Clark, a dark colored cow.

not responsible
    Notice by Walter Gustin of Colchester that he is no longer responsible for the debts of his wife, Elizabeth Gustin.
    ****

1773

From *The New London Gazette*, January 1, 1773

died
    Yesterday died here in New London, Mrs. Love Coit, wife of Captain Daniel Coit of this town.

slave boy for sale
    to be sold, a Negro boy about 13 years old, lately brought into the country. Inquire of printer.

notice of dissolution
Notice that the partnership between Elijah Backus and Joseph Otis in Norwich is dissolved.

strayed or stolen
from his stable of John Ripley of Windham, a brown mare belonging to Samuel H. Parsons of Lyme; it formerly belonged to Elisha Paine of Plainfield.

****

From *The New London Gazette*, January 8, 1773

to be sold
a likely Negro wench; about 21 years of age. She can be well recommended for her honesty. She has a female child of about three month old that will be sold with her. Inquire of Robert Niles at Norwich Landing.

prisoner released
Some days ago one James Sheels was taken up and committed in New York on suspicion of his being the person who had lately murdered a man near Saybrook ferry. But the master and mate of a sloop lately arrived, that the said Sheels shipped on at the island of Hispaniola and was aboard that ship until its arrival in New York on the third instant and he was discharged.

****

From *The New London Gazette*, January 15, 1773

captain washed overboard
An account of the misfortunes of the brig *Norwich Packet* and the loss of Captain Chester in the late commander as related by Douglas Woodworth, the chief mate ."We sailed out from the New London on the 21st of August and, on the 16th of September, in a gale of wind after midnight, the brig overset, upon which Captain Chester ordered the main mast be cut away. He and the mate were in the fore shrouds when the mast went over board. Captain Chester going to cut away the fore braces was washed over and, coming up under the vessel's stern, spoke to the people who that were on the quarter deck, who threw a line

to him, but whether he was hurt in going over it, he could not say it, and he disappeared immediately. The vessel lay on her ends for about three quarters of an hour before she righted.

harbor watch

We are informed that about eight nine days ago, a vessel from St. Euststia was seized at Newport by the Captain of a Man of War for having a six sets of cups and sauces on board. But upon application to the Honorable Board of Commissioners at Boston, they thought it proper to release the vessel.

We hear about Lt. Dudington, who lately commanded the *Gaspee* schooner, which was burnt at Providence, is daily expected at Boston with a Ship of War under his command, given him as a reward for his past services.

died

Last Saturday, died at Windham, Thomas Brown of that place. About three weeks before his death, he had the misfortune to break one of his thighs, which was in a fair way healing. But on Saturday evening last, he suddenly complained of feeling strangely and immediately expired.

accident

Yesterday morning, the widow Mary Bushnel, on a visit at her father's, Captain John Lefftingwell, coming down the stairs, she broke one of her thighs in such a manner that now her life is in great danger.

administration of estates

Notice by Noah Pomroy and Israel Kellogg, Commissioners, to the creditors of the estate of Asahel Strong, late of Colchester, deceased and represented insolvent, that a meeting will be held at the dwelling house of John Tainter in Colchester.

Notice by Elizabeth Lord, Administratrix, to debtors and creditors of the estate of Dr. Elisha Lord to settle accounts.

Notice by Bethiah Talman, Administrator, to the debtors and creditors of the estate of Samuel Talman, late of New London, to settle accounts.

strayed
out of the pasture of Jeremiah Ross of New London North parish, a mare.

escape
Broke out of the goal in New London, John Johnson, alias John Richardson, who was for the second offense convicted of burglary, received the punishment and was committed to said goal for cost. He is of middling stature; about 30 years of age; looks down; has had both ears cropped and branded in the forehead with the letter B. Notice given by Christopher Christophers, Sheriff of New London.

salmon dinner
Yesterday, a number of gentlemen dined in the London Coffeehouse in New London on salmon caught the day before in the Connecticut River.

list of letters in the Post Office at New London

Benjamin Billings, New London
Abigail Bolt, New London
Daniel Brown, New London
James Butler, Chesterfield
Samuel Billing, North Parish, New London
Jonas Belton, Groton
Joseph Colen, New London
Joseph Cashfield, Saybrook
John Denison, Groton
John Denison, Stonington
Richard Davenport, Coventry
David Douglass, Stonington
Jonathan Edgcomb, Norwich
Aaaron Eaton, Stonington
Henry Field, Norwich Landing
Thomas Fanning, Long Island
Samuel Gilbert, Hebron
Sarah Hallam, New London
Stephen Hempsted Jr., New London
Stephen Harrold, New London
Daniel Hodgins, North Parish, New London
Alexander Henry, Long

Island
David Kearney, New London
Nathan Kembell, Brookline
Peter Latimer, New London
Joseph Leach, New London
Aaron Lamphear, Stonington
Daniel Mecky, New London
Mr. Milson, New London
Thomas Miller, Lyme
Samuel Powers, New London
Aollis Pyner, New London
Nicholas Robinson, New London
William Rogers, New London
Giles Russel, Stonington
Elnathan Rossiter, Stonington
John Simpson, New London
James Smith, Norwich
Oliver Smith, Stonington
Isaac Sheffield, Stonington
Park Woodward, New London
Gideon Westcott, Norwich

****

From *The New London Gazette,* January 22, 1773

mill for sale in Lebanon
    A fulling mill and about one acre of land lying in Lebanon Second Society, about 1 1/2 miles from the Meeting House, being the real estate belonging to one Zilphs Newcomb of said town, a minor, and to be sold at public auction at the house of Mr. Asael Clark, inn holder. Notice given by Seth Wright, Guardian for said minor.

died
    Last Friday the morning, died at Millington in East Haddam the Reverend Diodate Johnson, minister of the Gospel at that place.

    Last Tuesday died of the smallpox at Groton, Mr. Samuel Palmer of that town. We hear about twenty persons have been of this same distemper in Groton and also a number in Stonington, where the distemper first broke out. But we did not learn that it has proven very mortal.

administration of estates

Notice Robert Dixon, Joseph Eaton and James Bradford, Commissioners of the estate of John Smith of Voluntown that a meeting of creditors will be held at the house of Phoebe Smith Voluntown, widow.

Notice from Bethiah Talman, Administratrix of the estate of Samuel Talman of New London to settle accounts.

Notice by Elizabeth Lord, Jr. to the debtors and creditors of the estate of Dr. Elisha Lord of Norwich to settle accounts.

taken up

by Joseph Baley of Groton, an old long boat.

Delaware Companies

Notice by Jabez Fitch Robert Dixson, Elisha Tracy and Isaac Tracy that a meeting will be at Azariah Lothrop's, innkeeper in Norwich, among the proprietors of the First and Second Delaware companies.

****

From *The New London Gazette*, January 29, 1773

died

Departed this life, the Rev. Diodate Johnson in the 28th year of his life, the sixth of his ministry, Pastor of the Church at Millington in East Haddam, after a slow and gradual decline with a consumptive disorder. The Rev. Stephen Johnson of Lyme, the father, preached the sermon.

New London land for sale

to be sold by Edward Robinson and Richard Law on behalf of Thomas Gardiner, a minor, land in New London that adjoins the street that leads easterly from the main street that runs past Joseph Packwood,s; sale at Edward Palmes, inn holder.

administration of estates

Notice by Julius Buck and Samuel Parmele to creditors of the estate of Jonathan Nicholson of Saybrook to settle accounts

Notice by Adam Shipley and Marvin Wait, Commissioners of the estate of George Gardiner, late of New London to meet at the dwelling house of Thomas Allen of New London

****

From The New London Gazette, February 5, 1773

fire

About ten days ago a large barn belonging to Thomas Randal of Groton was consumed by fire. It had ten fine shipping horses, a yoke of oxen and several loads of hay in it. The fire communicate itself to a stack of hay nearby which was also consumed . A Negro man belonging to Mr. Randal, we have heard, confessed to starting the fire purposely.

twins

The wife of Elias Farman of Preston was lately delivered of two sons at birth who were baptized by Mr. Park, one by the name of George Whitefield, the other Jeffrey Amherst. The same parents had two daughters in the same birth some years since who are still living.

died

at Groton of the small pox, Capt. Moses Fish, aged 90 who about three years since, and for many preceding years, was the representative of that town in the General Assembly.

Last week in Stonington, Mrs. Mary Chesebrough, wife of Amos Chesebrough, formerly of this town New London.

Last Monday night, Mr. Elijah Bishop of Norwich was at his door when stricken by a palsy and lies dangerously ill. This person won the 700 pound prize in the late Chelsea Bridge lottery.

Last Wednesday evening, the wife of Thomas Williams of Chatam was suddenly taken ill and died the next morning.

On Monday the 11th ultimate departed this life very

suddenly, Mrs. Betty Bottom, wife of James Bottom of Norwich. She was at a visit with Deacon Nathan Bushnell of that town and was in perfect health till struck. She continued, although senseless, for about twenty hours. She was of great public usefulness in the office of midwife and will be much missed. She was 59 years of age.

administration of estates
Notice by Peter Latimer and Picket Latimer, Executors of the estate of Peter Latimer of New London to all debtors and creditors to settle accounts.

Notice by Solomon Kellogg, Executor of the estate of David Debbie of East Haddam to creditors that there will be a meeting at the dwelling house of James Dixon, inn holder, East Haddam.

Notice by P. Mortimer, George Phillips and George Stocker, Commissioners of the estate of Capt. Julius Taylor, late of Middletown, to creditors that a meeting will be held at the dwelling house of Mr. Thomas Bigelow of Middletown.

strayed
from Andrew Lothrop from his pasture in Norwich, New Concord Society, a one year old steer.

from Nathan Crary in Groton, a bull.

runaway
from Joseph Kirtland, an apprentice name Jabez Bottom; about 20 years of age; light colored hair.

****

From *The New London Gazette*, February 12, 1773

earthquake
About 8 o'clock of last Saturday evening, a small shock of an earthquake was felt in this town (New London) attended with a considerable rambling noise.

died
On the 28th *ultimo,* Mrs. Mathabel Brainerd, widow of Capt. Joshua Brainerd of East Haddam, had her breakfast that morning with a good appetite. Upon rising from the table, she suddenly complained of a great pain in her head and was soon thereafter in great pain throughout her body, which held for about an hour when the pain entirely left her. In which condition she remained about an hour and expired in the 87th year of her life, after never having had a bit off sickness.

Last Sunday morning, Mr. John Parsons of Enfield got out of bed well and, as he was making a fire, dropped down dead in the hearth.

About six o'clock in the evening last Wednesday died here (New London), Mr. Hezekiah Huntington of Norwich in the 76th year of his life. We hear his remains will be carried to Norwich where he will be interred tomorrow by the Rev. Mr. Lord.

adultery
We hear that few days ago a man and woman were confined to the Litchfield goal for having broken the 7th commandment.[48]

agriculture
Middletown: Last Sunday was killed here by William Southward, a small cow which weighted 450 pounds.

farm for sale
with about 120 acres of land, a good dwelling house and a new barn thereon, lying on the road which leads from New London to the North Quarter of Lyme, about three miles from New London; inquire of Manassah Leach living on the premises.

strayed or stolen
from Lebbeus Peck of Lyme, a black horse.

administration of estate
   Notice to the creditors of the estate of Dan Hyde of Lebanon to present their claims at the house of Simon Gray in Lebanon or be barred.

****

From *The New London Gazette*, February 19, 1773

agriculture
   Last Wednesday, a cow was killed in this town by lighting which was raised by Peter Bulkey of Colchester. She was 4 years old at last spring, weighted 1,108 pounds and stood more than 16 hands and half high. She sold for about 20 pounds.

   Last week a hog was killed by a Mr. Post of Colchester which weighed 23 score, at only 22 months old.

died
   Last Friday died here, Mrs. Sarah Prentis, aged 53 years and widow of Captain John Prentis, who formerly commanded a ship of war in the colony service.

   Sunday last, died of small pox at his house at the Harbor mouth was Captain William Harris, aged 56.

   Yesterday died at his house at the head of the Niantic River, William Crocker, aged about 70.

married
   to Mr. Joseph Coit of Hartford to Miss Betsy Palmes of Norwich.

found
   on the road from New London to the Harbor mouth, a pocket book containing a sum of money. The owner may have the same by applying to Benjamin Hempsted of New London.

beach house for sale
   To be sold or let, a commodious dwelling house pleasantly situated at White Beach at the mouth of New London

Harbor with about 30 acres of land contiguous, having a good orchard and barn thereon, with a well of excellent water. Said premises have been improved a number of years for a Tavern. For particulars, inquire of Joseph Hurlbut of New London.

horse stolen

John Sydelman is a man about 46 years of age, of a low stature, bald headed with light colored hair which he combs backward. He is either a high Dutchman or Hanoverian. He speaks tolerable good English; he carried off a horse he was to deliver in New York; notice given by Henry Williams in Beaver Street, New York, and John Smith.

****

From *The New London Gazette*, February 26, 1773

a cold spell

Friday, the 19th instant at New London, near seven o'clock in the morning, by a thermometer of very inexact construction, the mercury was observed at seven degrees above the cypher[49]

Saturday, the 20th at 5
Sunday, the 21st at cypher
Monday, the 22nd at well below the cypher
Tuesday, the 23rd at 2 below
Wednesday, the 24 at 5 above the cypher
Thursday, the 25th at 18 above the cypher

births and deaths

We hear from Long Meadow in in Springfield that from January 23, 1772 to February 1773, there had been but three funerals in at that place, and one a woman aged 69, another woman aged 51 the third a still born twin infant. There was baptized there at the same time - 18.

jewelry for sale

Advertisement by John Champlin that he has, at his shop near the courthouse in New London, different types of jewelry for sale.

to be sold
    a farm containing 300 acres of choice land a good dwelling house, barn and other out houses thereon. The land is well portioned with wood, pasture and mowing land. Well watered, good orchard on which makes at least 100 barrels of cyder a year on average and produces 40 loads of hay.The situation is good for a tradesman, trader or tavern. It adjoins an excellent fish pond. Said premises lay in Chesterfield Society, six miles from the courthouse in New London and on the road to Colchester. For more particulars, inquire of Nicholas Fish, living on the premises.

administration of estates
    Notice that Sarah Brown and Thomas Brown have been appointed Administrators of the estate of Thomas Brown late of Windham.
,
    Notice that P. Mortimer and George Philips, have been appointed Commissioners of estate of Capt. Justus Taylor, of Middletown, deceased, and that a meeting will be held at the house of Thomas Bigelow, inn holder there.

                   ****

From *The New London Gazette*, March 5, 1773

shipping news
    Captain Elisha Hinman of this port (New London) is arrived at Stonington from the West Indies.

died
    Last Saturday died at the North Parish in this town New London, Mr. William Prince formerly of Salem, age 56.

    Departed this life, the widow Jane Ransom, late consort of Mr. Joseph Ransom, deceased, of a very short illness in the 84th year of her age. She lived respected and died lamented. She doubtless will be very much missed as she has officiated in the office of a midwife for 43 years. She was taken of a fit in the forepart of the day of which she recovered and was so well that she went out the door about an hour before she died, when she was taken with a second fit and expired in eight few moments. One thing was very remarkable. A few days before she died, she told a grand daughter who resided with her that she should not live out the month and, accordingly, prepared her own funeral. God in his Providence is daily crying in our ears. Be ye all ready.

agricultural
Notice by John Coult of Lyme that he killed one of an English breed of hogs that he had me bred, short of nine months old, which weighed 255 pounds.

pay up
Notice by Benjamin Kennedy that all persons indebted to him should make payments to Jeremiah Kinsman of Norwich.

newspaper delivery service
Notice by Nathan Bushnel, Jr and Aaron Bushnel to those *New London Gazette* subscribers who have their papers left at Preston City that the agreement is expiring and, if they want to settle up and re-up said service, they are notified that a year will expire on Friday.

administration of estates
Notice by John Prentis III that all persons who have accounts with the estate of Mrs. Sarah Prentis, late of New London, should bring in the same to him for settlement.

Notice by John Dean, Elnathan Rosseter and John Denison IV, Commissioners, to the creditors of the estate of Peris Palmer of Stonington that a meeting will be held at the dwelling house of Captain Giles Russel in Stonington.

Notice by Robert Dixon, Joseph Eaton, and James Bradford, Commissioners, to the creditors of the estate of John Smith, late of Voluntown, that a meeting will be held at the house of the Widow Phebe Smith in said Voluntown.
****

From *The New London Gazette,* March 12, 1773

shipwreck

Last Friday night, a small schooner belonging to this place (New London) in her passage from Rhode Island, ran on the rocks at the east end of Fisher's Island and was soon beat to pieces. She had only one hogshead of molasses on board which was lost.

died

In the West indies of smallpox Mr. Gideonn Stacy of this town, New London.

to be sold

by Samuel Gifford, Executor of the estate of Stephen Gifford, sundry lots of land lying about two miles from the town house in Norwich, adjoining to a public highway. Said land is part meadow and choice woodland. Sale to be held at the dwelling house of Azariah Lathrop, inn holder of Norwich.

administration of estates

Notice by Thomas Fanning, Administrator, to the creditors of the estate of Elisha Hurlbut of Windham to submit their claims and settle accounts.

runaway

from Pete Lester in Groton, an apprentice boy about 17 years old, named John Brunnuck; small of stature; dark complexion, brown hair with light eyes; a great tobacco chewer.

****

From *The New London Gazette,* March 19 1773

lost

Notice by Michael Felshaw of Hebron that he lost a leather pocket book on the road between New London and Hebron.

strayed or stolen

from the pasture of Ezekiah Bissel of Windham, a mare.

to be sold
   a farm belonging to the estate of Robert Crage of Norwich, about one mile from Norwich Landing; it is about 35 acres with a good new dwelling house, neatly finished, and a good new barn thereon and also a good orchard. Inquire of Daniel Spicer, living on the premises.

Susquehanna Company
   Notice by Eliphalet Dyer, Jediidah Elderkin, Nathaniel Wales Jr., Samuel Gray and Gershom Breed, Committee, of a meeting of the Susquehanna Company to be held in Hartford.

administration of estates
   All persons indebted to the estate of Daniel Rogers, late of Norwich, are asked to settle accounts; notice given by John Rogers and Alexander Rogers, Executors.

agricultural news
   On the second instant, Captain Walter Hyde of Lebanon killed a sheep, the four quarters of which, weighted 133 pounds. In the space of nine months, there was released from the same sheep 11 pounds and 8 ounces of wool.
   On the seventh instead was killed by Mr. Jedidiah Hyde of Norwich, a cow which weighed as follows: hide was 94 pounds; tallow was 136 pounds; forequarters 257 and 236 pounds and the hindquarters weighed 224 and 207, for a total of 1,154 pounds.

died
   Last Wednesday died in this town New London, after a few days illness of a pleurisy, Mr. John Prentis, aged 80 years. It is remarkable that this person lived as a bachelor until 16 months ago when he married a widow, aged 38, of whom he had a son born about three weeks ago. He has left a considerable land interests which had he died without a male issue, would have descended to a cousin. He has left a maiden sister near his age.

married
   at Providence, Captain James Munro of New London to

Miss Rebecca Snow, daughter of the Reverend Mr. Joseph Snow.

ran away
    from Elisha Williams of Stonington, an indentured Indian boy named David Job; about 15 years old; is likely and well made.

****

From *The New London Gazette*, March 26, 1773

day of fasting and prayer
    His honor Governor Trumbull has issued a proclamation appointing Wednesday the 21st day of April next to be observed throughout this colony as a day of fasting and prayer.

died
    at the Harbors mouth in New London of the smallpox, Mrs. Lester, wife of Mr. Eliphalet Lester.

shipping news
    Saturday evening last, put in to Newport, the Brig *Betsy*, Captain John Gordon, of this colony in a leaky condition. We hear all the crew has deserted for fear of an impress.[50]

    Sailing soon for London, the brig *Victory* James Rogers, Master, now lying in New London. She will sail in about 15 days. For passage or freight, apply to David Manwaring.

to be let
    A large and commodious dwelling house, situated in New London on Main street near the head of the mill, with four acres of land adjoining and a good barn thereon. Inquire of John Prentis 2d who has also to dispose of a likely Negro man about 23 years of age.

for sale
    beaver hats by Wheeler Coit of Preston.

strayed or stolen
    from the pasture of Jedidiah Beckwith in Lyme,

Chesterfield Parish, a mare.

small pox inoculations
Notice that Drs. John and Elisha Ely of Saybrook will begin their inoculation on Duck Island.

to be sold
by David Greenleaf of Norwich, Administrator of the estate of Mr. Jesse Williams in Norwich, First Society, a dwelling house with a large and excellent garden adjoining to said house; with a good well of water in said garden, near the door. Said house is large with two stacks up chimneys. Two stories high on the front which face the town street and three stories on the rear. It is well accommodated for two families and situated near the store of Christopher Leffingwell.
****

From *The New London Gazette,* April 2, 1773

burglary
Whereas the store of Mr. James Mumford in New London was broken open on the night following the 12th day of February last and again on the night following the 15th day of this month and sundry goods, previously seized by James Ayscough, Commander of his Majesty's sloop the *Swan*, thence stolen and carried away by persons unknown.[51]

postscript
A cow mentioned in the *Gazette* in number 488, killed by Jedidiah Hide, we are desired to say, was raised and fattened by Jeremiah Kinsman of Norwich.

shipwreck
On Friday last, a small sloop was discovered to be overset or foundered in the Sound off of Fisher's Island. The people supposed to be all drowned. The owner may have what is saved by applying to Elisha Perkins of Groton.

farm in Pomfret for sale
Notice by Stephen Keyes of Pomfret that a farm

containing about 68 acres and a convenient dwelling house and barn, standing about half a mile north of Mr. Ebenezer Grosvenor on Woodstock Road. It has on it a good orchard well wooded and well situated.   **********

From *The New London Gazette,* April 9, 1773

runaway
    from Joseph Neff in Weathersfield, an indentured servant named James Grant; he is about 30 years of age; lusty and well set; has a Roman and hooked nose and sullen countenance. A blacksmith, was born in Scotland and has lived since in Saybrook.

shipping news
    Bound for Nova Scotia, *Indian King,* now lying at Norwich Landing; William Andrews, Master.

    Bound for Nova Scotia, the schooner *Two Brothers,* Thomas Rochford, Master, lying at Norwich Landing.

Sag Harbor house to be let
    by Nathan Fordham Jr. at Sag Harbor a good house, barn and garden, two storehouses, one suitable for a merchant with dry goods; likewise, a bake house and gristmill and salt meadow adjoining sufficient to the house to cut four or five loads of good salt hay and a pasture for 3 or 4 cows.[52]

reward offered
    Notice by Duncan Stewart, Collector and Thomas Moffat, Comptroller of Customs House, that a reward is offered for information regarding the store of James Mumford in New London, being twice broken into and sundry goods previously seized by James Ayfcough, commander of His Majesty's Ship Swan, were taken.

Susquehanna company
    Notice given by Eliphalet Dyer, Jed. Elderkin, Nathaniel Wales, Samuel Gray and Gershom Breed that a meeting is to be held in Hartford regarding matters of the Susquehanna Company.

for rent: house in New London town
    To be let, a large and commodious dwelling house pleasantly situated on New London main street, near the head of the mill cove, with four acres of land adjoining and a good barn thereon; inquiries to John Prentis, II.

follow up
    The sloop mentioned in our last paper to been overset and lost near Fishers Island belonged Mr. Wait Still Cary of Chatham in this colony. She came the same morning from that place down to Millick River or to New London. She was only about 10 tons. The names of the persons that were drowned in her were Nathaniel Talbut, Ebenezer Talbut and Jonathan Babbit. Ebenezer Talbut lived in Goshen, the others at Chatham. Each of them a left a widow and a number of small children.

lightning
    Se'nnight, one Zechariah Bates was killed by lightning at Litchfield.

****

From *The New London Gazette,* April 16, 1773

farm for sale in Lebanon
    To be sold, a good farm containing 133 acres of choice land lying within one mile of the meeting house in the First Society in Lebanon with a dwelling house and a barn thereon; well watered and wooded and under good improvement. Inquire of Elkanah Tisdale, living near or David Fanning living on the premises.

****

From *The New London Gazette,* April 23, 1773

died
    T. Potter departed this vane and transitory life with a consumption in the 52nd here of her age.

    Mrs. Zerviah Fitch of Lebanon, consort to Captain Joseph Fitch of that place. She was kind, courteous and affable in her disposition.

ran away
   from Script Watter, an indentured servant names named Phineas Hide in Mansfield. He is about 53 years of age; lusty and well set. He has a considerable red blaze in his face.

whipped
   Notice by Daniel Corning that a transient mulatto, who calls himself James Hammond, was taken up, condemned by authority and very decently whipped ten stripes on his naked body for stealing sundry articles from the shop of William Coit of Norwich. Said James pretends to be a free man, but is as black as a Negro; he says he was born in the Rhode Island government, near Poqutuck bridge, where he lived until fourteen years of age and that he has served ten years in the Army. He is about five feet and ten inches high and slim built; he is now assigned in service to Capt. Daniel Corning of Norwich for the space of eight months to pay damages and costs of prosecution.

administration of estates
   Notice to the creditors of the estate of John Cone, late of East Haddam, that a meeting will be held to receive claims. Notice given by Noadiah Gates, Joseph Spencer and Elisha Cone, Commissioners appointed by the Court of Probate.

for stud service
   Horse *Scrip;* apply James Clark at his dwelling house in Lebanon.

   Horse *Young Weldaire*; apply to John McCurdy of Lyme.

apprentice wanted
   An apprentice to the printing business in Norwich wanted: an active a sprightly lad about 14 years old, who can read well and write a tolerable hand. Inquire at the house of Mr. Benjamin Dennis at Norwich Landing; also wanted a journey man printer that is a steady good work man. Such a person applying to T. Green will meet with good encouragement.

****

From *The New London Gazette,* April 30, 1773

punishment for polygamy
    At the Superior court held at Norwich, in and for the County of New London, one Robert Burch, alias Benjamin Burch and Benjamin Robert Burch, was convicted of the crime of polygamy and sentenced to be whipped 20 stripes, to be branded with the letter A on the forehead and to wear a halter around his neck during his continuance in this colony. The above sentence was put into and execution when he was recommitted to goal for costs.

shipping news
    Captain Daley, who sailed from this port (New London) in the severe weather we had in February last, is safe arrived at Guadalupe.

triplets
    This morning the wife Gilbert Fanning of Stonington Harbor was safely delivered of three daughters, who are all well and likely to live.

accident
    A melancholy accident happened in the Second Society of the Town of Windham on Friday. Deacon Thomas Stedman of that Society, age about 75 years, was riding on the tongue of his cart between his oxen, when his oxen took a sudden start and set out on a run, by which means the Deacon was thrown down between the wheels and so bruised that he expired in about a quarter of an hour.

died
    here in New London, much lamented, the youngest son of Captain Zeb Butler, aged five years and five months.

just imported
    by Nathaniel Backus Jr. in the ship *Rosamond,* Captain Miller, from London via New York, a neat assortment of English and European goods.

administration of estates
    Notice given by Ann Hancock, Admintratrix, to creditors of the estate of Capt. William Hancock to settle all accounts.

runaway
    from John Foster of Southampton, a Negro man Cush, 26 years old was born in Stonington; is about five feet, nine inches high; rather slim built; is a straight limbed and likely fellow; not very black; has one or two of his fore teeth out and a scar on one of his ears.

    Notice by Roger Gibson of New London for the return of a female Negro child named Suzanne, four years and six months old and small for her age; she is bandy legged, pert and speaks plain. She was carried off by her mother, who had run away from her new master Joseph Miner of Colchester to whom the subscriber had sold her and her male child now ten months old. The said Negro wench is named Lilley and man child Toney. She is supposed to be about 39 years of age; is likely; of a slender middle stature; can read; has a proud and affected air; is cunning, subtle and insinuating; pretends that she is free and it is possible may have some forged papers.

list of letters left at New London Post Office

Benjamin Arnold, Plum Island
Thomas Bolles, New London
Hannah Buell, New London
Captain Chester, Groton
Ebenezer Fitch, Norwich
Gilbert Fanning, Stonington
Jeremich Gilbert, New London
Stephen Harold, New London
John Hopkins, New London
Phineas Hyde, Norwich
Denson Palmer, Stonington
Joseph Peabody, Lebanon
Ephraim Woodbridge, New London
Ebenezer Whiting, Norwich

General Assembly elections
    The following gentlemen are chosen representatives to sit in the next General Assembly for:

New London: Col. Gurdon Saltonstall, William Hillhouse
Colchester: Henry Champion and Daniel Foot
Groton: William Ledyard and William Avery
East Haddam: Daniel Brainerd and Capt. Dyar Throp
Chatam: Silas Dunham and Ebenezer White
Middletown: Jabez Hamlin and Richard Alsop
Weathersfield: Silas Deane and Thomas Belding
Norwich: Rufus Lathrop and Benjamin Huntington
****
From *The New London Gazette*, May 7, 1773

ship seized
Last Saturday, the cruiser sloop of war off Block Island took Captain Stephen Tucker in a schooner in from the West Indies and has carried her into Newport.

died
at Litchfield, Colonel Ebenezer Marsh.

at Glastonbury, John Kimberly.

at Hanover in New Hampshire, Col. Alexander Phelps, lately of Hebron.

in New Haven of the smallpox, Captain Ebenezer Riley.

shipping news
Bound for Nova Scotia, the schooner *Indian King*, William Andrus, Master. Now lying at Norwich landing. For freight or passage, apply to Captain Moses Pierce at Norwich or Robert Avery at Lebanon.

stud services
The stud *Black Turk* by Samuel Hassard, Jr. in Colchester.

administration of estates
Notice to the creditors of the estate of the Joseph Rose, late of Coventry, to make payment to Timothy Demmock or

Samuel Rose, Jr. in Coventry and that a hearing will be held at Timothy Demmock's dwelling house.

house in Lyme for sale
　　For sale, a handsome well finished, dwelling house with good gardens, situated in the First Society in Lyme, near the Saybrook ferry. It is very near to all branches of the Connecticut River and on the Post Road, one mile from the Meeting House in said Society. Apply to Elisha Merrow of Lyme.

saddles for sale
　　Enoch Bolles Jr. of New London has for sale of a quantity of saddles pricking irons and awls, which are new. He continues the saddler's business as usual.
　　　　　　　**********

From *The New London Gazette,* May 14, 1773

London Coffee House
　　Opened by Thomas Allen where genteel entertainment is continued for gentlemen travelers; also to be sold, for cash only, and in order to accommodate the sick and weakly, a variety of wines and old spirits.

runaway
　　from Isaiah Bolles, in New London, an Indian woman, a slave,[53] named Mary; about 45 years old; is very large made; limps as one of her legs is sore and much swelled.

just published
　　and to be sold by Green & Spooner in Norwich and by T. Green in New London a funeral sermon for the Honorable Hezekiah Huntington, who died in New London on February 10, 1773 by Benjamin Lord, A.M.

taken up
　　by Jonathan Gilbert of Chesterfield Parish in Lyme, an old brown mare.

drowning
Last Monday, the be dead body of a man was seen floating between Fishers Island and the Hommocks. It is supposed he is one of the people who were drowned in the sloop lately mentioned in this paper to have been overset near said place.

died
at Hanover in Norwich, Matthew Perkins, aged about 60 years.

pay up
Notice by Ephraim Brown of New London to owe those who owe him to settle accounts.

****

From *The New London Gazette*, May 21, 1773

drowning
Last Friday, the body of a man was found floating in the Connecticut River near East Haddam and towed to shore. He had on a checkered shirt, a jacket without sleeves, a pair of the silver buckles on he shoes and silver sleeve buttons.

died
The same day, the Reverend Mr. Daniel Kirtland of Norwich, aged 72 years; he was seized with a fit and died on Monday night greatly lamented. His funeral was attended on Tuesday by a great number of people when a sermon suitable to the occasion was preached by the Reverend Mr. Levi Hart.

In Windham Second Society on the 10th of May, died suddenly Mrs. Mehetabeel Holt, wife of Paul Holt of that place. She was any just about 53 years. She arose in the morning as well as usual and laid out a large day's work in wash and bake. As she stood at her wash tub, she fell down and expired in a few minutes with out speaking a word. She has left husband and seven children to lament their loss.

sale adjourned
    The sale of delinquent proprietors interests in the Township of Canaan in the Province of New Hampshire to be held at the dwelling house of John Scovels in said Canaan has been adjourned. Notice given by George Harris.

strayed or stolen
    from Ichabod Spencer in the Lyme, North Society, a dark brown mare; reward given to anyone who brings the horse to Mr. Griffing, inn holder in said Lyme.

****

From *The New London Gazette*, May 28, 1773

drowning
    On the 21st of last month, being a fast day, one Hugh Watkins, a transient person, supposed to be a deserter from his Majesty's service, went in the morning to divert himself by fishing in a small brook in Mansfield. As he had no settled place of abode, no inquiry was made for him until Saturday morning when he was found a drowned in a small Creek of the said brook. It is supposed he fell into the same in a fit.

accidents
    Last Wednesday se'nnight, as Alvan Fosdick of Norwich with his wife were riding down a hill at Lebanon Crank in a carriage, some of the tacking gave way. When the carriage shot forward against the horses, they took fright and immediately set out upon a run. Mr. Fosdick in attempting to jump from the carriage, caught his leg in the foot stool, when his head and shoulders were dragged upon the ground between 30 and 40 rods before the horse could be stopped. This has wounded him in such a terrible manner that his life is in the most imminent danger. Mrs Fosdick happily jumped out of the carriage without receive any considerable hurt. The young couple had been married but about 10 days

    And on Saturday last, the following melancholy accident happened at Norwich. As Thomas Waterman was washing a sheep in the River near his house, in company with his brother and a Negro man, he fell into a hole about 2 rods in circumference and six or seven feet deep where he unfortunately drowned. A number of people in a few moments collected at the place and the various expedients were made use of, but since the body was not found for near an hour, to no avail. His funeral was attended the next day by a great concourse of people. He was in the 39th year of his age; a son to Mr. Asa Waterman of Norwich. He was a dutiful son, a kind husband and indulgent parent and a good neighbor. He left a widow and five children.

shipping news
    Notice is hereby given that Samuel Smith Jr. has an excellent new passage boat with which he determines to ply between New London and Norwich as often as the wind and weather will permit.

stolen or strayed
    from the pasture of John Jones is East Hartford, a red roan mare; notice by Lemeul Soughton of Windsor.

taken up
    by William Chrough a sorrel horse, at Gales Ferry in Groton.

runaway
    from William Gardiner of Groton, an apprentice boy, James Jeffords.

    from Thomas Truman of Norwich, a Negro woman named Lettice; of middling height and slender built; born on Long Island; speaks good English; very sprightly.

for sale
    a farm of 100 acres on Oyster Pond Point Southold, Long Island; contact Stephen Veil on premises.

found
    by Jabez Avery in Norwich on the road to Norwich, a woman's crimson colored coat.

lost
on the road from Norwich Landing by Oliver Coit of Preston, a leather purse with money; reward, if returned to Oliver or William Coit at Norwich Landing.

****

From *The New London Gazette,* June 4, 1773

drowned man found
Last Sunday was drove on the beach at Westerly, the dead body of a man who, to appearances, had been drowned for a considerable time. He was buried in the same day, near the place where he was found.

died
Last Sunday night, Mr. Benjamin Cornwell of Middletown, suddenly in a fit and at his house in that place.

Monday last, Mr. Enoch Bolles Jr. of this town (New London); he was seized with a convulsive fit and died very suddenly.

Wednesday, died here New London, Captain Michael Phillips who in the late war was commander of a privateer out of this port.

shipping news.
Captain Oakerman, who is arrived in Boston from Dominica, spoke with Captain Hezekiah Smith of this port (New London) in the sloop *Ranger,* now bound to St. Vincent's. All is well on board.

Committees of Correspondence and Inquiry
From the House of Representatives of the Colony of Connecticut: This house, taking into consideration the contents of a letter from the Speaker of the House of Burgesses of the colony of Virginia, containing certain resolutions entered into by said house, are of the opinion that they are weighty and important in nature and designed, calculated and tending to produce happy and salutary effects in securing and supporting the ancient legal

and constitutional rights of this and the colonies in general and do hereby approve of, and adopt the measure.

Whereupon a standing committee of correspondence and inquiry be appointed to consist of nine persons: Ebenezer Silliman; William Williams, Benjamin Payne, Samuel Holden Parsons, Nathaniel Wales, Silas Deane, Samuel Bishop, Joseph Trumbull and Erasmus Wolcott, Esquires.

The business of said committee shall be to obtain all such intelligence and to keep up and maintain any correspondence and communication with sister Colonies, respecting the important considerations mentioned and expressed in the aforesaid resolutions of the patriotic House of Burgesses.

RESOLVED that the speaker of this house shall transmit to the speakers of the different assemblies of the British colonies on this continent, copies of these resolutions.[54]

for sale
a quantity of good pine boards and plank to be sold by Joshua Starr at his wharf in New London.

****

From *The New London Gazette,* June 11, 1773

died
On the 12th of last month's died at Lyme, after a long and tedious illness, Mrs.Hannah Griswold, in the 79th year of he age, widow and relict of John Griswold, late of that place. She was charitable to the poor and a kind and tender parent. She was a woman of uncommon industry, prudence and virtue in the course of her life.

Died on his passage from the West Indies, Capt. Elijah White of East Haddam.

married
Mr. Ebenezer Douglas to Miss Nabby Baley daughter to Nathaniel Baley

****

From *The New London Gazette,* June 18, 1773

church news
We hear that about a fortnight since, the Reverend Mr. Benjamin Dunnington of Marlboro's Society in Hebron was by a Council of Ministers dismissed from his pastoral relation to the people of that Society in consequence of his own application for that purpose.

married
Last evening was married here in New London, Joseph Denison of Stonington to Mrs. Elizabeth Hallam of this town.

Also was married last evening at the North parish here, Guy Richards Jr. of this town (New London), Merchant, to Miss Hannah Dolbeare, daughter of Mr. George Dolbeare, deceased. She is an agreeable young lady with a handsome fortune.

strayed or stolen
from Nathaniel Walwa, Jr up of Windham, a light bay mare.

from Peter Smith of Ashford, a sorrel horse, 3 years old.

from Jonathan Starr of Norwich, a brown, two years old. It is about five weeks since the horse was missed. The last intelligence he has was that it was seen in Canterbury Woods between that place and Scotland.

ran away
from Azariah Palmer of Stonington, an apprentice boy named Roswell Stevens; about 18 years old, but very small for his age; wears his own brown hair.

shipwrights wanted
Two workmen at the ship carpenter's business may find encouragement on immediate application to John Wales of Glasonbury.

taken up
  by John Cooper in the First Society in Chatham, a small black mare.

administration of estates
  Notice by Daniel Lathrop, executor of the estate of Hezekiah Huntington of Norwich, to settle accounts. Executor also has a Negro boy to be sold.

  Notice by Justus Buck and Edward Shipman, Commissioners appointed by the Court of Probate for the District of Guilford to examine and adjust the claims of creditors to the estate of Matthew Coole, late of Saybrook, deceased and represented to be insolvent, that a meeting will be held at the dwelling house of Captain Edward Shipman, inn holder in said Saybrook.

     ****

From *The New London Gazette,* June 25, 1773

died
  On Sabbath evening last, departed this life William Metcalfe of this town (New London) in the 65th year of his age. He was a gentleman and for many years a principal merchant in this town. For upwards of 20 years, and at the time of his death, he was a Justice of the Peace for the County of Windham.

  Wednesday last week, died at Lebanon Joseph Fitch of that town.

British patrol
  The sloop of war, Captain Haowe, is on a cruise between Block Island and Montauk.

printing office moving
  The printing office in New London, which for the last 60 years has been kept at a north part of the town, will on Monday next be removed a few rods west of the courthouse.

runaway
 from Ezechiel Fox of the North parish in New London, one Jonathan Lee, who was lately bound in service for three years. He is about 40 years old, tall and large made, with a fresh countenance and a round face.

house for sale
 to be sold near Chelsea Meeting House in Norwich, a dwelling house, barn and 16 rods of ground with a well of water thereon; very convenient for a tradesman; inquire of Joseph Kelley.

     ****

From *The New London Gazette*, July 2 , 1773

lightning
 On Sunday the 30th of May last, the Orphans Asylum Academy in Georgia was burned down, occasioned by lightning.

war clouds
 A cruiser ship of war is lying off New Haven harbor.

small pox
 A number of persons in the North Parish of New London were taken down with small pox.

imported and for sale
 in the Sloop *Britannia,* Capt. Luther Elderkin, and to be sold in the Distil House in New London by Roswell Saltonstall, a quantity of middling, fine and superfine Maryland flour, corn, oats and ship bread for cash only.

 for sale the best of claret, frontinac, cordials; also choice rum by the gallon; inquire of the Printer.

 Just imported by Charles Chadwick and to be sold at his store in New London, choice indigo, rice, sugar, pitch, reeds and good Philadelphia flour.

 Just published and to be sold by the printer hereof and

also at the printing office in Norwich and by Nathan Bushnell, Jr. and Joseph Knight, Post Riders, the *Orations on the Beauties of Liberty or the Essential Rights of Americans* delivered at the Second Baptist Church in Boston.

administration of estates
  All people indebted to the estate of Jonathan Chester, late of Norwich, are advised to settle accounts; notice given by Asa Waterman Jr. and Freel Chester, Executors.

shipping news
  The schooner *Two Brothers*, Thomas Ratchford, Master, bound for Nova Scotia; for freight or passage inquire of John Baker Brimmer or the master at Norwich Landing.

business location for sale
  at Norwich Landing, a small but very convenient situation for any gentleman in the wholesale, retail or navigation way of trade; for further particulars, inquire of Phineas Holden, near the premises.

blacksmith
  John Landers, blacksmith, near the shop of Mr. Pember Calkins near the Court house in New London, shoes horses in the best manner; also engages in the farrier business.

    ****

From *The New London Gazette*, July 9 , 1773

large house for sale in Norwich
  to be sold at Norwich a large and commodious dwelling house, near Christopher Leffingwell's store; convenient for two families with a large garden spot around it; inquire for price and terms of Asa Waterman, Jr.

for sale
  Jeremiah Clement has for sale at his store in Norwich: Albany peas and wheat, bar iron, German steel, deer's leather, all sorts of clothes and goods suitable for the season.

runaway
    from John Mulford of East Hampton, Long Island, a Negro slave named Prince. He lived for about six years with Daniel Dennison of Stonington; is about 28 years old; of middling stature and bigness; tells various stories to prevent him for being taken as a runaway.

    from Charles Smith of Groton, an apprentice boy named Nathaniel Miner; between 18 and 19 years of age; is thick set; of middling height, dark complexion and short brown hair.

    from Ezchiel Root of of Pittsfield in Massachusetts Colony, two mulatto men slaves, one named Edward Peters, about 30 years old; has lost his foreteeth; very bushy hair; is about five feet six inches high; well set; has a down look; the other is Rufus Cooper about 25 years old; five feet ten inches high; very straight limbed and active; has remarkable white eyes for a mulatto.

drowning
    Monday evening a valuable Negro man belonging to Benjamin Dennis of Norwich Landing was drowned in the river at this place while bathing himself. Although a good swimmer, he died in only three feet of water.

cruiser ship of war
    Last Saturday the cruiser ship of war returned to Newport from a cruise up the Sound.

land and house for sale in Stonington
    Thirty four acres of land lying on the Post Road, near Mystic Meeting House in Stonington, having a dwelling house and orchard; the farm is well fenced; there is contiguous to said premises a tan yard, currying shop, mill house and bark house, all in excellent order to conducting the tanning and shoe making business; for further particulars inquire of David Dougal of that place or Capt. Giles Russel, inn holder in Stonington.

found
Last Friday, on the road between New London and Colchester, a pocket book; inquire of printer.

bees wax wanted
Cash given for bees wax; inquire of the Printer.

****

From *The New London Gazette*, July 16 , 1773

died
on the 4th instant in Saybrook, Mr. Joseph Lynde in the 70th year of his life. He was a son of Mr. Daniel Lynde of Saybrook, originally from Boston.

Friday morning last, departed this life, after a short illness, in the 43rd year of his age, James Wadsworth of Farmington.

burglary
One night last weeks, some villains broke into the house of Mr. Thomas Harris at the Harbor's mouth, took out his desk and carried it some rods from the house where they pillaged the same of about 9 pounds in money and made off undiscovered, leaving a number of articles of clothing which were in the drawer, strewn on the ground.

strayed
from Benjamin Huntington in Norwich, a three year old brown horse.

for sale
Elijah Lothrop has for sale at his father's Mills in Norwich choice wheat, Indian corn, flour etc.

To be sold by John Champlin, a Goldsmith in New London, molding sand, the black lead pots, and a good assortment of wire.

theft

Notice by Capt. William Morgan of New London of a theft from him of sundry articles by an old country, straggling fellow who said his name was Thomas Adams.

lottery

Notice of a lottery in Colchester in the sum of 700 pounds. Messrs. Gershom Buley, Henry Champlin and Joseph Isham Jr., all of Colchester, are appointed Managers of said lottery.

****

From *The New London Gazette*, July 23, 1773

storm

On the third instant, there was considerable fall of rain at East Haddam attended with thunder and lightning which killed a cow belonging to Mr. Timothy Brainerd, near his house. It also greatly damaged the roof of a barn belonging to Mrs. Ann Selden. An Indian, who was asleep in the barn, was almost suffocated with the sulphurous smell which attended the lightning.

sinking of ferry

Last Friday, the ferry boat in passing the River to this place (New London) was suddenly struck by squall of wind which overset her. There were five persons on board, who before the boat sunk, were taken off without receiving any damage than being thoroughly wet.

vineyards

Accounts from South Carolina mentioned the thriving state of the vineyard yards in that province. They all well furnished with grapes and that next year a great deal of wine will be made there.

died

On the 19th of this month died of a lingering disorder which he bore with Christian fortitude and resignation, Daniel Coit, aged 75 years. He was a gentleman distinguished for a long and uninterrupted course of public usefulness, having for 50 years been a commissioner of the peace, town clerk and clerk of the County court, besides other public offices.

On the seventh of July in Georgetown Maryland, died George Mumford, son of Mr. James Mumford of this town (New London) in the 28th year of his age.[55]

farm for sale
Good farm for sale lying in the northwest corner of Canterbury in the Society of Brookline, about three miles from the Meeting House. It contains 270 acres, 70 of which are under a good improvement with a good house and orchard. For further particulars, inquire of Increase Hewit living on said farm.

administration of estates
Notice by Adam Shapely and William Adams, Jr., Commissioners, to the creditors of the estate of Enoch Bolles Jr., late of New London, deceased and represented insolvent, that a hearing will be held at the house of Captain Edward Palmes; Marvin Wait is Administrator.

shipping news
A schooner lying at Norwich Landing, burthen around 50 tons, fit for immediate use except for some light repairs . For further particulars, apply to Jabez Dean at said Norwich Landing.

****

From *The New London Gazette,* July 30, 1773

town meeting
At a town meeting held in New London on Monday last for the special purpose of choosing a town clerk in the room of Daniel Coit, deceased, Mr. James Mumford was chosen into that office.

died
In Pomfret, on Saturday last, departed this life in a sudden and afflicting manner, the very amiable consort of the Reverend Mr. Aaron Putnam of this place in the 36th year of her age. She

had been unwell for some years and, for the promoting of health, had been riding out with the Rev. Putnam in a chair and, in returning back, she desired him to stop and take some useful herbs, which she observed as they were passing along. He accordingly did, (apprehending no danger) got out of the chair to do as she proposed at which time the horse suddenly started and ran over a rock, by which she was thrown out and received such a shock, that, notwithstanding the doctors who were providentially nigh at hand, proved her death in about three hours. She was the daughter of the Reverend Mr. David Hall of Stockton.

At Woodstock, Doctor Parker Morse, Jr
****

From *The New London Gazette*, August 6, 1773

administration of estates
  To be sold at public venue by order of the Court of Probate for the District of Windham, all the real estate of Mr. Dan Hide, late of Lebanon, deceased, which consists of about 70 acres of choice land with a good house and barn; notice given by Samuel Hide, Jr., Administrator.

  Notice by Ephrim Herrick, Executor, to the creditors of the estate of Mr. Nathan Lester, the late of Preston, deceased, to settle accounts.

First Delaware Companies
  Notice given to the proprietors of the Township of Huntington in the First Delaware Purchasers to meet at the dwelling house of Mr. Ebenezer Fitch, inn holder in Norwich, to hear the report of their committee to survey and lay out said Township; notice given by Jonathan Huntington, Clerk.

not responsible
  Notice by Samuel Bolles that his wife Mary has deserted his bed and board through the bad advice of evil counselors. This is to forbid all persons to harbor or trust her on my account for I am determined to paying no debt of her contracting.
****

From *The New London Gazette,* August 13, 1773

whipping
Last Saturday, a transient fellow, who called himself Thomas Adams, was whipped at the public post in this town (New London) for stealing a number of articles from Captain William Morgan, as was lately advertised in this paper.

died
Mr. James Mumford;

Elizabeth Leach, 84, widow of Capt. Clement Leach;

at New Haven Capt, James Minet, aged 49, son of Hon James Minet of Concord in Massachusetts Bay;

at Colchester Capt. Solomon Kellogg;

at Norwich on the 4th instant of consumption, Mr. Burril Lothrop, aged 24, from which he labored under for four months.

****

From *The New London Gazette,* August 20, 1773

died
at Preston this week, Mrs. Mott, wife of Mr. Edward Mott and Mrs. Barnes wife of Elijah Barnes. They were sisters who lived in the same neighborhood and died in a few hours of each other.

at Norwich, Captain John Leffingwell in an advanced age. For many years he had a house of public entertainment in the that town.

at Hartford, Mr. John Skinner, aged 76 years.

for sale
at Church & Hallam in New London, choice rock salt for cash or goods or flax seed. Also cash given for bees wax.

William Stewart has just imported choice a rock salt which he will exchange for flax seed. Those who do not want salt he will give cash for their seed and he will barter for rum, sugar, molasses or any kind of dry good for oats or beans; he will want to quickly a few likely young horses.

taken up
  in a suffering condition, by John Hebberd of Canterbury and notice given in the town record within 14 days as the law directs, a dark roan mare. The owner may have her by paying reasonable charges. Otherwise she will be sold as the law directs.
****
From *The New London Gazette*, August 27, 1773

town meeting
  At a special meeting of the Freeholders all of the town of the New London held at the court house, Col. Gurden Saltonstall, was chosen to the office of the town clerk by the selectmen for that town in the place of James Mumford, deceased. There were present 294 voters, a greater number than was have been known to convene in the town on any alike occasion.

benefits of sea air and bathing
  We hear of that Sir William Johnson by advice of his physicians he has taken a house at Montauk Point on the East end of Long Island, for the benefit of the sea air and of bathing in the salt water. It is expected he will shortly arrived here in New London.

immigrants from Ireland
  The distressed circumstances of the middle and low class of people in Ireland, it is said, has occasioned upwards of eighteen thousand emigrating from their native country since January last to settle in different parts of America.

outbreak of fatal fevers in Preston
  Last Monday morning at about four o'clock departed this life, Mrs. Sarah Mott, in the 29th year of her age. She was the amiable consort of Edward Mott, Merchant. She has left behind

her a disconsolate husband, six small children, two of them are twins, but eighteen days old. She was the daughter of Mr. Joseph Kinne, was born and brought up in this town and was early taught and instructed in the principal rules of Christianity. She was a beautiful child, a kind and loving wife, a tender parent, a good neighbor of a peaceable, free and generous disposition, ready to communicate to the necessities of the poor a bright and shining example; in the Church of Christ, she lived happily and cheerfully and died calmly and peaceably.

    The same day, at about three o'clock in the afternoon, died Mrs. Lucy Barns in the 31st year of her age. She was the wife of Mr. Elijah Barns and sister to Mrs. Mott. There was but 20 months difference in their age and they lived and died about 40 rods distance from each other. Mrs. Barns was also a woman of the same character but the writer of these lines, not having been acquainted with her, cannot mention particulars.

    On Tuesday, the remains of the two sisters were both carried to the Meeting House attended by all the ministers of the town and a vast concourse of people. The Reverend Mr. Hart made the first prayer. Rev. Mr. Park preached a sermon suitable to the occasion. At the close of the exercise, the ordinance of baptism was administered to Mrs. Mott's two children who are baptized by their names of Kizie and Desire. After this, a solemn procession passed to the House appointed for the living where the remains of the two deceased sisters went decently interred.

    It has been for several weeks past a very distressing time in the neighborhood. Six persons have died in the three weeks all adults and in the prime of life. Twenty seven persons are now sick with a very distressing fever within a quarter of a mile of Mrs. Mott's and even more at some distance.

murder suspect caught

    A transient fellow is taken up at Norwich, who is suspected to be the person that murdered James Johnson at Saybrook in the month of October. He is committed to goal.

estate notice

    Notice to the creditors of the estate of Silas Newcomb, deceased, that they are requested to make speedy payments to his

Administrators, Silas and Paul Newcomb, at the dwelling house of his widow, Submit Newcomb, in said Lebanon.

settlement on the Mississippi
Whereas the gentlemen of the Committee, appointed by the Company of Military Adventurers to reconnoiter the lands on the Mississippi River, have now returned and ready to make their report to the company; and whereas there are many things to communicate wherein the company is deeply concerned and a speedy meeting of the company being necessary to prevent the loss of every advantage they expect from said lands (and there is now a large tract of land in reserve for said company for a certain time which, unless by them soon taken up, will be disposed of to others) and there being a great number of persons from Europe and America continuing making settlements in that country, all members of the company hereby are desired to meet at the courthouse in Hartford on the first Wednesday of October next to consider what they will do about making a settlement on said lands; notice given by the committee P. Lyman, Alex Wolcott, Elihu Humphrey and Daniel Bull.

lottery tickets for sale
Tickets in the Colchester lottery, which are now selling off fast, may be had from T. Green.
****
From *The New London Gazette,* September 3, 1773

died
Yesterday, Captain Joseph Packwood arrived here in a brig from Hispaniola and stated that a few days before he sailed, Eliphalet Mason of this town (New London) died on board the vessel.

at Hartford, Thomas Gross and Mrs. Burr, wife of William Burr, merchant.

at Tolland, Elisha Steel.

shipping news
   Since our last, Sir William Johnson arrived at Fisher's Island from Montauk Point.

   Arrived the sloop *Nancy*, Jeremiah Tryon, Master, from Barbados, with whom came, as passengers, Capt. John Olcott, Capt. John Bigelow and Mr. John Caldwell, all hearty and in good spirits.

administration of estates
   Notice to creditors of the estate of Daniel Coit to settle accounts; notice given by Wm. Coit and Samuel Belden, Executors, New London.

   Notice by Commissioners Uriah Brigham, Josiah Babcock and Caleb Stanley, appointed by Probate Court of Windam, to the creditors of the estate of Joseph Rose, late of Coventry, deceased and represented to be insolvent, that a meeting will be held at the house of Ephraim Root Esq in Coventry; payments should be made to the estate to Timothy Dimick and Samuel Rose Jr., Administrators.

for sale
   on board the brig *Hero,* now lying at the London Coffeehouse Wharf, choice rock salt imported from Turk's Island for cash or flax seed. Notice given by C. Chadwick, New London.

   by Ebenezer Way at his store in New London rock salt or cash or flax seed.
.
found
   at a tavern in town, a woman's crimson colored short cloak, something the worn. Inquire of the Printer.

strayed or stolen
   from William Mudge in Windham dark brown mare
   ****

From *The New London Gazette,* September 10, 1773

shipping news
  By Joseph Packwood from Port au Prince, we are informed that a number of the English vessels have lately been seized by French Guards from that place, in all about 20 vessels, for breach of the acts of trade. They principally come from the Carolinas and Jamaica.
  Captain Packwood also advisers that he left the ship Charming Nancy, Captain Charles Bill whose hands were all sick

Sir William Johnson
  Yesterday, arrived the from Fishes Island, Sir William Johnson, Baronet.

strayed
  from Benjamin Lothrop in Norwich, a black mare

  from Thomas Fanning of Windham, a black horse, three years old.

ran away
  from John Annable of East Haddam, an apprentice named Daniel Booge; about 18 years old.

to be sold
  by Thomas Fanning, a general assortment of English and West India goods at the store lately improved by Mr. Elisha Hurlbut of Windham.
     ****

From *The New London Gazette,* September 17, 1773

died
  On the eighth instant, died at Windham, Dr. Ebenezer Gray in the 76th year of his age. He was born in in Boston, October 31, 1697. He took his first degree at Harvard College in 1716. He spent the chief of his life in the practice of physick and died in the firm belief of the promises of the Gospel and his own salvation.

Sir William Johnson
    Friday night Sir William Johnson set out from hence by land for his seat at Johnson Hall. We hear that some advices which he received in the post relating to Indian affairs occasioned his sudden departure.

accident
    Last Tuesday se'nnight, as a number of persons were raising a steeple of the new Meeting House in Enfield, two feet of the mortices fell over and came to the ground. Although several people were in imminent danger, yet providentially no lives were lost or limbs broken.

    Wednesday se'nnight, one Strong, a young man belonging to Middle Haddam accidentally fell from a boat into the River near that place and was drowned.

codfish
    Wednesday a schooner arrived here from a fishing voyage having caught 1,100 quinal of codfish.[56]

died
    in Windham, Jonathan Huntington formerly for several years, Chief Justice of the County court for Windham county.

    at Preston Mr. Asher Rosseter, Jr.

elections
    The following gentlemen are chosen representatives in the General Assembly to be held at New Haven on the 14th of October next:

New London - Richard Law, William Hillhouse
Lyme - Major Samuel H. Parsons, William Noye
Saybrook - Capt William Worthington, Mr. Chalker
Groton - Capt. William Morgan, Thomas Mumford
Norwich - Isaac Tracy, Benjamin Huntington
Stonington - Major Charles Phelps, Capt. Daniel Fish

evening school
An evening school will be opened in the new schoolhouse at New London for the education of youth, of either sex, in which will be concisely taught the most useful branches of literature by Thomas Smith. Note well: Those who first apply will be admitted as the master is resolved not to crowd the school.

for sale
Daniel Jennings will repair and will sell all kinds of utensils for repairing clocks and watches at the store of John Champlin, near the courthouse in New London.

administration of estates
Notice to the creditors of the estate of Capt. Barnabas Tuthill, late of Lyme, deceased, are desired to come in and settle their accounts. Notice given by Abia Tuthill and Marsh Parsons, Administrators.

ran away
from his masters Joseph Leech and William Lyman in Lebanon, an apprentice boy named John Tiffaney a saddler by trade; 5 feet 9 inches high; in his nineteenth year; has a round face, high forehead and short brown hair; with a fresh complexion.

also ran away at the same time and place, an apprentice boy named Rowland Swift; a shoe maker and tanner by trade; in the 20th year of his age; 5 feet nine inches high; of a pale complexion; short; he had short, light colored hair.

from Daniel Corning of Norwich Landing, a mulatto indented servant man, who calls himself James Hammond. He is about five feet ten inches high; a well built fellow; his hair curled and bushy.

strayed
from the pasture of Captain Dennis Bemont of Enfield; a dark brown mare; notice given by Elisha Lillie.

****

From *The New London Gazette,* September 24, 1773

shooting in Southampton
   We hear from Southampton on Long Island that last Thursday sen'nnight, one Stephen Pierce, an inhabitant of that town, being in liquor, took his gun, which was charged with shot, and went into the street, next to the house of Mr.Uriah Rogers, who was his next neighbor and at whose chamber window sat four young gentleman. Observing Pierce to stand a considerable time in this street exercising his musket, they spoke to him in a jeering way, upon which Pierce deliberately raised his piece and discharged it at them. Two shots went through the head of Capt. William Hallock and another entered his face just below one eye, which wounded him considerably. Part of the charge went over the house and broke a window in another house near 10 rods distant. Pierce was immediately brought before a Magistrate and committed to goal.

accident
   Last Tuesday, when some boys were running and diverting themselves with a chimney sweep in town, one of them fell with an open jack knife in his hand, which entered his belly and wounded him in such a manner that his life is in danger.

strayed
   or it is more likely supposed, stolen, out of the pasture of the Reverend David Ripley of Pomfret, a sorrel mare.

   from the pasture of Gershom Breed in Chelsea, a black horse belonging to the Rev. Nathaniel Whitaker D.D. of Salem.

to be sold
   a good farm containing about 120 acres of land, lying within one mile and three quarters of the Meeting House in the First Society in Ashford, with a convenient dwelling house and barn thereon; it is well watered and under good improvement. Said farm lies on the main road that leads from the First to the Second Society in Ashford. For terms and particulars, apply to Thomas Knolton living on the premises.

taken up
    by Samuel Chapman of East Haddam, a young heifer.

    by Joseph Palmer in Windham, about 30 sheep, marked by a square crop of the left ear. The lambs are not marked.

administration of estates
    Notice to debtors to the estate of William Prince, late of New London, deceased, to settle accounts; notice given by Mary Prince, Executrix.

gold and silversmith
    Notice by John Hallam that, at his shop near The Sign Post in New London, he makes and sells all kinds of gold and silversmith work. He will take country produce in payment: beef, pork, cheese, butter, grain, bees' wax, Bayberry tallow and flax seed the same as cash.

married
    at Boston, Rev. Elijah Parsons of East Haddam to Miss Elizabeth Rogers, daughter of Mr. Gamiel Rogers.

died
    On the 18th instant, Lodowick, son of Dr. Fosdick of this town (New London). He exchanged a transitory to an immutable life in the 17th year of his age. He was honored with a great concourse of sympathizing followers, perhaps more than we have ever seen on a mournful occasion in this town.

    Mrs. Elizabeth Howard, widow of Mr. Ebenezer Howard
    ****

From *The New London Gazette,* October 1, 1773

outbreak of fevers
    We hear from Preston in that ever since the first of July last a very violent fever has raged in the First Society of that town. The patients, when first seized with it, in almost every instance, complain of a severe pain in the head and neck and in the small of the back with weakness in the knees and feeling

faint. The fever is most instantaneous, has frequent intermissions or rather remissions for several days with intermediate sweating, and then becomes more of a continued fever. In the course of it, the different patients are very diversely affected. In some, it will change into a slow fever and the patient in about 20 or 30 days recovers. In the others, the nerves are very much affected which proves very fatal. In some, it puts on the face of what is commonly called the Long Fever and in some instances proves mortal, but what is common to all the patients is that the force of the distemper seats mostly in the head with a violent pressing of vaporary difficulties, with many sweating turns some violent purgings; others directly the reverse. It very much exhausts the juices of the body and appears to be very contagious. It is now spreading more over of that town and some of the towns adjacent. This account together with the following account of the progress of this calamity and the deaths have been in the compass of about 2 miles in the center of that parish chiefly between the ninth of July in the 17th of September was sent to us by a gentleman of the neighborhood.

Those who died in outbreak were:
Widow Abigail Fobes, senior person in the parish
a child of Benjamin Brewster, 2 ½ years old
Mr. Seth Starkweather, aged 23 years
Mr. Nathan Geer, left a widow and three children
Edward Bowdish, age 18
Mrs. Mary Sabin, wife of Seth Sabin; left five children
Mrs. Sarah Mott, wife of Edward the Mott, left six young children
Mrs. Lucy Barns, wife of Elijah Barns, left five young children
an infant son of Mr. Peter Bowdish
Mrs. Abigail Bowdish, wife of Peter Bowdish, left six children
Mr Asher-Sherman Rosseter, aged 26
Mrs. Amy Ames, wife of Mr. Cyrus Ames; left three children
widow Martha Hewit, aged about 34 years
Samuel L. Treat, left young children, fatherless and motherless.
Mr. Tree's wife died a year before her husband in childbirth.

Twenty three more died in this parish within a year exclusive of the above named; about a hundred persons have been sick with his fever, some very dangerous.

accident

On the 16th of last month the only son of Edward Mott, about five years old, fell into a well that was digging, fractured his skull very much and is dangerously ill.

shipwreck

Wednesday se'nnight in the evening, the sloop *Patty*, Capt. Jeremiah Harris, being bound from this port (New London) to Boston anchored in the sound under Fisher's Island shore and, during the night, drifted upon some rocks where she lay part of the next day and received so much damage that she returned on Friday to unload.

drought

There has not been perhaps in the memory of the oldest person among us of a more severe and distressing drought that has been felt in this and the neighboring towns upon the seacoast as has for the summer past and especially for the last two months. Numbers of people have been in a large to fodder their cattle. A great part of the streams and wells of water have dried up. Almost every grist mill within 30 miles of this place has been entirely stopped for several weeks. Many persons obliged to pound their grain in mortars and others to go 10 or 15 miles to a grist mill. In short, never were the people in general been seen more dejected nor their apprehensions more gloomy. But it has pleased God within these past few days greatly to change the prospect. Wednesday afternoon we had several refreshing showers and it has continued to rain a great part of the time since.

for sale

salts of lye by Christopher Leffingwell at his store in Norwich. He also has for sale excellent dry codfish, smoked and pickled salmon.

taken up

in the pasture of James Sherman in New London, a dark brown mare.

desertions
    Notice by T. Willson, master of the sloop *Sally*, of the desertion of Jacob Croo, New England born; dark complexion; about five feet three inches tall; marked in the face with smallpox; black curled hair, clubbed behind;
    Also deserted from the same sloop, James Barn, Irish born about five feet eight inches high; square shoulders; down look; short black hair; dark complexion.

          ****

From *The New London Gazette,* October 8, 1773

died
    On the 15th of last month died at Windham of a putrid fever in the 78th year of his age, the Honorable Jonathan Huntington, an eminent and noted physician and formerly one of the assistants of this colony and Chief Judge of the Inferior Court in the County of Windham.

bankruptcy notices
    Report by Elias Worthington and Joseph Isman, Jr., Trustees to the creditors of the bankrupt estate of Amasa Jones, insolvent debtor of Colchester, that a meeting will be held at the Tavern of Mr. John Taintor in Colchester.

    Report by Charles Foot and Joseph Isman, Jr., Trustees to the creditors of the bankrupt estate of insolvent debtor Jonas Wilds of Colchester, that a meeting will be held at the Tavern of Mr. John Taintor in Colchester.

    Report by Elias Worthington and Joseph Isman, Jr., Trustees to the creditors of the bankrupt estate of John Clark, insolvent debtor of Colchester that a meeting will be held at the Tavern of Mr. John Taintor in Colchester.

ran away
    from William Avery of Groton, an apprentice boy named Joseph Brown; 14 years old; black eyes and hair.

strayed or stolen
> from pasture of Cullick Ely of Lyme, a sorrel horse.

> from the pasture of Darius Morgan in New London, a black mare.

to be sold
> at the house of Azariah Lothrop in Norwich, the dwelling house belonging to Ebenezer Backus, deceased, and the shop where said Backus dwelt with the land containing about 60 rods lying between two streets;
> also about 2 3/4 acres of land with a dwelling house thereon on the North East side of the town street near Samuel Wheat's land;
> also land on the opposite side of the street with a barn, corn house and buildings, thereon bounded South East on the land of Mr. Joseph Post;
> also 60 acres of land on the South side of the quarter near the town plat by John Edgerton's land;
> also 10 acres of land in the West Sheep Walk by the South West corner of the land lately belonging to William Lothrop;
> also 15 acres and 50 rods of pasture land near Daniel Douglas' on Shetucket River near the landing place;
> also four acres of land in the home lot bounding South East Pond by Simon Colkin's land;
> also a handsome dwelling house shop, barn, out houses and land that now in the occupation of Mr. Ebenezer Lord, near the Meeting House in Norwich;
> also two tracts of land, the first containing about 20 acres which formally belonged to John Edgerton, the second about seven acres which lately belonging to Dr. Elisha Lord; for particulars as to the purchase of the above lands apply to Samuel Huntington of Norwich.

****

From *The New London Gazette,* October 15, 1773

taken up
> by John Cobb of Canterbury, a yearling of red color.

church matters
　　We hear from Ripton that the Church and Society of that place have invited Mr. David Ely to settle with them in the gospel ministry.

patrol boat
　　Wednesday, one of His Majesty's cruisers, probably from Newport, passed this harbor (New London) and went up Sound.
　　　　**********
From *The New London Gazette,* October 22, 1773

drought in Long Island
　　a letter from a gentle man at Long Island, dated the 23rd of last month, says the appearance there is melancholy beyond imagination or description. The face of the earth is stripped entirely of herbage except here and there, some useless and noxious weeds. There is nothing green to be seen, unless in some low bottoms and meadows but many of the trees are scorched and withered. The gardens are most of them quite dried up and every species of vegetables weathered. On a great part of the ground, the turf is wholly consumed as well as the herbage. But in the midst of judgment, God has mercifully remembered them with respect to the Indian corn that has strangely been preserved through that distressing season and they think they shall have at least a half crop thereof.

thanksgiving
　　Thursday, the 25th of November, is appointed to be observed as a day of public Thanksgiving through the colony.

coal mines discovered
　　Any number of coal mines are this founded on the East Branch of the Susquehanna; the quality of the coal is said to be much superior to any heretofore discovered in America.

pay up
　　Notice by David Adams that all those persons who are indebted to him should set out their accounts with Experience Robinson of Scotland. In cases of dispute, he will attend at the

house of Richard Kimball or Abner Flint of Scotland.

ran away
 from Joseph Miner in Stonington, a Negro woman slave named Peg; she is about 40 years old; has lost the sight of one or her of her eyes.

found
 a black Tassety apron was found in Chatham about 2 miles east of Middletown's ferry. The owner may have it again by applying to John Ames of said Chatham and paying charges.

just published
 and to be sold by T. Green in New London or by Green and Spooner in Norwich *Freebetter's Connecticut Almanac* for the year 1774.

    ****

From *The New London Gazette,* October 29, 1773

fire
 We hear from Pomfret that on the 18th of this month, a barn belonging to D. Lord of that town was consumed by fire, together with a considerable quantity of grain. The fire, we are told, was occasioned by his sons shooting a firearm in the barn and not being careful to extinguish the wadding.

died
 Last Friday died at East Hampton, Mrs. Abigail Tinker, wife of Captain Sylvanus Tinker.

 Mr. Daniel Jennings, watch maker.

administration of estates
 Notice by Elijah Tredway, Nathaniel Brown and Elisha Starr, Commissioners appointed by the Court of Probate for the District of Middletown to the creditors of the estate of Captain Samuel Rockwell, late of Middletown, deceased and represented insolvent, that a meeting will be held at the dwelling house of Ephraim Finne, Inn keeper in said Middletown.

to be sold
    on reasonable terms, a farm containing 200 acres lying in the East Society in Lyme with a good house and barn thereon; three orchards and a good quantity of plow and Meadow land, well watered and wooded. Inquire of Amos Lay living on the premises.

strayed or stolen
    from Peter Sluman of Charleston, a brown colt.

taken up
    in my pasture, a three year old steer; notice by Joseph Churchville of Chatham.

          ****

From *The New London Gazette,* November 5, 1773

religious news
    Wednesday se'nnight, the Reverend David Ely was ordained to the ecclesiastical office over the Church and Society at Ripton in Stratford.

storm at sea
    The cruiser *Snow*, Captain Howe, lately met with a storm off the Capes of the Delaware in which she had a great part of her sails blown away and was obliged to throw all her guns overboard.

King is unhappy
    We hear that, in answer to a petition from the Massachusetts Assembly respecting the appointment of judges, His Majesty declared his intention of supporting the supreme authority and rights of the British Parliament to make laws binding on the Colonies and expressed his deep displeasure that principles repugnant to this rights should be set forth in the petition.

died
    Mrs. Lovet, wife of the Reverend Joseph Lovet.

At Stonington, Samuel Prentice.

On last Saturday evening in the 62nd year of his age Captain Daniel Morgan after a very distressing illness of seven days which he bore with Christian Patience and Fortitude.

fire

On Sunday night last, a large new dwelling house well furnished in the occupation of Thomas Dyer of Windham was consumed the a fire when everything therein, except a few article in a lower room. By Mrs. Dyer's providentially awakening while the house was in flames, the family had just time to escape out of the upper windows.

town meeting

At a town meeting held in Stonington last week for the purpose of choosing a town clerk in the place of Samuel Prentice deceased, P. Cheseborough was chosen into that office. We hear that there were present nearly 300 voters.

goods and services

Ebenezer Douglas has for sale at his shop near the courthouse and directly opposite the printing office, a neat assortment of glass ware.

Amos White, gold smith and jeweler, has his shop at East Haddam.

Watches mended and cleaned by Edward Palmes.

The clothier's business is carried on by Nathan and Ebenezer Wales at Elderkin's Bridge in Norwich.

theft

Notice by Abraham Page of North Branford that one Joshua Chappel stole money from him out of his boat at Glastonbury.

strayed
out of the pasture of Elisha Scovel in Colchester; a horse. Return to Silas Deane or Joseph Webb is Wethersfield.

****

From *The New London Gazette,* November 12, 1773

lottery
The lottery at New Haven will commence on the 20th day of December at the Statehouse. All who may have any tickets unsold are desired to return them by that time.

died
in Stonington, of a lingering and complicated disease, Samuel Prentice of this place in the 70th year of his age, universally lamented. He was buried with the greatest decency and respect and his funeral was attended by a numerous assembly of all parts of the town and neighborhood when a sermon was preached by the Reverend Mr. Fish. He had been born at Lancaster in the Province of Massachusetts of worthy and religious parents and moved to Stonington when his son was a youth. He has left a sorrowful widow and six sons and three daughters.

for sale
Connecticut law looks to be sold by T. Green.

shipwreck in Connecticut River
Last Friday as a schooner, belonging to Piscataqua and loaded with salt, sugar and English goods, was going up the Connecticut River between Wethersfield and Hartford, she struck a sunken log with such force as to bilge her and she sank so suddenly that the people had but just time to save themselves in their boat.

died
after eight few days of an illness of a malignant disorder, Joseph Hurlbut, Jr. of New London.

Benjamin Brown

medicines for sale
    Dr. Seth Holmes of New London, North Parish has invented and prepared medicines which infallibly cures all those disorders mentioned by Dr. Anthony Veldall in his late advertisement. They are made up in the same manner and sold at a moderate price.

cash given
    for small furs, beeswax, old brass, copper and pewter by David Gardiner Jr. at his shop near the courthouse in New London, who has to sell a good assortment of ship chandlery ware and groceries of all kinds.

runaway
    from Daniel Clark in Plainfield a boy named Elias Thomas about 17 years old; of a light complexion and slim built.

taken up
    in the pasture of Nathaniel Bishop in Norwich, a spotted black and white yearling steer.

just published
    and to be sold by T. Green, a narrative of the captivity sufferings and removal of Mrs. Mary Rowlandson, who was taken prison by the Indians with several others and treated in the most barbarous and cruel manner by of those vile savages.

                ****

From *The New London Gazette,* November 19, 1773

died
    Last Lord's Day morning, died at the North parish in this town, after a long illness, Mrs. Patience Jewet, consort of the Reverend Mr. David Jewet and, on Tuesday, her remains were decently interred with a sermon preached by the Reverend Mr. Throop of Norwich.

agricultural news
    A gentleman in town (New London) has raised in his garden this season a crop of Indian corn produced from seeds of

this year's growth. The ears of each crop is full-grown. Samples of it may be seen at the printing office.

religious news
 We hear that John Blanchard is now preaching in a neighboring town.

married
 at Hartford, the Reverend Mr. Brick of Springfield to Mrs. Dorr, widow of the late Reverend Mr. Dorr of Hartford.

ran away
 from Gabriel Sistarr in New London, a Negro man named Peter; 37 years old; speaks English, French and Spanish; is about 6 foot high and well set. The sinews of his right wrist are contracted and his head declining downward. He has a scar on his forehead over his left eye.

sailing to New York
 Jeremiah Clement is at Norwich Landing and is bound in the good sloop *Bridget* to New York and perhaps up the Hudson River; burthen about 40 tons; whoever wants to send freight or take passage must be ready in three or four days from the date hereof, as the season is far elapsed.

court delayed
 Whereas the public Thanksgiving happens to be appointed on the first week of the County court's sitting, which will render it inconvenient and expensive to the parties and to the public for the court to sit and do business the first week, it is therefore thought advisable to acquaint the public that the court proposes only to meet and immediately open and adjourn to the Monday the next following. Notice by Richard Raw, Judge, sitting in Norwich.

stop thief
 Whereas the shop belonging to Asahel Clark Jr. in Lebanon was broke open during the night after the sixth of November and sundry articles stolen from thence, a reward is

offered for the apprehension of the thief or thieves and the return of the articles stolen.

for sale
John Hallam at his shop in the Sign Post in New London makes and sells all kinds of gold smith, silver smith and jeweler's work as cheap as can be had in this colony. He will take country produce in payment, *viz* beef, pork, cheese, butter, grain, beeswax, Bayberry tallow and flax seed the same as cash.

Just come to hand and to be sold by Peabody Clement at his store, lately improved by John B. Brimmer, at Chelsea, European goods suitable for the season.

****

From *The New London Gazette,* November 26

bankruptcy notice
Notice by William Coit, Thomas Shaw and George B.. Hurlbut, Commissioners appointed to hear examine and report upon a petition by John Braddick of New London for an act of insolvency and advising all creditors to meet at the dwelling house of Edward Palmes of New London.

administration of estates
Notice by John Avery and J. Halsey, Commissioners appointed by the Honorable Jabez Huntington, Judge of the Probate Court for the District of Norwich, to the creditors of the estate of Mr. Samuel Branch late of Preston, deceased and represented to be insolvent, of a hearing at the dwelling house of Robert Crary, inn holder in said Preston; all persons indebted to said estate are desired to make speedy payment to Hannah Branch, Adminstratrix of said estate.

new laws enacted
The following acts were passed by the last session of the General Assembly

an Act regulating and governing the goal or workhouse in the town in Simsbury and for the punishment of certain atrocious crimes and felonies.

An Act for the suppression of Mountebanks.[57]

an Act in addition to an act for preventing and suppressing of lotteries.

An Act establishing a brand for horses in Cornwall.

new British patrol boat
The new *Gaspee* ship, having lain at this harbor New London for several days, came to sail on Tuesday and stood to the eastward.

died
at Glastonbury, Mrs. Eells, wife of the Reverend Mr. John Eells.

for sale
Pursuant to the order of the superior court to be sold by public vendue the real estate of William Bowdoin, late of Roxbury deceased, a valuable farm in Leicester, containing about 500 acres, more or less, with a good dwelling house and barn thereon. A great part of it is under good improvement, well fenced and watered with a fish pond and a great quantity of wood growing thereon.. It is presently in the occupation of William Gillers.
Also, real estate in the occupation of Mr Nathaniel Richardson, about half a mile from Mr. Jonathan Sargeant, inn holder in Leicester and about 50 miles from Boston.

****

From *The New London Gazette,* December 3, 1773

land to be sold
at public sale, by order of the Court of Probate for the District of Windham, the real estate of Mr. Jonathan Clark, Jr. late of Lebanon. The estate consists of about 85 acres of land with a good house, barn and orchard thereon. Notice given by John Clark, Administrator.

tax sale
      To be sold at public venue, by order of the General Assembly, such a part of the real estate of Mr. John Spencer, late of Windham, as will raise the sum of 120 pounds. The sale is to be at the house of Eleazer Cary, inn holder in Windham. Notice given by Zebulon Hebard.

just imported
      from London and to be sold as cheap as in New York by Simon Wolcott at his shop near the courthouse in New London, a fresh and general assortment of drugs and medicines.

wanted
      a school master to take charge of a school in New London who is qualified to teach the Latin and English tongues, writing and arithmetic. The school consist of only 31 boys. $220 per annum wages will be given in quarterly payments. None need offer but those whose characters will bear the strictest inquiry. It is requested that such as apply will send a specimen of their writing, with their age and place of abode and whether married or not.

Susquehanna
      Notice is hereby given to all the proprietors of the Township now called by the name of Warwick, in the Susquehanna Purchase, lately surveyed and laid out by Zachariah Lothrop of Norwich, to meet at the dwelling house of Azariah Lothrop, inn holder in Norwich, to hear the report and see the survey and to choose proper officers for said town and to conduct any of the business proper. Notice given by David Hough, Proprietors Clerk.

thieves
      Stolen from Capt. Oliver Smith of Stonington by one James M'Donald, an Irishman, and John Lappineer, who appears to be to be a Frenchman, a Moses Boat of 14 feet with different articles on board.

strayed or stolen
    from the pasture of Samuel Belden of New London, a dark bay horse.

    from the pasture of subscriber James Thomson in New London, a horse.

    from the pasture of Ebenezer Goddard of New London, a young, small red cow

died
    We hear from New Concord in Norwich that Mrs. Elizabeth Lothrop, relict of Deacon Samuel Lothrop, late of that place, was taken with an apoplectic or fainting fit and unhappily, being near a large fire, fell into it and was awfully burned before she was discovered, the family being providentially all absent at the time period. It is most probable she had no sense of the disaster as there were no signs of the least motion or struggle from falling into the fire. She was a person of strict virtue and eminent piety, highly esteemed while living and her death is much lamented.

    On Friday the last, Mrs. Ann Whiting, wife of Deacon William Whiting, living in weakness and confinement, was taken with a sudden disorder which put an end to her life in about ten hours. She had been long way waiting and wishing for the happy release from the world of sin and sorrow.

Boston people's opposition to tax on tea
    Our latest advices from Boston are that the spirits of the people in that town with regard to the detestable East India Company's tea was amazingly high, that Faneuil Hall could not contain the people who collected there on Monday last but that the meeting was adjourned from there to the old South Meeting House where it was voted to opposes the landing of the tea and send it back.[58] It is thought they could carry their point.

    We hear that Admiral Montague declares that he has received no instructions with regard to the tea and that he will not inter meddle in the affair.

fever outbreak in North Carolina
Letters from North Carolina mention that a "billious fever rages there very violently of which many persons have died."

arms broken in accidents
The following casualties happened at East Haddam last week, namely, on Wednesday, Job Wheeler fell from an upper loft of a store and broke one of his arms.

On Thursday, Timothy Brainerd, being on horseback, a young woman in attempting to jump on the horse behind and accidentally pulled him off. In the fall, he broke one of his arms.

And on Friday, as two men were wrestling, one of them named Samuel Barney was thrown and had one of his arms broken in two places.

One day last week, a boy named Tucker fell about 50 feet from the mast of a sloop at Saybrook onto the vessel's deck and broke his arm in two places.

ran away
from Daniel Yeamans in Lebanon, an apprentice boy in the clothier's business named William Whitley; in the 21st year of his age; of middling stature; dark bushy hair.

lost
a white Holland apron was found about half a mile from Poquatanuk. The owner may have it again on by applying to Jesse Williams of Norwich.

****

From *The New London Gazette,* December 10, 1773

Boston tea
From a letter from Boston "part of the detested tea has at length arrived and the people resolved that it should all be sent back without paying a farthing of duty. The consignees, who would not comply with those terms, have taken refuge at the Castle. The commissioners of the customs have once more quit town and gone to the Castle. The Governor, they say, is there too. The tea is now in the hands of the people. Whether they really

will ship it back or not is, as yet, in doubt. Most probably they will follow the example of New York and house it.

low water
    By reason of the lowness of water in the Connecticut River, a number of sea vessels have, for ten or twelve days, been prevented from coming down.

married
    at Norwich John Chester of Wethersfield to Mss Elizabeth Huntington, daughter of Col. Jabez Huntington.

died
    in Lyme, after a short illness, Elisha Moor, aged 28, the only son of Asa Moor .

    at Fairfield, David Burr, Justice of the Peace for Fairfield County and for many year a representative from that town to the General Assembly.

drowning victim saved
    On Sunday last, a child, the grandson of John Marson of Westerly, had the misfortune to be drowned, but, on being taken out of the water (how long it had been in it is uncertain) and, although without the least appearance of life in the child, its jaws set and limbs stiff, by rubbing, rolling and embracing the body with salt and camphoronated spirits, there appeared some symptoms of life so that, on bleeding, it was perfectly restored again.

              ****

From *The New London Gazette,* December 17, 1773

strayed or stolen
    from the pasture of Jeremiah Hubbard in Middletown, a reddish brown horse

not responsible
    Notice from Jonne Butelere that his wife Marjare has eloped and gone away from his bed and board and that he

forewarns all he will not be responsible for any debts she undertakes.

wanted
    Cash given for clean linen rags at the Printing Office.[59]

religious news
    The First Church and Society of Wethersfield have chosen Rev. Mr John Marsh to be their pastor in the place of the Reverend Mr. James Lockwood, deceased

accident
    Last Tuesday, as a Negro man of John Tainter's was assisting in the scalding of hogs at his master's house in Colchester, he accidentally fell backwards into a large tub of the hot water which scalded him in so terrible a matter that he died yesterday.

married
    Thursday se'nnight was married at Stonington, Captain Henry Hunter of Newport to Miss Rebecck Eells , daughter of the Reverend Nathaniel Eells.

deaths at sea
    Thursday s'ennight, a sloop arrived at Stonington from the West Indies. Captain Joshua Rathbun, master, died on the passage of a fever as did one of the hands.

settle accounts or be sued
    All persons indebted to Russel Hubbard, by book or note, whose debts are more than one years standing are desired to settle their respective accounts without delay or they may depend on being sued at the next court. He expects that this will be as sufficient a warning as if he wrote to each person separately.

wanted
    a journey man cabinet maker by Jonathan Starr Jr. in New London

ran away
    from Joseph Allen of Scotland in Windham County, an apprentice boy named JohnTuff; about seventeen years old; has black straight hair and a brown complexion.

taken up
    in the pasture or of William Westcote of New London Great Neck, a yearling bull.

****

From *The New London Gazette,* December 24, 1773

To the printer
Sir:
    in reading a little essay upon newspapers in a book which I picked up a few days ago I find among other advantages of these periodicals the author mentions the public benefit of the advertisements as being by no means the most inconsiderable and instead of complaining of there being so common in all businesses wishes rather that they were extended to more of the different arts, professions, wants and losses etc. of mankind. I was so pleased with this proposal that I could not help throwing the following advertisements together which may serve as models for some of your correspondents who have more leisure and inclination to pursue this invaluable of public intelligence

Was lost
    A character. It is the worse for wear and has been patched in several places. Whoever finds he said character and returns it to me shall be handsomely rewarded

Was stolen
    A character quite new. It will be useless to anybody except the owner.

Was lost
    A friend. He disappeared immediately after a jest and has not been heard of since. $1000 Reward

Was lost
A friend. He disappeared immediately after asking a favor from him.

Was lost
A memory. The person who has met with this misfortune has received innumerable benefits which he cannot recollect so as to thank his benefactors for them.

Was lost
A heart bloated on one side with vanity and mortified on the other with pride.

Wanted
A husband and accomplished rake would be most agreeable, provided he can bring proper certificates of his health.

Wanted
A housekeeper for a bachelor. She must understand housewifery perfectly well and be able to turn her hand to any thing.

Were lost
The seven last years of a lady's life. They were seen frequently in the Playhouse, in the streets and in the assembly room.

Settle up
Whereas the partnership between religion and morality entered into above 1700 years ago is now dissolved, all persons indebted to them are requested to pay off their accounts immediately to the letter or they will be put into a lawyer's hands

Just imported
from the Moon in the shape of *Airy Castle* 150 likely sets of servants of both sexes; among them are lovers, schemers, horse jockeys, jobbers etc.

For Sale for gold

At the State House, the schooner *Extravaganza*, Howard Spendthrift, Master, the cargo of which consist of new fashioned furniture, a quantity of plate, new clothes and English horses.

Made to their escape
a husband's affections. They disappeared immediately after seeing his wife with her face and hands unwashed at breakfast.

To the public
Whereas my wife, AMERICAN LIBERTY, has lately behaved in a very licentious manner and run me considerably into debt, this is to forewarn all persons from trusting her.
LOYALTY

To the public
Where as my husband LOYALTY has in the late advertisement forewarned all persons from trusting me on his account, this is to inform the public that he derived all his fortune from me and, by our marriage, articles he has no right to proscribe me from the use of it. My reason for leaving him was because he behaved in an arbitrary and cruel manner and suffered his domestic servants, grooms, fox hunters etc. to direct and insult me.
AMERICAN LIBERTY

for sale
Jeremiah Clement has to sell bar iron in the best kind and all sorts of hats, beaver, beverett, castor and felts.

administration of estates
Notice by Eleazer Baldwin, Josiah Babcock and Aaron Hovey, Commissioners appointed by the Court of Probate in Windham to the creditors of the estate of William Cummings, late of Mansfield, deceased and represented to be insolvent, that a meeting will be held at the dwelling house of widow Mirium Cummings in Mansfield.

died
  Last Sunday evening died at Stonington, Nathaniel Williams of that place. About 10 o'clock he was heard to say, just before he went to bed, that the weather felt very cold and that he felt a touch of his old disorder that is the swelling which he had been subject to for several winters past. A few minutes after he got into bed, his wife going to bed to him put out the candle, she heard him make an uncommon noise and stretched himself out. She immediately called to him but receiving no answer said she called to the people then in the kitchen to bring in a candle and, the candle brought in, he was seen only to make a gasp without any other motion. He had enjoyed his health extremely well for some times before.

  Yesterday died at Norwich West Society in the seventy ninth year of his life, the eminently worthy and much respected in this town, Thomas Willes. A sermon, ,suitable to the solemnity, was delivered at the funeral by the Reverend Benjamin Lloyd of Norwich.

Boston Tea Party
  The substance of the following concise account of what happened in Boston on Thursday last may be depended upon as fact.
  On that memorable day, a number of the inhabitants of the town of Boston and other neighboring towns to the amount of between two and three thousand met, via an adjournment, at the old the Fourth Meeting house in Boston. After reading some animated letters from the country towns, from New York and one from Plymouth. Mr. Rotch, part owner of one of the tea ships, appeared before the body and protested against the custom house for not clearing out his ship so it could sale with the tea for London. Immediately upon which a number of persons, in seamen's habits, who were in the porch, blew their whistles and a shouted around through the whole building and the body dissolved. Soon after that, a number of persons entered Rotch's ship, took the chests of the tea out of the hold, stove than and threw the tea overboard. From thence, they proceeded to Bruce's and Coffin's two vessels and behaved in the same manner so that

every bit of the East India Company's tea which was in harbor of Boston, is utterly destroyed. It is the first part of 2000 chests of tea sent out by the East India Company. The [fates of] the second and third parts, we expect, will soon be published in New York and Philadelphia.

First Delaware Purchase

Notice by Jonathan Huntington, Clerk to the proprietors of the Township of Huntington in the First Delaware purchase to meet at the dwelling house of Azariah Lothrp in Norwich to consider and act upon such matters relative to said township.

****

From *The New London Gazette,* December 31, 1773

lottery

Notice by Joshua Lathrop, Samuel Tracy and Rufus Lathrop, Managers for the new lottery for finishing and completing the Great Wharf Bridge at Chelsea in Norwich.

to be sold

a likely Negro woman; about 26 years of age who understands all kinds of household work. Also, two likely Negro boys, one of them six and the other two or three years of age. Inquire of Bridgett Harris, widow of Captain William Harris, in New London.

administration of estates

Notice by Joseph Hewit, Joseph Champlin and John Hallam, Commissioners appointed by the Honorable Charles Phelps, Judge of Probate for the District of Stonington, to the creditors of the estate of David Hillard, 2d, late of Stonington, deceased and represented insolvent, that a meeting will be held at the dwelling house of Captain Giles Russel, inn holder in Stonington.

strayed

from the pasture of Flavel Moseley in the parish of Canada in Windham, a deep black horse, two years old.

hogs
    Last Friday was killed by Mr. Richard Ransom of Lyme, two hogs which were both of one litter and no more than 18 months old. One of them weighted 20s score and 10 pounds and the other 20 score and eight pounds.

bad weather
    We hear that a schooner was drove ashore at Stonington in in the late gale and that a number of boats in different places are likewise ashore. And from the severity of the gale, it may be expected that we shall soon here of considerable damages.

    Yesterday morning, there was considerable ice in the River Thames.

    There is so great a freshet in the Connecticut River, that the meadow was overflowed ad and had been considerable ice in the River prevents the passing of boats at both of the ferries.

****

ENDNOTES

1. Jesuit Bark, or Powder, was first introduced to the European population by Jesuit missionaries. They had encountered its use by the Peruvian Indians in South America. It was a remedy for malaria and is the source of today's quinine

2. Packet ships carried mail between Britain and her colonies as well as among the colonies. The letters sometimes became the source of news items.

3. "Consumption" is the old name for what we now know as tuberculosis or TB". The earlier name was descriptive of how the illness wasted away or consumed its victims. It has been around since at least the time of the ancient Greeks and Hippocrates. A bacterial infection it was highly contagious and fatal most of the time.

4. "Se'nnight" is an abbreviation of the fuller phrase "seven nights", hence a week. Popular in colonial days, it is rarely, if ever, used today. Its cousin, "fort night" meaning fourteen nights or "two weeks is still occasionally seen.

5. Freshet" is another word, which was once an everyday term in colonial America, but is never used today. It referred to a flood resulting from heavy rain or a spring thaw, especially one from snow and ice melt in rivers and feeder streams.

6. "Moon cursers" was a term for smugglers, who apparently preferred darkness to moon light.

7. Cape Nicola Mole is on the island of Santo Domingo, in northwest Haiti.

8. The Delaware and Susquehanna companies were land companies formed in Eastern Connecticut in the early 1750s for the purpose of developing the Wyoming Valley and Susquehanna territories in

Pennsylvania. Connecticut's charter stipulated that the colony's western boundary to be northeast Pennsylvania. A tract of land was purchased from the Indians in 1754 by John Henry Lydius, a Dutch trader, and preparations were made for development. However, a massacre of settlers in Pennsylvania in 1763 triggered , a proclamation by Connecticut Governor Fitch prohibiting further settlement, until the Indians were pacified. In the meanwhile, Eliphalet Dyer of Windham was sent to England in an unsuccessful attempt to secure confirmation of the land grant. It was 1769 before any definite settlement was made. Soon, the settlers became embroiled with rival settlers from Pennsylvania, who claimed the lands. The dispute as to ownership continued through 1782 when it was resolved in favor of Pennsylvania.

9, The word :"manufactories" has an awkward sound to it while the shortened version of the word "factories" is a familiar one. It is a plant consisting of one or more buildings with facilities for manufacturing.

10. Non importation agreements were boycotts of imported British goods. They proved to be a very effective, economic pressure against British control. A weapon of the Sons of Liberty, they appeared as early as 1766 and had a major effect on the repeal of the Stamp Tax Act. Boston passed the first one and every port city and nearly every region adopted one like it, including New London and Southeast Connecticut. In 1774, the first Continental Congress would pass a colony wide prohibition against any trade with Great Britain.

11. Mad dogs are mentioned on a regular basis in the *Gazette*. The term refers to dogs infected with the rabies virus, a disease that can occur in mostly all warm blooded animals. As the dog disease advances, the dog is affected by showing the aggressive and furious behavior associated with rabies and what earns it its name of " mad dog." For a good example of "mad dogs" see *The New London Gazette*, March 8, 1771, *infra*.

12. The island of St. Eustatius, or Statia as it is commonly called,, is volcanic in origin. During colonial days it was once one of the busiest and most powerful commercial ports in the Caribbean. To avoid the British blockade during America's Revolutionary War, most goods destined for the new colonies flowed into St. Eustatius. Today it today a part of the Netherlands Antilles but, over its history, it has changed hands more than 20 times.

13. Norwich Landing or Chelsea or, as it was sometimes called, was the name for a section of what is now Norwich, situated at the head of navigation of the Thames river, the junction of the Shetucket and Yantic rivers.

14 As the name implies, the Committees of Inspection sniffed into the efforts of elite merchants to evade colonial boycotts. It was particularly active and effective in discouraging merchants from paying the Tea Tax of 1773.

15. Flushing, Otter Creek was another effort to settle Connecticut's claimed western lands. Unfortunately, the Province and people of New York disagreed. Colonel Reid and his settlers were brutally forced to leave and the settlement burned by a mob of a hundred men in August 1773.

16. These documents were in possession of John Winthrop's, who received the Royal grants in the first years. It was hoped would establish Connecticut boundary claims in the West.

17. There are any number of advertisements for "fat horses" and other livestock which would be shipped to the Carribean colonies. There are also many references in news items to that stock being swept overboard over board in gales.

18. A rod is a unit of measure equal to 5.5 yards, 16.5 feet or 5.03 meters.

19. Chelsea was also known as Norwich Landing. See endnote 13, *supra*

20. "Before you can say Jack Robinson" or "quicker than you can say Jack Robinson" does nor refer to the famous Brooklyn Dodger player who broke the color barrier in major league baseball. The expression originated in the 1700s, but the identity of Jack Robinson has been lost. A 1785 dictionary says he was a man who paid such brief visits to acquaintances that there was scarcely time to announce his arrival, before he had departed, but it gives no further documentation.

21. The pages of the *Gazette* contain any number accounts of whipping as a punishment. At least in Southeastern Connecticut, it seemed more utilized than the other corporal punishments relied upon by Colonial American, from the pillory to the ducking stool. Branding on the

forehead and cropping of ears were close seconds. Punishment was exacted in public in a ceremonial fashion, intended to humiliate on as much as to inflict physical pain. Most common offenses that lead to whipping, branding and the cropping of the ears were theft, fornication, blasphemous expression, running away, adultery, and lewd .

22. T. Allen was a colonial entrepreneur of the waterfront. After beginning the London Coffee house, which was a misnomer as it was an inn/tavern, not an early Starbucks, he expanded his operations to running the London Coffee House Wharf. In fact, in the 1773, he was "sponsoring" the *Gazette's* weekly list of vessels which "entered into" and "cleared out of" the Harbor.

23. Potash was a cash crop of sorts for colonial farmers. It was refined from the ashes of hardwood trees. The trees themselves were the by products of the farmers clearing their wooded land for crops. The easiest way to clear it was to burn it. Ashes from trees could then be used to make lye, which could either be used to make soap or as potash.

24. This goes back to New London's earliest days into the claims of the parties to a certain large tract of land in Hebron, anciently granted by John Mason, assignee of Uncas, Owaneco and Joshua, Sachems.

25. Elementary education was widespread in New England. Reading was necessary to study the Bible, so children were taught early. The literacy rate among men was nearly 100%. Each town was required to pay for a primary school. Of course, boys generally stayed on the family farm or became apprentices to artisans, so higher education was not a priority. In fact, it was the churches in New England which established colleges to train ministers.

26. What exactly were "fulling mills"? Unknown to most these days, they were found on streams in every village in colonial times, continuing in America an art, practiced since medieval times in Europe. Fulling mills cleaned woolen cloth and shrunk it somewhat thicker. Villages were self supporting then. Life's basics-- food, clothing, and shelter, were produced locally. Wool was the principal fabric for clothing but handwoven woolen cloth made on a loom is not very tight and the wool still contains too much grease and oils. It needed to be fulled., a process which involves beating the cloth by a pair of wooden mallets, powered by a water wheel, in a wooden tub

with some water and soap. often for days. This process shrinks the cloth to perhaps half its original size. Then the fulled cloth needs to be stretched and dried, which was done on a "tentering" frame.

27. In colonial New England almost every farmer had his own orchard and harvesting the apples was as much a part of the annual cycle as was haying or collecting wood for winter's heat. Apples could be stored in barrels in the cellar, where they would ripen over the winter for personal consumption. A part of the crop was converted to cider, alcoholic and not. The cider could be sold or bartered making it at times a cash crop as well.

28. Spinning wool begins with shearing the sheep. Skirting the fleece is next which involves removing the unspinnable stuff, wool that is too short or too greasy. Scouring the wool follows whereby the wool goes into a vat, cover the wool with water several times, letting the dirty water drain out a hole in the bottom of the vat. A warm water wash removes excess lanolin, then the wool is spread it out and dried. A wool carder, using wire bristled cards, gets all of the burrs out of the wool and the two cards and brush them together to make the wool soft and fluffy. The more a carder could do, the more a spinner, who got it next, could convert the fibers into a continuously twisting yarn. Next the wool goes to the fuller. See endnote 26 above.

29. "Side Leather" refers to leather made from one half, or "side", of a full hide. It typically refers to leather whose top grain (outermost layer) has been left intact.

30. Batteau" is a French term for "boat" and in colonial America, meant any flat-bottomed, shallow-draft vessel that was pointed at both ends. It was the mainstay of inland shipping.

31. Small pox was not only a killer but it scarred the survivors for life. In New Jersey, over 15% of the notices seeking the return of runaway servants, deserters, escaped prisoners and thieves are descriptions like "pock mark'd" or "pox fretten", reflecting how many of the survivors of this disease were permanently scarred by it. An outbreak of small pox was to be feared and efforts, even primitive inoculations, were taken to avoid its spread through the population. The New London region does not seem to have been afflicted with it in the 1760s, although Boston was, as the *New London*

Gazette of April 13, 1764 reports: "The small pox having broke out in Charles Town last week, the inhabitants of that town and others have been given leave by the Selectmen to be inoculated there until the 25th of this month and no longer. Such surprising success has attended the present method of inoculation that it is said that nearly 3000 persons of all age, from a months until 50 years old who received the inoculation in that way are already recovered or out of danger but few instances of mortalities, ten to a dozen, only who died from it and those chiefly afflicted with other disorders from which they died."

32. This probably refers to Paul and Barnabas, missionaries to the Gentiles in Galatians 2:1-10). The two had been given "the right hand of fellowship" by highly esteemed leaders of the Christian community on Jerusalem "when they recognized the grace given to them." The Right Hand of Christian Fellowship is a practice performed by many sects of Christian as an extension of brotherhood into the church.

33. The barrel of petroleum oil and that of the whale oil barrel are not related. The petroleum barrel contains 42 gallons. Whale oil barrel ranged from 30 to 35 gallons. It has been suggested that in the early days of the fishery, the ship's carpenter might have decided the size of actual whale oil barrels, if they were made at sea, especially in the last months of the whaling season when perhaps only scraps were left.

34. Until the early 1700s, whales (usually right whales), entered Long Island Sound in large numbers, and remained from November to April. First, Indians hunted them by using canoes to drive them to shallow water where they could be killed and butchered. The early colonists improved on this by using long boats to chase the whales within the waters of the Sound. Whales being intelligent creatures responded by leaving the Sound and going into the Atlantic. The colonists followed. Open sea whaling became common. Sloops of sixty to eighty tons replaced the canoes and open boats of earlier. They would seek out the whale (usually the sperm) at sea, and after a capture, would carry the blubber to shore to extract the oil by boiling.

By 1761 vessels carried on board try works for extracting the oil from the blubber, enabling the vessels to remain at sea for long periods of time. The American Revolution brought all such activities to a sudden halt.

But, in the 1800s, whaling resumed but on a grander scale. New

London became such a center it as to earned the name "The Whaling City".

35. Made of wood and bound with iron, the carriages, wagons, and riding chairs that navigated rugged colonial roads had to be strong and tight.

36. The custom of appointing a special day known as a fast day has been in vogue in New England since the Puritans and was fairly must limited to the region. They had brought with them from England the custom of appointing special days for fasting and prayer. Originally, it was set by the clergyman from the pulpit for his congregation. Then, the Governor selected a date for all in the colony to observe and proclaimed in the newspapers.

37. Lackwack or Lackawack township might refer to a region of the New York Catskill Mountains in present day Sullivan county. It would not be settled under any claim of right but as an investment –buy the property and put a town there.

38. Pomfret at Otter creek was a settlement similar to Flushing, also on Otter Creek. See endnote 15, supra.

39. Thousands of North Carolinians were cross with the local North Carolina officials whom they considered cruel, arbitrary, tyrannical and corrupt. The local officials were supported by the Governor. The effort to eliminate these abuses became known as the Regulator War. Some argue it was one of the first acts of the American Revolutionary War. Others say it was not aimed at the Crown but local authority. Many of the insurgents were to become patriots in the Revolution, however. Governor William Tryon was a special target of the dissatisfied. His lavish home built in 1770 in New Bern became one of the main points of resentment for the Regulators, who were already paying substantial taxes.

This news item reported in the Gazette in April 1771 was precursor to the Battle of Alamance on May 16, 1771, the only real battle in the war. Casualties were about the same for both sides, although some rebels were hung afterwards.

40. Dropsy is an old term for the swelling of soft tissues due to the accumulation of excess water. It is more a symptom than the cause.

For example, some may have dropsy because of a heart condition.

41. Also called nard, nardin, and muskroot, Spikenard (*Nardostachys grandiflora*); is native to the Himalayas of China, India and Nepal. Nard oil is used as a perfume, an incense, a sedative, and an herbal medicine said to fight insomnia, birth difficulties, and other minor ailments, since the days of the ancient Greeks.

42. Girls attended formal schools, but most were able to get some education at home or at so-called "Dame schools" where women taught basic reading and writing skills in their own houses.

43. Quorum is derived from Latin and was adopted in Middle English. Literally, it translates "of whom" from the wording of the commission formerly issued to justices of the peace.

44. Fairfield was only a "stop along the way in the history of the town of Woodstock in Grafton County, New Hampshire. In 1763, Colonial Governor Benning Wentworth named the town Peeling after an English town. However, many of the first colonists were originally from Lebanon, Connecticut. In 1771, the name was changed to Fairfield, after Fairfield, Connecticut. The town was renamed Woodstock in 1840.

45. The HMS *Gaspee had* ben sent by King George III to Rhode Island waters in March of 1772 to prevent smuggling. She and her commander, Lt. William Dudingston, harassed ships that had properly passed custom inspection in Newport.
 That was the case in the item in the *Gazette*. On June 9, 1772, the sloop *Hannah* had left Newport bound for Providence, when the *Gaspee* gave chase, *Hannah's* Captain Lindsey (deliberately, some say) lured her across the shallows off what is now known now Gaspee Point. The *Gaspee* ran aground and, stranded on a sandbar, was unable to move until the next flood tide. Before that, however, eight longboats with muffled oars to the stranded ship. Lt. Dudingston and his crew were removed and, near daylight on June 10th, the *Gaspee* was burned to the waterline and then exploded.
  Despite the offer of a considerable reward, Britain could never identified the culprits. Public sentiment was on "the people's side". Throughout all the colonies, this incident became something of a symbol in the percolating unrest.

46. An embargo is a prohibition against exporting certain products.

Here it was apparently done out of necessity. It was withdrawn a couple of weeks after "when it appeared to them that there was a sufficient supply in the colony for the support of its inhabitants."

47. In 1765, Boston had a population of 15,520 living in 1676 houses. Hiller B. Zobel, *The Boston Massacre* at 5

48. In the Protestant and Hebrew Bibles, the Seventh Commandment prohibits adultery. It is the Sixth Commandment in the Catholic Bible.

49. Zero degrees

50. A meaning of the word "impress" in a broad sense means taking someone by force for the public service. On the waterfront, an "impress gang" was, a party of men, with an officer, which compelled merchant seamen to serve on ships of war.

51. Was this an ordinary burglary or soon to be Patriots, but now smugglers, retaking what was taken from them?

52. In colonial days, towns were often settled based on their proximity to salt marshes due to the importance of salt meadow cordgrass. Formally named *spartina patens,* but known as salt hay it a species of cordgrass native to the Atlantic coast of North America. It was harvested for bedding and fodder for farm animals and for garden mulch.

53. While rarely associated with slavery, there was a sizeable population of Indian --Native American -- slaves, especially through the 1740s. Captured by other tribes in raids, they were sold by their captors into slavery. The victims were from South Carolina and Georgia (referred to as "Carolina slaves"), from Florida ("Spanish Indian slaves") and from the west, as far as Texas. See Alan Gallay in his *The Indian Slave Trade: the Rise of the British Empire in the American South* (1670 -1717) .The Chickisaw were major dealers in the trade, assisted by the British.

54.Committees of Correspondence, as the name implies, were bodies organized by the local governments of the colonies so as to collect and coordinating written communication from outside of the colony. They can be traced back to Boston in 1764 and emerged periodically when the need arose. Not only did they "spread the word" at a time when communication between regions were slow and uncertain, they also rallied opposition on common causes and set idea for collective action. They were the beginning of what ultimately became a formal political union among the colonies, known today as The United States of America.

The resolutions involved here were prompted in part by the *Gaspee* Affair in March 1773 (see endnote 45 *supra)*. A permanent Committee of Correspondence was formed by the Virginia House of Burgesses on March 12, 1773.

55. The summer of 1773 was not kind to James Mumford. The July 23 issue of the *Gazette* reports his son's death. The July 30 issue announces that he has been selected to replace the lately deceased Daniel Coit as Town Clerk of New London. Two weeks late, the *Gazette* tells that James Mumford himself had died and the August 27 issue announces that Col. Gurdon Saltonstall has been appointed his successor as New London's Town Clerk.

56. One quinal is 220.462 lbs.

57. A traveling salesman of sorts, a hawker of quack medicines who attracts customers with stories, jokes, or tricks. It has come to connote a charlatan or fraud.

58. Passed by Parliament in May of 1773, The Tea Act would spark the revolutionary movement in Boston. Oddly enough, the Tea act was not intended to raise revenue in the American colonies, but to prop up the financially floundering East India Company which had eighteen million pounds of tea to unload. This tea was to be shipped directly to the colonies and sold cheaply. The East India Company was a monopoly supported by a powerful lobby in Parliament. The direct sale of cheap tea, via British agents, would have undercut the business of local merchants and was viewed by many as an attempt to emasculate their boycotts and non importation agreements against British goods. Colonists in Philadelphia and New York turned the tea ships back to Britain. In Boston, however, a stubborn Governor held the ships in port, where the colonists would not allow them to unload. What happened can be seen in the December Eve issue of the Gazette.

59. Before wood pulp, cotton and linen rags were the "pulp" needed to make paper. It took a lot of time and work First, rags had to be collected from several sources: including "rag pickers" who went from house to house, asking for rags, which they then sold to paper mills

and ads in the newspapers, such as this one, offering to buy them. Then the rags were cut up and placed in a vat full of a special solution, where they soaked until the solution had broken down the cloth fibers to only tiny pieces. A framed screen was lowered into the vat and gathered the matted fibers and then left it to dry. This made a single sheet of paper!

INDICES

PEOPLE

A

ABBE, Shubal - 6/15/70
ABBOT, Israel - 9/13/71; 3/27/72; 4/3/72
ABELL, Thomas - 7/17/72
ABRAHAM - 2/28/72
ADAMS, David - 10/22/73
ADAMS, Michael - 5/4/70l; 9/14/70; 1/11/71
ADAMS, Pygan - 2/22/71
ADAMS, Thomas - 3/13/72; 7/16/73; 8/13/73
ADAMS Jr.. ,William - 4/3/72; 7/23/73
AITCHISON, John - 8/31/70
ALDEN, Mrs. Elizabeth - 1/12/70; 9/7/70; 9/28/70; 10/11/71 ;10/18/71; 11/22/71
ALDRIDGE, Mrs. Gershom - 9/14/70
ALGAR, Capt. Benjamin - 8/3/70
ALGT, George - 7/20/70
ALLEN, Caleb - 10/18/71
ALLEN, Elizabeth - 7/6/70
ALLEN, Joseph - 12/17/73
ALLEN, T.- 4/20/70 ; end note 22
ALLEN, Thomas 10/12/70; 1/29/73; 5/14/73
ALLEN, Capt. - 9/18/72
ALSOP, Richard - 7/19/71; 4/30/73
AMES, Mrs. Amy - 10/1/73
AMES, Cyrus - 10/1/73
AMES, John - 10/22/73

ANDREW, Mrs. Elizabeth - 11/8/71
ANDREW, Samuel - 11/8/71; 9/11/72
ANDREWS, William - 4/9/73
ANDRUES , Samuel - 6/22/70
ANDRUS, William - 4/3/72; 5/7/73
ANDRUS, Zebediah - 4/3/72
ANDRUS JR., Zebediah - 8/24/70; 9/7/70
ANGELL, James - 5/10/71
ANNABEL, Cornelius - 1/11/71;11/6/72; 11/13/72
ANNABLE, John - 9/10/73
APLIN, Mrs. - 8/23/71
APPLETON; Captain Benjamin - 12/4/72
APTHORP, Charles Ward - 11/8/71
ARCHIBALD, Edward - 3/16/70
ARCHIBALD, Francis - 3/16/70
ARCHIE; - 6/14/71
ARNOLD, Benjamin - 4/30/73
ARNOLD, Enoch - 10/4/71
ARNOLD, Mrs.- 10/4/71
ASHER, Rosseter, Jr.,- 9/17/73
ASPENWALL, Nathaniel - 11/13/72
ATSATT, Mr.- 10/30/72
ATTEN, Capt. - 9/18/72
ATTUCKS, Crispus - 3/16/70
ATWELL, Captain - 3/29/71
ATWOOD, Samuel - 3/16/70
AUSTIN, Mrs. Dorothy - 7/17/72

AUSTIN, Captain Richard - 7/17/72
AUSTIN, S. - 12/4/72
AVERY, Amos - 8/14/72
AVERY, Gideon- 8/2/71
AVERY, Humphrey - 9/14/70
AVERY, Jabez - 3/29/71; 2/7/72; 5/28/73
AVERY, James - 2/23/70; 9/14/70
AVERY, Lieutenant John - 6/12/72 ; 11/26/73
AVERY, Jr. John - 6/1/70; 9/13/71
AVERY, Robert - 5/7/73
AVERY, Samuel - 7/12/71
AVERY, Simeon - 7/26/71
AVERY, Theph - 5/4/70
AVERY, William - 5/22/72; 4/30/73; 10/8/73
AYER, Joseph - 1/3/72
AYER, Timothy - 1/3/72
AYSCOUGH, James - 4/2/73; 4/9/73

B

BABBIT, Jonathan - 4/9/73
BABCOCK, Amos - 1/19/70
BABCOCK, Josiah - 9/3/73; 12/24/73
BABCOCK, Stephen - 1/11/71
BACKUS, Ebenezer - 6/29/70; 8/3/70; 8/21/72; 10/8/73
BACKUS, Jr., Ebenezer - 12/4/72
BACKUS, Elijah - 9/14/70; 1/1/73
BACKUS, John - 8/21/72
BACKUS, Nathaniel - 2/16/70; 9/6/71
BACKUS Jr., Nathaniel - 4/30/73
BACON , Peirpont - 6/14/71;12/11/72;11/13/72;
BAILEY, Nathan -11/22/71 ;3/6/72
BALDWIN, Ebenezer - 1/5/70; 10/5/70; 2/22/71;-2/21/72; 3/27/72
BALDWIN, Eleazer - 12/24/73
BALDWIN, Jacob - 1/5/70
BALDWIN, John - 10/18/71; 12/25/72;10/23/72
BALDWIN, Mary - 10/23/72 ; 12/25/72
BALDWIN, Timothy, - 12/11/72
BALEY, Joseph - 1/22/73
BALEY, Miss Nabby - 4/11/73
BALEY, Nathaniel - 4/11/73
BALL, Elijah - 7/10/72
BANCROFT, Benjamin - 1/5/70
BANNING ,Mr.5/31/71
BANNISTER, John - 7/6/70
BARBER, Dr. Abner - 1/31/72
BARBER, Thomas - 5/4/70; 9/14/70; 7/12/71
BARKER, Ephraim - 12/14/70
BARKER, Ignatius - 7/5/7 1
BARKER, Dr. John - 2/16/70
BARKER, Rev. Nemihiah - 3/27/72
BARN, James - 10/1/73
BARNEBY, Thomas - 6/12/72
BARNET, David - 7/20/70
BARNEY, John,- 7/12/71
BARNEY, Samuel - 12/3/73
BARNS, Elijah - 8/20/73; 8/27/73; 10/1/73
BARNS, Mrs. Lucy - 8/20/73; 8/27/73; 10/1/73
BARROWS, Jr. Jabez - 6/12/72
BARROWS, Lemeul - 6/12/72
BARRY, Moses - 11/6/72
BARTLET, Icabod - 7/12/71
BARTLET; Seth - 3/27/72

BATES, Zechariah - 4/9/73
BAUMAN, Martin - 5/10/71
BAYARD, William - 11/27/72
BAYLET, JR..,.Obidiah - - 1/5/70
BEATTY, Francis - 6/26/72
BECKNELL, Zechariah - 11/1/71
BECKWICH Sr., Rev. George W.- 7/27/70; 10/30/72
BECKWICH Jr., Rev. George - 7/27/70;10/30/72
BECKWITH, Jedidiah - 3/26/73
BECKWITH, Joshua - 5/25/70
BEEBE, Ebenezer- - 1/5/70
BEEBE, Eliphalet - 5/4/70; 11/22/71
BEEBE, Joel - 12/20/71
BEEBE, Zacceus - 7/12/71
BELDEN, Samuel - 11/1/71; 9/3/73; 12/3/73
BELDING, Thomas - 4/30/73
BELTON, Amos - 7/12/71
BELTON, David - 1/11/71
BELTON, Jonas - 6/26/72 ; 1/15/73
BELTON, Capt. - 9/14/70
BEMONT, Captain Dennis - 9/17/73
BENEDICT, Rev. Joel - 3/15/71
BENEDICT,, Rev. Noah - 10/11/71
BENT, John - 5/15/72
BERNARD, David -5/4/70; 6/29/70
BIGARANT, Peter - 9/14/70
BIGELOW, Capt John - 9/3/73
BIGELOW, Thomas - 2/5/73; 2/26/73
BILL, Captain Charles - 9/10/73
BILL, Lt. James - 1/25/71
BILLINGS, Benjamin - 1/15/73

BILLINGS, Samuel - 1/15/73
BILLINGS, Stephen - 8/2/71
BILLINGS, Lucretia - 5/4/70
BILLINGS ,William - 10/2/72; 3/29/71
BIRCHARDE, Matthew - 5/3/71
BISHOP, Clement - 9/6/71
BISHOP, Captain Daniel - 2/16/70
BISHOP, Elijah - 2/5/73
BISHOP, Nathaniel - 11/12/73
BISHOP, Samuel - 6/4/73
BISSEL, Ezekiah - 3/19/73
BISSLE, Hez.- 2/16/70
BLACKSEE; Enos - 10/2/72
BLAKSLEY, Ebenezer - 7/12/71
BLANCHARD, John - 11/19/73
BLISS, Jedidiah - 9/28/70
BLISS, John - 5/18/70
BOARDMAN, Rev. Mr.8/10/70
BOCKWAY, Captain William - 8/31/71
BOGUE, Elisha - 9/13/71
BOLLES, Sr. Enoch - 11/15/51
BOLLES Jr., Enoch - 7/19/71; 5/7/73; 6/4/73; 7/23/73
BOLLES,, Isaiah - 5/14/73
BOLLES, Jonathan - 10/26/7 ; 4/10/72; 6/26/72
BOLLES,, Mary - 8/6/73
BOLLES,, Samuel - 8/6/73
BOLLES, Thomas - 4/30/73
BOLLES, Zedediah 12/13/71
BOLT, Abigail - 1/15/73
BOOGE, Daniel - 9/10/73
BOOTH, Henry - 5/3/71
BORROUGHS, Rev.- 3/15/71
BOSTON, slave 8/10/70; 8/16/71
BOTTOM, Mrs. Betty - 2/5/73
BOTTOM, Jabez - 2/5/73
BOTTOM, James - 2/5/73
BOUGHMAN, Martin - 11/15/51

BOWDISH, Mrs. Abigail - 10/1/73
BOWDISH, Edward - 10/1/73
BOWDISH, Peter - 10/1/73
BOWDOIN, William - 11/26/73
BOWLES, Captain John - 6/14/71
BOWLS, John - 9/14/70
BRADDICK, John - 1/11/71; 5/22/72; 11/26/73
BRADDICK, Captain - 4/10/72
BRADFORD, Alexander - 11/8/71
BRADFORD, James - 1/23/73; 3/5/73
BRADFORD, John- 9/20/71
BRAINERD, Daniel - 4/17/72; 4/30/73
BRAINERD, Capt Joshua - 2/12/73
BRAINERD, Mrs. Mathabel - 2/12/73
BRAINERD,, Othaniel - 12/25/72
BRAINERD, Timothy - 7/23/73; 12/3/73
BRAMAN, James - 11/27/72
BRANCH, Hannah, - 11/26/73
BRANCH, Samuel - 11/26/73
BRECK, Lord - 3/2/70
BREED, Gershom - 2/16/70; 5/18/70; 10/5/70;2/22/71;8/16/71; 8/23/71; 2/21/72; 3/27/72; 3/19/73; 4/9/73; 9/24/73
BREED, John MClarren - 11/1/71
BREWSTER, Benjamin - 10/1/73
BREWSTER, Comfort - 1/3/72
BREWSTER, Elijah - 2/16/70
BREWSTER, Samuel - 7/3/72
BRICK, Reverend Mr.- 11/19/73
BRIDGES, Mr.- 5/1/72
BRIGHAM, Uriah - 9/3/73
BRIMMER, John Baker - 3/23/70; 7/5/71; 11/8/71; 4/24/72; 7/10/72 ; 7/2/73; 11/19/73
BRINK, Mr. - 8/23/71
BRINTNELL, Capt.- 10/9/72
BROCKWAY, Elihu 5/31/71; 8/31/71
BRONNUCK, Robert - 1/25/71
BROOKS, David - 1/11/71
BROOKS, Guy - 2/16/70
BROOKS, Joshua - 2/23/70
BROWN, Benjamin - 11/12/73
BROWN, Bryant - 1/11/71
BROWN, Daniel - 1/15/73
BROWN, David - 9/6/71
BROWN, Ephraim - 5/14/73
BROWN, Eunice - 7/24/72
BROWN, John - 9/14/70; 12/20/71; 3/27/72; 4/17/72; 6/12/72 ;7/24/72
BROWN, Jonas - 6/26/72
BROWN, Joseph - 7/24/72; 10/8/73
BROWN, Joshua - 5/15/72
BROWN, Nathaniel - 3/27/72; 4/3/72; 10/29/73
BROWN, Peter - 3/23/70
BROWN, Richard - 3/23/70
BROWN, Samuel - 3/23/70
BROWN, Sarah - 2/26/73
BROWN, Thomas - 1/15/73; 2/26/73
BROWN Jr., Thomas - 2/26/73
BROWN, Capt.- 3/8/71
BRUCE, Mr. - 12/24/73
BRUNNUCK, . John . - 3/12/73
BUCK, Justus - 6/18/73
BUCK, Julius - 1/29/73

BUCKLAND, Captain - 2/28/72
BUDINGTON, Oliver - 1/10/72
BUEL, William - 8/21/72
BUEL, Mrs.- 8/21/72
BUELL, Abel - 5/4/70; 11/22/71; 8/21/72
BUELL, Hannah - 4/30/73
BUGBEE, Benjamin - 12/6/71
BULEY, Gershom 7/16/73
BULKEY,, Daniel - 7/10/72
BULKEY, Captain Gershom - 11/6/72
BULKEY, John - 9/25/72
BULKEY, Peter - 2/19/73
BULKEY, Roger - 11/27/72
BULL, Daniel - 8/27/73
BULL, David -2/21/72
BULL, Mrs. Lydia -1/31/72
BULL, Samuel ,-1/31/72
BULLAN, Asa - 11/15/51
BURCH Benjamin - 4/30/73
BURCH , Benjamin Robert - 4/30/73
BURCH, Robert - 4/30/73
BURCH, Thomas - 3/2/70
BURNAM, Benjamin - 4/13/70
BURNAM, Daniel - 6/19/72
BURNET, Jacob - 9/6/71
BURNUM, Benj.- 4/13/70
BURR, David -12/10/73
BURR, John -8/9/71
BURR, William - 9/3/73
BURR, Mrs., - 9/3/73
BURROWs, Paul - 1/24/72
BUSHNEL, Aaron - 3/5/73
BUSHNEL, Alexander - 2/1/71
BUSHNEL, Widow Mary - 1/15/73
BUSHNEL Jr., Nathan - 3/5/73; 7/2/73
BUSHNELL Benajah - 3/23/70; 8/21/72
BUSHNELL, Handley - 4/26/71

BUSHNELL, Nathan 10/12/70; 2/5/73
BUSHNELL, Mrs. Zerviah - 3/23/70
BUSHNELL, Mrs. - 8/21/72
BUTELERE, Jonne - 12/17/73
BUTELERE, Marjare - 12/17/73
BUTLER, Amos - 3/8/71
BUTLER, Daniel - 5/17/71
BUTLER, James - 1/15/73
BUTLER, Moses - 6/12/72
BUTLER, Zebulon- - 1/5/70; 5/4/70; 4/30/73
BUTT, Nathaniel - 4/13/70
BUTTON, Eliphalet - 1/25/71

C

CADA, Charles - 1/5/70
CADY, John - 10/4/71
CADY, Stafford 10/12/70
CALDWEL, Charles - 1/19/70
CALDWEL, George - 1/19/70
CALDWEL, James - 3/16/70
CALDWELL, John - 9/3/73
CALKINS, Jonathan - 6/15/70
CALKINS, John - 3/13/72
CALKINS, Pember - 7/2/73
CALKINS, Samuel - 2/2/70
CAMPBELl, Mr.- 3/27/72
CAPRON, William - 5/18/70
CARDWELL, Elizabeth - 1/11/71;7/12/71
CAREY, Michael - 12/27/71
CARPENTER, Captain Ephraim 2/7/72
CARR, Robert - 11/27/72; 12/11/72
CARR, William - 1/5/70
CARSEY, John - 11/15/51
CARTER, David - 9/14/70
CARTEY, John - 7/24/72
CARY, Eleazer -2/16/70; 3/2/70; 3/9/70; 12/3/73

CARY, John - 9/11/72
CARY, Jr., John 10/12/70
CARY, Wait Still - 4/9/73
CASE, Zebulon - 7/6/70
CASEY, Samuel - 11/16/70
CASHFIELD, Joseph - 1/15/73
CHADWICK, C.- 9/3/73
CHADWICK, Charles 8/10/70;
6/26/72; 7/2/73
CHALKER, Stephen - 1/10/72
CHALKER, Mr.- 9/17/73
CHAMBERS, Robert - 6/19/72
CHAMPION, Henry - 6/21/71;
7/12/71; 4/30/73; 7/16/73
CHAMPLIN, Asa - 7/12/71
CHAMPLIN, Elizabeth - 9/14/70
CHAMPLIN, Captain George -
9/13/71; 9/11/72
CHAMPLIN,, John - 4/13/70;
2/7/72; 11/13/72; 2/26/73;
7/16/73; 9/17/73
CHAMPLIN, Joseph - 12/31/73
CHAMPLIN, Captain - 3/15/71;
3/6/72
CHANDLER, Peter - 7/20/70
CHAPEL, Edward - 7/12/71
CHAPEL, Chapel, Samuel -
7/26/71

CHAPIN, Benjamin - 6/15/70;
10/18/71
CHAPIN, Jonathan - 12/11/72
CHAPMAN, Isaac - 1/18/71
CHAPMAN, James - 11/29/71
CHAPMAN Jr., James - 7/20/70
CHAPMAN, Jeremiah - 6/14/71
CHAPMAN, Mary - 9/14/70;
7/12/71; 6/26/72
CHAPMAN, Samuel - 9/24/73
CHAPMAN, Zachariah - 9/18/72
CHAPPEL, Joshua - 11/5/73
CHAPPEL, Captain - 10/18/71; -
12/27/71

CHENCY, Jacob - 6/26/72
CHESEBOROUGH, Amos -
9/7/70; 1/11/71; 5/17/71;
11/8/71; 2/5/73
CHESEBOROUGH, Elihu -
7/12/71
CHESEBOROUGH, Mrs. Mary -
2/5/73
CHESEBOROUGH, P. - 11/5/73
CHESEBOROUGH,, Samuel -
5/17/71; 6/26/72
CHESEBOROUGH, Colonel- -
1/5/70
CHESTER, Freel - 7/2/73
CHESTER, Jonathan - 7/2/73
CHESTER, John - 7/19/7;
12/10/73 1
CHESTER, Thomas - 12/11/72
CHESTER, Uriah - 1/17/72
CHESTER, Captain - 1/3/72;
1/15/73; 4/30/73
CHEW, Joseph - 11/8/71;
11/22/71
CHEW, Captain Samuel -
5/3/71
CHEW, Captain - 9/13/71
CHILD, Capt. Elisha - 4/13/70;
9/13/71
CHRISTOPHERS, Christopher -
11/8/71; 1/15/73
CHROUGH, William - 5/28/73
CHURCH, Silas - 3/20/72;
8/28/72; 12/25/72
CHURCH JR., Silas - 12/20/71;
6/19/72
CHURCH, Singleton - 1/5/70;
9/14/70
CHURCHVILLE, Joseph -
10/29/73
CLARK, Amos - 8/28/72;
10/23/72
CLARK, Asael - 1/73/73
CLARK Jr., Asahel -11/19/73

CLARK, Benjamin - 9/14/70; 3/6/72
CLARK, Daniel - 11/12/73
CLARK, James - 7/6/70; 4/23/73
CLARK, John 10/12/70; 10/8/73; 12/3/73
CLARK, Jr. Jonathan - 12/3/73
CLARK, Silas - 12/25/72
CLARK, Mr. - 10/23/72
CLARKE, Thomas - 11/16/70
CLAY, Samuel - 12/14/70
CLELAND, Robert - 3/29/71
CLELAND, Mr.- 4/5/71
CLEMENT, Jeremiah - 7/9/73; 11/19/73; 12/24/73
CLEMENT, Peabody - 11/19/73
CLESS, Samuel - 11/13/72
CLESS, Mrs. - 11/13/72
CLEVE, Capt. M. - 3/9/70
CLEVELAND, Aaron.- ½6/70
CLIFT, Amos - 8/3/70
CLIFT, Mr. - 11/6/72
CLOUD, Daniel - 11/29/71
COBB, John - 10/15/73
COFFIN, Mr.- 12/24/73
COGSWELL, Miss Alex - 5/15/72
COGSWELL, Mrs. Alice - 4/17/72
COGSWELL, Reverend James - 3/20/72; 4/17/72; 5/15/72
COGSWELL, Rev. Mr.- 4/19/71
COIT, Daniel -2/14/72; 1/1/73;7/23/73; 7/30/73; 9/3/73; end note 55
COIT, Isaac 8/10/70
COIT, Joseph - 2/16/70; 2/22/71; 2/19/73
COIT Jr.- Nathaniel - 1/5/70
COIT, Mrs. Love - 1/1/73
COIT, Captain Nathaniel - 4/10/72

COIT, Oliver - 5/28/73
COIT William - 10/12/70; 12/20/71; 4/23/73; 5/28/73; 9/3/73; 11/26/73
COIT, Capt. - 1/19/70
COLEMAN, - John - 1/5/70
COLEN, Joseph - 1/15/73
COLKIN, Simon - 10/8/73
COLOME, Dr. William 5/31/71
COMSTOCK, Asa - 3/9/70
COMSTOCK, Curtis - 7/5/71
COMSTOCK, James - 5/4/70
COMSTOCK,, Jr, Nathaniel - 3/8/71
CONAHAN, Cornelius - 7/20/70
CONE, John - 4/23/73
CONE, Elisha - 4/23/73
CONEANT, Shubel - 10/25/71
CONKLING, Jeremiah - 3/9/70
CONVERSE , Benjamin - 6/28/71
COOK, Daniel - 6/15/73
COOK, John - 6/8/70
COOK, Richard - 8/23/71
COOLE, Matthew - 6/18/73
COOPER, Daniel - 10/9/72
COOPER, Elihu - 10/26/70
COOPER, John - 6/18/73
COOPER, Rufus - 7/9/73
COPP, Jonathan - 12/18/72
CORKERAN, John - 6/26/72
CORNELL, Gregory - 3/3/70
CORNING, Clark - 9/11/72
CORNING, Daniel - 4/23/73; 9/17/73
Cornwell, Benjamin - 6/4/73
CORWITHER, David- 6/14/71
CORY, Braddock - 5/15/72
COTTON, Mrs. Mary - 9/28/70
COTTON ,Samuel - 9/28/70
COTTON, Captain - 10/18/71
COULT, John - 3/5/73
CRAFT, Deacon Samuel -

4/13/70
CRAGE, Robert - 3/19/73
CRAIG, Robert - 5/15/72
CRANDALL, Jared - 1/11/71; 1/10/72
CRARY, Nathan - 2/5/73
CRARY, Robert - 4/13/70; 11/26/73
CRISP, Adam - 9/14/70
CROCKER, Captain David - 4/17/72
CROCKER, Freeman.- 10/19/70
CROCKER; Peter - 4/24/72
CROCKER, William - 2/19/73
CROCKER, Captain - 9/13/71
CROO, Jacob - 10/1/73
CROWELL, Capt. - 2/28/72
CUMMINGS, Mirium - 12/24/73
CUMMINGS, William - 12/24/73
CURTICE, Elizabeth - 6/28/71
CURTICE Jonathan - 6/28/71
CURTIS, John - 4/13/70; 7/13/70
CUSH;, - 12/11/72; 4/30/73
CUSHMAN,,Ephraim - 6/5/72 4/30/73
CUSHMAN, Mr.- 9/11/72
CYRUS, Indian man - 9/14/70

D

DALEY, CAPTAIN - 3/29/71; 9/13/71; 4/30/73
DARE, Thomas - 12/14/70
DARLING, Thomas - 6/28/71
DARROW; Ichabod - 4/24/72
DART, John - 11/15/51
DART, Solomon.- 12/18/72
DAVENPORT, Abraham - 10/25/71
DAVENPORT, Richard - 1/15/73
DAVIS, Mrs. Abigail - 12/7/70
DAVIS, Ezra - 5/25/70

DAVIS, , Capt.- 8/3/70
DAVISON, Captain - 4/12/71
DAWSON, Samuel - 11/15/51
DAY, David - 11/6/72
DE WOOLF, Steven - 7/10/72
DEAN, Jabez - 5/11/70; 3/27/72; 7/23/73
DEAN, John - 3/5/73
DEAN, Joseph - 3/2/70
DEAN, Nathan - 11/15/51
DEAN, Captain - 7/19/71
DEANE, Silas - 4/30/73; 6/4/73; 11/5/73
DEBBIE, David - 2/5/73
DEEN, Nathaniel - 7/12/71
DEIN, Samuel - 6/26/72
DEIVESON, Thomas - 6/26/72
DELAFERT, Abraham - 8/7/72
DEMMOCK [Dimick], Timothy - 5/7/73; 9/3/73
Dennison, Daniel - 7/9/73
DENISON,, Dennis - 1/18/71
DENISON, James - 1/18/71
DENISON, John - 3/2/70; 9/14/70; 11/8/71; 1/15/73
DENISON IV, John - 3/5/73
DENISON, Joseph - 1/11/71; 6/18/73
DENISON, 2d , Joseph - 9/14/70
DENNIS, Benjamin - 2/16/70; 4/23/73; 7/9/73
DENNIS Jr., Benjamin - 9/13/71
DENNISON, Daniel - 7/9/73
DENNIS, Capt. George - 6/8/70
DENIMORE, Samuel - 11/15/51
DENSON ,Palmer, - 4/30/73
DERSHON, Miss Sally - 9/21/70
DERSHON, Capt. John - 9/21/70; 12/20/71
DEVOTION, Rev. Ebenezer - 7/26/71; 10/4/71
DEVOTION, Reverend - 10/4/7; 3/20/72 1

DEWEY, Charles - 6/22/70
DIBBLE, Miss - 8/21/72
DICK, John - 8/23/71
DICKINSON, John - 3/2/70
DICKINSON, Rev. Mr., - 10/23/72
DIGGS, Daniel - 12/20/71
DISKEL, Job - 6/29/70; - 9/7/70
DIXON, James - 2/5/73
DIXON, Robert, - 1/22/73; 3/5/73
DIXSON, Robert - 1/22/73
DODGE, Joel - 11/9/70
DOGGETT, Captain Samuel - 10/4/71
DOLBEAR[E], George - 5/4/70; 1/11/71; 3/27/72; 5/22/72; 7/10/72; 6/18/73
DOLBEARE, Miss Hannah - 6/18/73
DOLBEARE, John - 5/22/72
DORR, Reverend Mr. - 11/19/73
DORR, Mrs.- 11/19/73
DOUGAL, David - 7/12/71; 6/26/72; 7/9/73
DOUGLAS, Daniel 10/8/73
DOUGLAS, Ebenezer - 4/11/73; 11/5/73
DOUGLAS, James - 8/2/71
DOUGLAS [DOWGLAS], Capt. Nathan - 1/26/70; 2/16/70; 11/23/70; 6/14/71 ;3/27/72; 5/29/72; 6/19/72
DOUGLAS Jr. Robert - 1/19/70; 7/31/72; 8/7/72
DOUGLAS Jr. Mr. - 7/31/72
DOUGLASS, David - 1/15/73
DOS UGLAS [DOWGLAS], , Captain John - 4/13/70; 9/13/71; 12/18/72
DOWGLASS, Jr., William - 3/2/70
DOWNER, Elizabeth - 1/11/71
DOWNER, James - 11/16/70
DRAKE, Samuel - 3/22/71
DREW, John - 2/7/72
DREW,Mrs. Mary - 2/7/72
DUDINGTON, Lt. William - 1/15/73; end note 45
DUFFY, Margaret - 1/5/70
DUNHAM, James - 10/5/70
DUNHAM, Cynthia - 10/5/70
DUNHAM, Silas - 4/30/73
DUNHAM, Mr. -8/9/71
DUNN, David - 9/18/72
DUNNING, Reverend Benjamin - 5/22/72
DUNNINGTON, Reverend Benjamin - 6/18/73
DUSSEL, Leonard - 11/15/51
DYER, Eliphalet - 5/18/70; 10/5/70;2/22/71; 9/27/71; 10/25/71;2/21/72; 3/27/72; 3/19/73; 4/9/73; end note 8
DYER, Johnon - 1/5/70
DYER, Thomas - 11/5/73
DYER, Mrs. - 11/5/73

E

EAMES, Ebenezer - 1/5/70
EATON, Aaron - 6/26/72; 1/15/73
EATON, Joseph - 1/22/73; 3/5/73
EDGCOMB, Jonathan - 1/15/73
EDGECOMBE, Jesse - 7/31/72
EDGERTON, Elijah -1/10/72; 6/26/72
EDGERTON, JOHN 10/8/73
EDWARDS; Bilade - 7/5/71
EELLS, Reverend Edward - 7/12/71; 5/22/72
EELLS, Reverend Mr. John - 11/26/73

EELLS, Rev. Nathaniel - 1/5/70; 9/14/70; 12/17/73
EELLS, Miss; Rebecck - 12/17/73
ELDERKIN, James - 2/16/70
ELDERKIN, John - 1/5/70; 5/4/70
ELDERKIN, Jedidiah 10/5/70; 2/22/71; 9/27/71;2/21/72; 3/27/72; 3/19/73; 4/9/73
ELDERKIN, Capt. Luther - 7/2/73
ELIOT, Jacob - 1/25/71
ELIOT, Zebulon - 3/8/71; 4/13/70; 11/16/70
ELLIOT, Mr. - 3/9/70; 4/13/70
ELLIS, Christopher - 1/10/72
ELLIS, Captain Joseph - 6/14/71
ELMOR, Timothy - 11/13/72
ELRIDGE, Charles - 9/14/70
Ely, Cullick 10/8/73
ELY, David- 10/15/73; 11/5/73
ELY, Elisha -3/6/72; 3/26/73
ELY, Dr. John - 3/26/73; - 5/31/71 -5/31/71; 3/6/72
ENGLISH, John - 9/14/70
ENGLISH, Richard - 6/26/72

F
FANNING, David - 4/16/73
FANNING, Gilbert - 5/4/70; 4/30/73
FANNING, Thomas - 1/15/73; 3/12/73; 9/10/73
FARGO, Mrs. Moses - 1/26/70
FARNHAM, Daniel - 5/8/72
FARNHAM, Elias - 2/5/73
FARNHAM, George Whitefield,- 2/5/73
FARNHAM, Jeffrey Amherst - 2/5/73
FARNSWORTH, Samuel -

7/19/71
FELCH, John - 9/13/71
FELSHAW, Michael - 3/19/73
FERIBAUL, Joseph - 11/15/51
FIELD, Henry - 1/15/73
FINK, Barney - 9/7/70
FINNE, Ephraim - 10/29/73
FISH, Capt. Daniel - 9/17/73
FISH,, John - 9/13/71
FISH, Joseph - 7/12/71
FISH, Capt. Moses - 4/13/70; 2/5/73
FISH, Nathaniel- 7/12/71; 11/15/51
FISH, Nicholas - 2/26/73
FISH, Reverend Mr. - 11/12/73
FISHER, Nathan - 5/3/71
FITCH, Abraham - 11/22/71
FITCH, Capt. Azel - 1/12/70; 9/7/70; 1/17/72
FITCH, Caleb - 3/2/70
FITCH, Ebenezer - 4/13/70; 4/30/73; 8/6/73
FITCH, Eleazer - 1/17/72
FITCH, Elisha - 2/16/70; 4/13/70; 9/14/70
FITCH, Ichabod - 10/4/71; 5/29/72; 6/19/72
FITCH, Jabez - 4/13/70; 7/13/70; 9/13/7; 3/20/72; 1/22/73
FITCH, Jonathan - 3/13/72
FITCH, Josephus - 3/8/71; - 4/23/73; 6/25/73
FITCH,, Lemuel - 9/7/70
FITCH, Pelatiah - 5/4/70
FITCH, Hon. Thomas - 10/25/71
FITCH, Mrs. Zerviah - 4/23/73
FITCH, Governor - end note 8
FITKIN, William - 10/25/71
FLINT, Abner 10/12/70; 4/12/71; 10/22/73

FLINT, James - 6/15/70; 9/4/72
FLITCHER, Seth - 10/5/70
FOBES, Widow Abigail - 10/1/73
FOOT, Charles 10/8/73
FOOT, Daniel - 1/5/70; 4/30/73
FOOT, Deacon - 8/23/71
FORBES, John - 1/17/72
FORBES, Ruth - 1/17/72
FORDHAM Jr. Nathan - 6/7/71; 4/9/73
FORDHAM, Mr. - 3/9/70
FORSTER, James - 4/5/71
FORSYTH, Jonathan - 9/6/71; 6/19/72
FOSDICK, Alvan - 5/28/73
FOSDICK, Lodowick, - 9/24/73
FOSDICK, Dr. Thomas - 1/5/70
FOSDICK, Dr. - 9/24/73
FOSTER, Daniel - 3/13/72
FOSTER, George - 3/13/72
FOSTER, John - 6/14/71 ; 12/11/72; 4/30/73
FOSTER, William - 1/5/70
FOSTICK, Alexander - 4/10/72
FOWLER, Dyah - 6/5/72
FOWLER, Rev.Joseph - 6/14/71
FOX, Ezechiel - 6/25/73
FOX, John - 11/16/70
FOX, Samuel - 1/12/70
FRANK, John- - 1/5/70
FREELOVE, Lewis - 7/12/71
FRIEND, John - 9/14/70; 7/12/71
FRIEND, Captain - 10/25/71
FULLER, Ezra - 1/5/70
FULLER, Rev John,- 3/13/72; 4/24/72
FULLER, 2d, Thomas - 7/6/70
FULLER, Rev. Mr.- 3/15/71

G
GALE, Benjamin - 9/14/70

GALE,, JOSEPH - 11/15/51
GALLUP, CAPT. BENADAM - 4/13/70; 9/14/70; 8/2/71
GALLUP, ELISHA - 1/11/71
GALLUP, JOSEPH - 9/14/70; 1/11/71; 7/12/71
GALLUP, Nathan - 9/13/71; 4/17/72
GALLUP, Thomas Prentice - 10/2/72
GAMBELL, Nathan - 12/27/71
GAMBELL, Mr.- 3/27/72
GARDINER, Abraham - 6/12/72
GARDINERJr., David - 5/18/70; 10/25/71; 3/6/72 ;4/3/72; 8/7/72; 10/16/72; 11/12/73
GARDINER, Elizabeth - 10/16/72
GARDINER George - 9/11/72; 1/29/73
GARDINER, Nathaniel - 1/5/70
GARDINER, Thomas - 1/29/73
GARDINER, William - 5/28/73
GATES, Noadiah - 4/23/73
GAY, Joel - 9/7/70
GAYLORD, Lucy - 11/22/71
GEER, Nathan - 10/1/73
GEER, Capt. Robert - 9/14/70
GEORGE, Captain John - 10/25/71
GEORGE, the Third, - 4/20/70; end note 45
GEORGE - 5/8/72
GIBSON, Roger - 11/20/72; 4/30/73
GIFFIN, Wlliam - 12/11/72
GIFFORD, Gale - 10/18/71
GIFFORD, Stephen - 3/12/73
GILBARTT, Joseph - 7/5/71
GILBERT, Gilbert, Jeremich - 4/30/73
GILBERT, Gilbert, Jonathan - 5/14/73

GILBERT, Gilbert, Samuel - 6/19/72;1/15/73; 3/12/73
Gilbert, Mr.- 7/19/71
GILLERS, WILLIAM - 11/26/73
GILMOR, Rev. Geo. - 9/14/70
GLEASON, Capt - 1/31/72
GODDARD, Ebenezer - 9/14/70; 7/12/71; 11/15/51; 12/3/73
GOODWIN, Jacob - 9/13/71
GORDON, , Duchess of - 11/27/72
GORDON, CAPTAIN JOHN - 3/26/73
GOULD, Sarah - 11/15/51
GOULD, Thomas - 6/7/71
GRANT, JAMES - 4/9/73
GRAVES, Reverend Mr.- 2/7/72
GRAY, GRAY, EBENEZER - 2/23/70; 9/17/73
GRAY, GRAY, SAMUEL - 2/2/70; -3/2/70; 3/9/70; 3/16/70; 5/18/70; 10/5/70;2/22/71; 6/7/71; 2/21/72; ; 3/19/73; 4/9/73
GRAY, Simeon -10/18/71; 5/29/72; 6/19/72; 12/25/72; 2/12/73 3/19/73;
GREEN, Joseph - 9/13/71
GREEN, Timothy - 3/9/70; 1/24/72; 9/4/72; 4/23/73; 5/14/73; 8/27/73; 10/22/73; 11/12/73
GREEN, Mr. - 4/6/70
GREENFIELD, James - 1/11/71
GREENFIELD, Starr Archibald - 1/5/70
GREENLEAF, David - 3/26/8/6/73 73
GREENLEAF, Stephen - 5/4/70
GREENWOOD, Mr. - 3/16/70
GREY Jr., Eben - 2/16/70
GRIFFING, Jasper - 1/10/72

GRIFFING, Mr. - 5/21/73
GRINDAL, Mr.- 11/6/72
GRISWOLD, Mrs. Hannah - 4/11/73
GRISWOLD, John - 4/11/73
GRISWOLD, Matthew - 10/25/71
GROSS, Thomas - 9/3/73
GROSVENOR, Ebenezer - 11/20/72; 4/2/73
GROVES, Richard - 11/15/51
GUSTIN, Elizabeth - 12/25/72
GUSTIN, Walter - 12/25/72

H
HALE, Deacon Richard - 4/13/70
HALL, Daniel - 5/17/71; 5/31/71
HALL, Reverend David - 7/30/73
HALL, Ephraim - 6/12/72
HALL, John - 4/17/72
HALL, Joshua - 7/24/72
HALL, Robert - 1/10/72
HALL , Stephen - 3/27/72
HALLAM, Edward - 6/19/72 ; 10/23/72
HALLAM, Eliza - 6/22/70
HALLAM, Elizabeth - 6/19/72; 6/18/73
HALLAM, Nicholas - 6/22/70; 6/19/72
HALLAM, Sarah - 1/15/73
HALLIE, Capt.- 2/2/70
HALLOCK, Capt. William - 9/24/73
HALSEY, J. - 11/26/73
HAMBLIN, Captain - 9/13/71
HAMLIN, Jabez - 6/22/70; 10/25/71;
HAMMOND, JAMES - 4/23/73; 9/17/73

HANCOCK, Ann - 4/30/73
HANCOCK, Benjamin - 1/5/70
HANCOCK, William - 5/15/72; 2/19/73; 4/30/73
HANCOX, Edward - 3/2/70
HANLY, John - 5/4/70; 6/29/70
HARDING, Mary - 12/14/70
HAROLD, Stephen- 4/30/73
HARRIS, Bridgett - 12/31/73
HARRIS, George - 5/21/73
HARRIS, Capt. Jeremiah - 10/1/73
HARRIS, John - 7/19/71
HARRIS Jr., Joseph - 7/12/71
HARRIS, Widow - 9/14/70
HARRIS, Mary - 5/4/70; 5/11/70; 11/22/71; 12/4/72
HARRIS, Capt. Peter - 11/23/70; 11/27/72
HARRIS, Richard - 1/5/70; 2/2/70; 5/11/70; 11/22/7;12/4/72
HARRIS, Thomas - 9/14/70; 7/16/73
HARRIS, Captain William - 7/12/71; 2/19/73; 12/31/73
HARRISON, John - 1/18/71
HARRISON, Peter - 11/27/72
HARRISON, Thomas - 11/27/72
HARROLD, Stephen - 1/15/73
HART, Reverend Mr. Levi - 10/11/71 5/21/73; 8/27/73
HART, Rev. William - 7/27/70
HART, Rev. Mr. - 3/15/71; 5/15/72
HARTSHORN, Ebenezer - 2/16/70
HASSARD, Jr., Samuel - 5/7/73
HATCHE, Captain - 12/20/71
HAUGHTON, James - 10/16/72
HAVENS, Henry 6/7/71
HAWK, Mr. - 5/15/72
HAZARD, Oliver - 8/17/70

HEBARD, Gideon 10/12/70
HEBARD, John - 8/20/73
HEBARD, Zebulon - 12/3/73
HEDESON, William - 11/27/72
HELLARDH, Ambrous - 3/2/70
HEMPSTED, Benjamin - 2/19/73
HEMPSTED, John - 9/14/70; 12/25/72
HEMPSTEAD, Joshua - 1/5/70; 3/16/70
HEMPSTED Jr., Joshua - 3/16/70
HEMPSTED, Jr., Stephen - 1/15/73
HENRY, Alexander - 1/15/73
HENRY, Eleanor - 1/10/72
HENSHAW, Joshua - 3/27/72
HERN, Elizabeth - 3/13/72
HERRICK, Ephraim - 8/6/73
HERROLD, Stephen - 1/11/71
HERTTEL, John H.- 5/22/72
HEWIT, Increase - 7/23/73
HEWIT, Joseph - 6/26/72 ; 12/31/73
HEWIT, Martha - 10/1/73
HIDDEN,- Noah 9/27/71; 5/15/72
HIDE, [see HYDE] Captain Daniel - 12/28/70; 2/12/73; 8/6/73
HIDE, see HYDE] Jedidiah - 8/31/71; 3/19/73; 4/2/73
HIDE Jr., Samuel - 8/6/73
HIDE, [see HYDE] Jr., Samuel - 1/12/70; 9/7/70
HIDE [Hyde] Phineas - 4/23/73; 4/30/73
HIGGINS, Capt. - 3/2/70
HILL, Esther - 8/21/72
HILL, Jonathan - 8/31/71
HILL, Nathaniel - 11/22/71
HILL, William - 11/16/70;

11/22/71; 2/14/72; 8/21/72;
9/11/72;10/16/72
HILLARD, 2d, David - 12/31/73
HILLDRUP, Thomas - 12/4/72
HILLHOUSE, James Abraham -
10/25/71
HILLHOUSE, William - 4/13/70;
9/14/70;7/5/71;9/13/71;
4/17/72; 12/25/72; 4/30/73;
9/17/73
HINMAN, Elisha - 3/5/73
HINMAN, Noble - 1/5/70;
6/26/72
HIPPOCRATES - end note 3
HIRT ,Reverend Levi - 4/24/72
HITCHCOCK, - 10/18/71
HODGEHDEN, Benj. - 7/12/71
HODGINS, Daniel - 1/15/73
HOFMER, Rev.- 7/6/70
HOLCOMB, Mr. - 7/24/72
HOLDEN, Parsons, Samuel -
9/14/70
HOLDEN, Phineas - 7/2/73
HOLLEY, William - 6/22/70
HOLMES, Seth - 9/20/71;
11/12/73
HOLMES, Rev. Stephen -
2/9/70
HOLT, Ebenezer - 5/17/71
HOLT, Mrs. Mehetabeel -
5/21/73
HOLT, Paul - 5/21/73
HOMES, Doctor - 7/12/71
HOOKER, Rev. Nathaniel -
6/15/70; 10/2/72
HOPKINS , John - 4/30/73
HOSMER, David - 6/28/71
HOSMER, Manassah - 4/13/70
HOUGH, David - 12/3/73
HOVEY, Aaron - 12/24/73
HOWARD, Abigail - 9/14/70
HOWARD Howard, Ebenezer -
9/24/73

HOWARD, Elizabeth -
9/14/70; 9/24/73
HOWARD, John 10/12/70
HOWARD, Mr. - 4/17/72
HOWE, George - 1/5/70;
5/4/70
HOWE, Joseph - 11/27/72
HOWE, Captain - 6/25/73;
11/5/73
HOWELL, William - 4/24/72
HOWELL, Stephen - 12/7/70
HOWLAND, Joseph - 12/20/71;
7/24/72
HUBBARD, Daniel - 6/8/70
HUBBARD, Jeremiah -
12/17/73
HUBBARD, Captain Richard -
7/19/71
HUBBARD, Russell - 5/4/70;
5/10/71; 9/13/71; 9/4/72;
12/17/73
HUBBARD, William - 6/8/70;
4/5/71; 9/13/71; 7/3/72; 9/4/72
HUDSON, Robert - 6/14/71
HUELL, Jacob - 3/27/72
HUGHES, John - 1/12/70
HULKSEY ,John - 3/27/72
HUMASTON, Caleb - 8/16/71
HUMPHREY, Elihu - 8/27/73
HUNGERFORD, Greene -
11/22/71
HUNTER, Captain Henry -
12/17/73
HUNTINGTON, Benjamin -
1/5/70; 8/17/70; 6/28/71;
9/13/71; 4/17/72 4/17/72;
7/10/72; 4/30/73; 7/16/73;
9/17/73
HUNTINGTON, Eleazer -
12/6/71
HUNTINGTON, Miss Elizabeth -
12/10/73
HUNTINGTON, Reverend Enoch

- 11/6/72
HUNTINGTON, Ezra - 11/20/72
HUNTINGTON, Hannah 12/13/71; 10/4/71
HUNTINGTON, Col. Hezekiah 10/25/71; 12/13/71; 2/12/73; 5/14/73; 6/18/73
HUNTINGTON, Jabez - 2/16/70; 12/28/70; 9/13/71; 9/27/71; 10/25/71; 12/13/71; 5/15/72; 11/26/73; -12/10/73
HUNTINGTON, Jedidiah - 2/16/70; 5/11/70; 6/28/71; 7/3/72; 9/4/72;2/28/72
HUNTINGTON, John - 12/25/72
HUNTINGTON, Jonathan - 8/6/73; 9/17/73; 10/8/73; 12/24/73
HUNTINGTON, Reverend Joseph - 10/4/71
HUNTINGTON, Joshua 12/13/71
HUNTINGTON, Samuel - 8/3/70; 4/3/72;10/8/73
HUNTINGTON, Rev. Mr.- 3/20/72
HUNTLEY, William - 2/14/72
HURLBUT, Daniel - 7/20/70
HURLBUT, Elisha -8/9/71; 8/16/71;3/12/73; - 9/10/73
HURLBUt, George B.. - 11/26/73
HURLBUT, Joseph - 3/29/71; 2/19/73
HURLBUT Jr. Joseph - 2/28/72; 1/12/73
HURLBUT, Capt. Titus - 1/19/70; 2/16/70; 4/6/70; 5/31/71; 6/14/7;5/29/72; 6/19/72 1
HUTCHINS, Captain Silas - 6/26/72
HUTCHINSON, Nehemiah -

2/16/70
HYDE, Captain Daniel [see Hide] - 2/16/70; 11/23/70;5/29/72; 6/19/72 ;12/25/72
HYDE, Hyde, Walter - 1/18/71; 11/1/71;5/29/72; 6/19/72; 3/19/73

I
INSTEAD, Samuel - 5/1/72
ISHAM Jr., Joseph 7/16/73; 10/8/73
ISAACS, Ralph - 6/5/72

J
JACKS, William - 2/28/72
JEFFARS, Charles - 1/11/71
JEFFERY, Charles. - 5/18/70; 6/8/70
JEFFORDS, James - 5/28/73
JENNINGS, Daniel - 9/17/73; 10/29/73
JENNINGS, Zephaniah - 3/22/71
JEPSON, Mrs. Susanna - 1/10/72
JEPSON, William - 6/28/71; 1/10/72
JERON, Stephen - 7/12/71
JEWET, Reverend Mr. David - 11/19/73
JEWET, Mrs. Patience - 11/19/73
JEWETT, Joseph - 12/25/72
JEWETT; Rev. Mr.- 3/27/72
JOB; David - 3/19/73
JOHNSON, David - 7/5/71
JOHNSON, Rev. Diodate - 1/22/73 ;1/29/73
JOHNSON, John - 10/4/71; 10/9/72
JOHNSON, James - 10/23/72; 8/27/73

JOHNSON, Elisha - 5/22/72
JOHNSON, Reverend Jacob - 4/24/72
JOHNSON, John - 1/15/73
JOHNSON, Reverend Samuel - 1/17/72 1
JOHNSON, Rev. Mr. Stephen - 4/20/70; 4/27/70; 7/27/70; 1/4/71;7/17/72; 1/29/73
JOHNSON, Dr. William Samuel - 10/4/71; 11/15/71; 10/9/72
JOHNSON, Sir William - 8/27/73; 9/3/73; 9/10/73; 9/17/73
JOHNSON, Rev. Dr. - 4/26/71
JONES, Abijah - 7/3/72
JONES, Amasa - 6/21/71; 10/8/73
JONES, Gidron - 3/13/72
JONES, Henry - 1/11/71; 7/12/71
JONES, - 5/28/73
JORDAN, Richard - 4/13/70; 7/20/70
JOSHUA, Sachem - 6/22/70; end note 24
JUDD, Daniel - 3/15/71
JUDSON, Rev. Ephraim - 10/11/71;4/24/72
JUDSON, Mr. - 4/19/71

K
KAYE, Isaac - 5/10/71
KEANE, Aaron - 1/11/71 7/12/71;
KEARNEY, David - 1/15/73
KELLEY, Joseph - 6/25/73
KELLOGG, Jr., Aaron - 5/10/71; 11/15/71; 5/15/72; 9/25/72
KELLOGG, Elijah - 8/21/72
KELLOGG, Israel - 1/15/73
KELLOGG, Martin - 2/1/71; 10/2/72

KELLOGG, Mary - 9/25/72
KELLOGG, Solomon - 9/14/70; 2/5/73; 8/13/73
KELLOGG, Capt.- 10/25/71
KELLY, Benjamin - 4/19/71
KELLY, Sarah Kelley - 4/19/71
KEMBELL, Nathan - 1/10/72; 1/15/73
KENEDY, Dennis - 6/26/72
KENNEDY, Benjamin - 3/5/73
KENNEDY, Jonathan - 10/26/70
KEYES, Stephen - 4/2/73
KIMBALL, Richard - 10/22/73
KIMBERLY, John - 5/7/73
KINE, Rev. Mr.- 3/15/71
KING, John - 3/23/70
KINNE, Rev. Aaron - 9/14/70; 10/11/71; 4/24/72
KINNE, Joseph - 8/27/73
KINSMAN, Jeremiah - 3/5/73; 4/2/73
KIRTLAND, Reverend Mr. Daniel - 5/21/73
KIRTLAND, Joseph - 2/5/73
KNIGHT, Joseph - 11/9/70; 7/2/73
KNOLTON, Thomas - 9/24/73
KRUPA, William - 4/24/72

L
LABOR, Jeremiah - 12/25/72
LAMB, Daniel,- 9/6/71
LAMB, James - 2/22/71
LAMBERT, Jonathan - 3/13/72
LAMPHEAR, Aaron - 1/15/73
LAMPHERE, Elijah - 6/5/72
LAMPHERE, George - 6/5/72
LAMPHERE, Levi - 3/2/70
LANDERS, John, - 7/2/73
LANE, Jr., Nathaniel - 7/12/71
LAPPINEER, John - 12/3/73
LARABE, Thomas - 6/19/72
LATHAM, Davis - 1/11/71

LATHAM, Edward - 1/5/70
LATHAM, Elizabeth -5/4/70; 6/29/70
LATHAM; Peter - 2/7/72
LATHAM, Captain - 9/11/72
LATHEN, Ruth - 6/26/72
LATHROP, Dr. Daniel - 3/3/70; 4/24/72; 7/3/72; 9/4/72; 6/18/73
LATHROP, Elisha - 2/16/70; 4/13/70; 5/29/72
LATHROP, John - 11/20/72
LATHROP, Joshua - 2/16/70; 4/24/72; 12/31/73
LATHROP, Rufus - 4/17/72; 4/30/73; 12/31/73
LATHROP ,Samuel - 7/17/72
LATHROP, Mr.- 2/16/70
LATIMER,, Amos - 7/19/71
LATIMER, Demmen - 6/14/71
LATIMER, Lydia - 3/23/70
LATIMER, Peter - 6/21/71;11/13/72; 1/15/73; 2/5/73
LATIMER, Jr., Peter - 2/5/73
LATIMER, Picket - 2/5/73
LATIMER, , Capt. Robert - 2/9/70; 3/23/70
LATIMER, Reuben - 6/14/71
LATIMER,, Samuel - 11/22/71; 12/4/72; 12/11/72
LATIMER, Jr Samuel - 6/15/70
LATIMER, Capt. - 1/5/70
LAW, Rev. Benjamin - 10/11/71 LAW, Rev. Benjamin - 10/11/71
LAW, Richard - 9/14/70; 11/22/71; 1/29/73; 9/17/73
LAY, Amos - 10/29/73
LAY 2ND, Joseph - 4/13/70
LEACH, Capt. Clement - 8/13/73
LEACH, Elizabeth - 8/13/73

LEACH, Harr - 6/26/72
LEACH, Isaac - 9/14/70
LEACH, Jonathan - 9/14/70
LEACH , Johnson - 5/4/70 ????
LEACH, Joseph - 1/15/73
LEACH, Manassah - 2/12/73
LEDLIE, Hugh - 2/9/70 ; 2/16/70; 3/3/70; 8/24/70; 6/28/71
LEDYARD, Ebenezer - 2/9/70 ; 5/4/70; 6/29/70; 4/17/72
LEDYARD, John - 9/13/71
LEDYARD, William - 4/30/73
LEE, Abner - 7/12/71
LEE, Cyrus - 1/11/71
LEE, Elisha - 6/28/71
LEE, John - 1/5/70
LEE, Jonathan - 6/25/73
LEE, Levi - 6/28/71
LEECH, Joseph,- 9/17/73
LEECH, Jr., John - 3/16/70
LEEDS, Capt.- 6/28/71
LEETE, Widow - 7/20/70
LEFFINGWELL, Christopher - 2/16/70; 4/13/70; 5/18/70; 3/29/71; 11/1/71; 12/6/71; 3/26/73; 10/1/73 7/9/73;
LEFFINGWELL, Elisha - 2/1/71; 4/24/72
LEFFINGWELL, Hez. - 2/9/70 ; 2/23/70
LEFFINGWELL, , Captain John - 1/15/73; 8/20/73
LEFFINGWELL, Capt. Samuel - 2/16/70; 3/3/70; 11/15/51
LESTER, Eliphalet - 3/26/73
LESTER, Nathan - 8/6/73
LESTER, Peter - 3/12/73
LESTER, Simeon - 10/30/72
LESTER, Timothy - 9/13/71
LESTER,, Mrs. - 3/26/73
LETTICE - 5/28/73
LEWIS, Deborah - 1/12/70

LEWIS, Francis - 1/12/70
LEWIS, Mr. 5/31/71
LILLEY, Captain - 1/10/72
LILLEY - 4/30/73
LILLIE, Elisha - 9/17/73
LIMAN, Mr.- 3/27/72
LIMERICK, Dean of 4/26/71
LINDSEY, Captain - end note 45
LITTLE, Rev. Mr. Ephraim - 11/6/72
LITTLE, Rev. Mr.- 6/14/71
LIVINGSTON, Mr.- 6/22/70
LLOYD, Rev. Benjamin,- 12/24/73
LOCKWOOD, Isaac - 10/23/72
LOCKWOOD, Reverend James - 7/24/72;12/17/73
LOCKWOOD, Reverend Samuel - 10/4/71
LOCKWOOD, Reverend - 5/1/72
LOGAN, James - 8/23/71
LOOMIS, Jonathan - 8/21/72
LOPER, James - 6/26/72
LORD, Benjamin - 5/14/73
LORD, D.- 10/29/73
LORD; Ebenezer - 10/8/73
LORD, Eleazer - 12/25/72
LORD, Dr. Elisha - 8/21/72; 1/15/73; 1/22/73; 10/8/73
LORD, Elizabeth - 8/21/72; 1/15/73; 1/22/73
LORD Lord, Ichabod - 5/22/72
LORD, Jabez - 1/11/71
LORD, Jeremiah - 6/22/70
LORD, John - 7/12/71
LORD Mrs. Patience - 5/22/72
LORD Samuel - 1/10/72
LORD Jr., Samuel - 6/26/72
LORD, Rev. Mr. - 11/15/51; 2/12/73
LOTHROP, Andrew,- 2/5/73

LOTHROP, Azariah - 1/22/73;3/12/73 10/8/73; 12/3/73; 12/24/73
LOTHROP, Benjamin - 9/10/73
LOTHROP, Burril - 8/13/73
LOTHROP, Elijah 7/16/73
LOTHROP,Mrs. Elizabeth - 12/3/73
LOTHROP, Joseph - 12/21/70
LOTHROP, Deacon Samuel - 12/3/73
LOTHROP, William 10/8/73
LOTHROP Jr., William - 7/17/72
LOTHROP, Zachariah - 12/3/73
LOVELAND, Abel - 5/22/72
LOVELAND, Chloe - 5/22/72
LOVELAND, Eliphas - 5/22/72
LOVELAND, Robert - 5/22/72
LOVELAND,- 5/22/72
LOVERING, William - 7/24/72; 8/28/72
LOVET, Reverend Joseph - 11/5/73
LOVET, Mrs. - 11/5/73
LUMIS, Tithy - 9/14/70
LUNKHORN, Mrs.- 6/22/70
LYDIUS, John Henty - 2/23/70; 10/12/70; 4/12/71; Lydius, end note 8
LYMAN, John - 10/11/71
LYMAN, P. - 8/27/73
LYMAN, William - 9/17/73
LYNDE, Daniel 7/16/73
LYNDE, Joseph 7/16/73
LYON, Caleb - 4/27/70 ; 6/1/70
LYONS, James - 7/12/71

M

M'DONALD, James - 12/3/73
MACK, Jonathan - 1/12/70
MACK, Josiah - 1/12/70

266

MAIBONE, Colonel Godfrey - 8/23/71
MAKCOW, Daniel - 6/26/72
MALL, Daniel - 10/4/71
MALLESON, Benjamin - 10/11/71
MANAWARING, David - 9/13/71; 3/13/72; 6/5/72; 3/26/73
MANWARING, Mrs. Eleanor - 8/14/72
MANWARING, Richard - 8/14/72
MANWARINNG, William - 11/23/70
MARSH, Colonel Ebenezer - 5/7/73
MARSH, Rev. John - 12/17/73
MARSH, Reverend Mr. Jonathan - 10/30/72
MARSH, Mr.- 9/25/72
MARSHAL, John - 4/6/70
MARSON, John -12/10/73
MARTIN, John - 3/1/71
MARVIN, Elisha - 8/31/71
MARY - 5/14/73
MASON, Rev. Elijah - 2/9/70
MASON, Eliphalet - 9/3/73
MASON, John- 6/22/70; end note 24
MASON II, Samuel - 11/8/71
MATHER, Dr. Eleazer - 9/14/70
MATHER,, Capt. Joseph - 4/13/70
MATON, William - 5/4/70
MATSON, Nathaniel - 7/12/71
MAVERICK, Samuel - 3/16/70
MAVERICK, Widow - 3/16/70
MAY, Ezra - 8/21/72
MAYNARD ; James - 6/21/71
MCALPINE, Captain - 10/25/71
MCCOY, Daniel - 9/11/72

MCCURDY, John - 8/3/70; 11/15/71; 5/1/72; 7/3/72; 4/23/73
MCNEILL, Alexander - 1/11/71; 7/12/71
MEAD, Amos - 6/12/72
MECKY, Daniel - 1/15/73
MELALLY, Elizabeth - 6/8/70
MELALLY, Capt. - 3/9/70; 12/21/70
MERCHANT, William - 3/16/70
MERILS, Alexander - 1/11/71
MEROTT, Captain Abial - 6/12/72
MERRIMAN, Theophilus - 11/2/70
MERROW, Elisha - 5/7/73
METCALFE, William - 6/5/72; 6/25/73
MILLER, Elisha - 1/5/70
MILLER, Jeremiah - 2/16/70
MILLER, John - 2/23/70; 5/4/70
MILLER Jr., Noah - 12/27/71
MILLER, Thomas - 1/15/73
MILLER, Captain - 4/30/73
MILSON, Mr. - 1/15/73
MINER, Clement - 7/20/70;
MINER, Jr. Clement 1/11/71
MINER, Henry - 1/11/71
MINER, Joseph - 6/28/71; 4/30/73; 10/22/73
MINER, Nathaniel - 1/5/70; 5/4/70; 7/12/71;11/15/71; 7/9/73
MINER Jr., Nathaniel - 1/11/71
MINER, Jr., Mr. - 1/5/70
MINER, young man - 11/1/71
MINET, Capt, James - 8/13/73
MOFFATT, Thomas - 12/14/70; 4/9/73
MONTAGUE, Admiral - 12/3/73
MOONEY,William - 12/11/72

MOOR, Asa -12/10/73
MOOR, Elisha -12/10/73
MOOR, Lemeul - 4/24/72
MOORE, Lemuel - 3/8/71
MOREDOCK, John - 4/13/70
MORGAN, Benjamin - 3/27/72
MORGAN, Darius 10/8/73
MORGAN, Captain Daniel - 11/5/73
MORGAN, Captain John - 5/17/71; 8/2/71
MORGAN, Samuel - 1/12/70
MORGAN, Shan -ap - 3/3/70
MORGAN,, Shapely - 5/17/71
MORGAN, Reverend Solomon - 4/24/72
MORGAN, Theophilus - 9/14/70; 3/8/7; 11/22/71
MORGAN, Thomas - 9/20/71
MORGAN, William - 2/22/71; 7/16/73; 8/13/73; 9/17/73
MORGAN, General - 1/11/71
MORRIS, Josiah - 11/15/51
MORSE, Deacon Jedidiah - 9/13/71
MORSE, Jr., Doctor Parker - 7/30/73
MORTIMER, P.- 2/5/73; 2/26/73
MORTON, Captain - 3/16/70
MOSELEY, Flavel - 12/31/73
MOSELEY,Thomas - 7/6/70
MOSES; Ebenezer - 11/27/72
MOSES; Mr. - 2/14/72
MOTT, Desire - 8/27/73
MOTT, Edward - 8/20/73; 8/27/73; 10/1/73
MOTT, Kizie - 8/27/73
MOTT, Samuel - 9/4/72
MOTT, Mrs. Sarah - 8/20/73; 8/27/7; 10/1/73
MUDGE, William - 9/3/73
MULFORD, John - 7/9/73
MUMFORD, George - 1/5/70;7/23/73
MUMFORD, J. - 9/13/71;3/27/72
MUMFORD, James - 1/5/70; 2/9/70; 8/24/70;12/25/72;4/2/73; 4/9/73; 7/23/73; 7/30/73; 8/13/73; 8/27/73; end note 55
MUMFORD, John - 5/4/70
MUMFORD, Thomas - 2/9/70 ; 9/17/73
MUNRO, Captain James - 3/19/73
MUNSELL, Jr, John - 2/1/71

N

NEFF, Joseph - 4/9/73
NEWCOMB, Paul - 8/27/73
NEWCOMB, Silas - 8/27/73
NEWCOMB, Jr., Silas- 8/27/73
NEWCOMB, Submit - 8/27/73
NEWCOMB, Zilphs - 1/73/22
NEWTON, Roger - 1/25/71
NICHOLAS, John - 11/27/72
NICHOLSON, Jonathan - 1/29/73
NILES, Robert - 1/8/73
NILES, ThomasNp.- 7/5/71
NOBLES, Jonathan - 2/7/72
NORRIS, Henry - 9/7/70
NORWORTH, T. 12/13/71
NOYE, William - 9/17/73
NOYES, Joseph - 9/14/70; 1/10/72
NOYES, Samuel - 1/17/72

O

OAKERMAN, Captain - 6/4/73
OCCOM, Rev. Samson - 9/14/70; 11/15/71; /10/72; 6/26/72; 11/6/72
OGDEN, Captain - 8/23/71
OLCOTT, Capt. John - 9/3/73

OLIVE - 6/19/72
OSBORN, Benjamin - 11/8/71
OSBORN, Jedediah - 12/11/72
OSGOOD, John - 12/7/70
OTIS, Joseph - 1/1/73
OTIS, William - 8/14/72
OWANECO, Sachem - 6/22/70; end note 24

P
PACKER, Daniel 5/4/70
PACKWOOD, Captain David - 10/25/71
PACKWOOD, Mrs. Elizabeth - 8/14/72
PACKWOOD, Captain Joseph - 8/14/72; 1/29/73; 9/3/73; 9/10/73
PACKWOOD, Captain William 7/27/70; 5/3/71; 8/2/71; 10/30/72
PAGE, Abraham - 11/5/73
PAGE, John - 3/2/70
PAINE, Elisha - 1/1/73
PALMER, Mrs. Abigail - 4/24/72
PALMER,, Amas - 4/24/72
PALMER, Azariah - 6/18/73
PALMER, Elijah - 1/11/71
PALMER, Jabish - 11/15/51
PALMER, Joseph - 9/24/73
PALMER, Nathan - 9/14/70
PALMER, Peris - 3/5/73
PALMER, Samuel - 1/22/73
PALMES, Captain Andrew - 4/24/72
PALMES Miss Betsey - 2/19/73
PALMES Edward - 11/26/73
PALMES, Captain Edward - 1/18/71; 2/22/71; 6/14/71; 11/22/71 ;12/20/71; 12/27/71; 2/14/72; 12/4/72; 1/29/73; 7/23/73; 11/5/73

PALMES, Miss Mary - 12/27/71

PALMES, Miss Rebecca - 12/20/71
PARK, John Adam - 12/28/70
PARK, Reverend Joseph - 10/30/72
PARK, Rev. Mr.- 2/5/73
PARK, Mrs. - 10/30/72
PARKER, Amos - 7/12/71
PARKER, Mary - 7/17/72
PARKER, Lt. Nicholas - 7/17/72
PARKER, Captain - 6/26/72
PARKS, James - 5/4/70
PARMELE, Samuel - 1/29/73
PARSONS, Daniel - 9/28/70
PARSONS, Rev. Mr. Elijah - 10/16/72; 11/6/72;9/24/73
PARSONS, John - 2/12/73 -
PARSONS, Samuel H.-
PARSONS, Marsh - 9/17/73
PARSONS, Samuel Holden - 4/17/72; 1/1/73; 6/4/73; 9/17/73
PATRICK, Robert - 5/11/70
PATTENGALL, Lemuel - 3/27/72
PAUL, Moses - 11/6/72
PAYNE, Benjamin - 6/4/73
PAYSON, John - 1/4/71
PEABODY, Joseph - 4/30/73
PEASE, Captain - 10/11/71; 11/1/71
PECK, Elijah - 12/27/71
PECK, Jedidiah - 12/27/71
PECK, Joseph - 1/5/70; 2/28/72
PECK Lebbeus - 2/12/73
PECK, Mather - 7/19/71
PECK, Peter - 12/27/71
PEG - 10/22/73
PENDERSON, Catherine - 5/4/70
PENDERSON, Ebenezer - 5/4/70

PENN, Governor - 11/27/72
PERKINS, Elisha - 4/2/73
PERKINS, Capt. Jabez - 2/16/70; 12/20/71; 5/29/72
PERKINS, James - 1/18/71; 4/24/72
PERKINS, Jr, Joseph - 6/19/72
PERKINS, Luke - 5/4/70; 1/11/71
PERKINS, Captain Matthew - 2/16/70; 5/14/73
PERKINS,s, Rev. Nathan - 10/2/72
PERKINS, Rufus,- 5/22/72
PERKINS, Captain - 4/12/71; 12/27/71
PERRY, Reverend Joseph - 10/30/72
PETER - 11/19/73
PETERS, Edward - 7/9/73
PETERS, James - 1/10/72
PETERS, Mr. - 8/23/71
PETTICE, James - 12/11/72
PETTICE, Peter - 12/11/72
PETTICE, Oliver - 12/11/72
PETTICE, Samuel - 12/11/72
PETTIS, [see PETTICE], Olive - 7/31/72
PHELPS, Col. Alexander - 5/7/73
PHELPS, Charles - 4/13/70; 9/14/70; 8/2/71; 10/23/72; 9/17/73; 12/31/73
PHELPS, Silas - 11/22/71
PHILIPS, George - 2/5/73; 2/26/73
PHILIPS, Jeremiah - 1/10/72
PHILIPS, Captain Michael - 6/4/73
PHILIPS, William - 12/27/71
PHILLLIMORE, Benjamin - 8/2/71
PICKET, James - 12/25/72

PIERCE, John - 4/13/70; 9/13/71
PIERCE, Capt. Moses - 8/17/70; 5/17/71; 8/23/71; 4/24/72; 5/7/73
PIERCE, Stephen - 9/24/73
PIERCE, Timothy - 3/13/72
PINE, Jr., Seth - 9/28/70
PITCHER, Elijah - 9/14/70
PITCHER, Capt. Jonathan - 3/3/70
POMEROY, Reverend Mr. Benjamin - 11/6/72
POMEROY, Rev. Seth - 7/13/70
POMP , - 11/9/70
POMROY, Noah - 1/15/73
POOL, David - 1/11/71
PORTER, Daniel - 2/9/70
POST; Joseph 10/8/73
POST, Mr.- 2/19/73
POTTER, T. - 4/23/73
POTTER,William - 11/15/51
POWELL, Captain Joseph - 10/18/71
POWER, Avery - 11/23/70
POWERS, Samuel - 1/15/73
POWERS, Capt. William - 11/1/71
POWERS, Mr. - 3/9/70
PRATT, Phineas - 7/3/72
PRENTICE, Jonas - 12/21/70
PRENTICE, Samuel - 11/5/73; 11/12/73
PRENTICE, Thomas -3/6/72
PRENTIS, Mrs. Sarah - 2/19/73; 3/5/73
PRENTIS III, John - 3/5/73
PRENTIS, Captain John ,- 2/19/73; 3/19/73
PRENTIS 2d ,John - 3/26/73; 4/9/73
PRESTON, Captain - 3/16/70
PRIDE, Absalom - 4/5/71

PRINCE, Mary - 9/24/73
PRINCE, William - 3/5/73; 7/9/24/
PRINCE - 7/9/73
PRIS, Joseph - 6/26/72
PROCTOR, John - 9/14/70
PROCTOR, Mrs. Lucretia - 9/14/70
PUNDERSON, Cyrus - 7/12/71; 11/15/71; 5/15/72
PUTNAM, Reverend Aaron - 7/30/73
PUTNAM, Mrs. - 7/30/73
PYNER, Aollis - 1/15/73

Q
QUACHEETS.- 5/10/71
QUACO - 11/6/72

R
RANDAL, Rufus - 8/3/70
RANDAL, Thomas - 2/5/73
RANSOM, Jane - 3/5/73
RANSOM, Joseph - 3/5/73
RANSOM, Richard - 12/31/73
RATCHFORD, Thomas - 10/2/72; 7/2/73
RATHBON, William - 6/26/72
RATHBUN, Captain Joshua - 12/17/73
RAUGHMANEN, Frederick - 5/10/71
RAW, Richard - 11/19/73
RAWSON, Reverend
RAYMOND, Eliakim - 11/15/71; 1/10/72
RAYMOND, John - 6/22/70
RAYMOND, Joshua - 11/1/71
RAYMOND, Sarah - 11/1/71
READ, Cornelius - 11/15/51
REED, Alexander - 1/11/71
REED, Temperance - - 1/5/70
REID, Colonel - end note 15

REVES, Joseph - 9/14/70
REYNOLDS, Elisha - 11/16/70
REYNOLDS, William - 11/16/70
RICE, James, - 5/4/70
RICHARDS, Daniel - 12/27/71
RICHARDS, Capt. Guy - 11/23/70
RICHARDS Jr., Guy - 6/18/73
RICHARDS, John - 9/14/70; 12/20/71; 7/10/72
RICHARDS, Pyrus - 7/6/70
RICHARDS, William - 3/27/72
RICHARDS, Captain - 10/25/71
RICHARDSON, John - 10/4/71; 10/9/72, 1/15/73
RICHARDSON, Nathaniel - 11/26/73
RIGGS, Samuel - 11/2/70
RILEY, Captain Ebenezer - 5/7/73
RINE ,John - 7/20/70
RINEY, John - 5/4/70
RIPLEY, Rev. David - 9/24/73
RIPLEY, Elijah - 7/19/71
RIPLEY, John - 6/19/72; 9/4/72; 1/1/73
RIPLEY, Rev. Mr.- 3/20/72
ROBBINS, David - 2/23/70
ROBERTS, Ebenezer - 3/9/70
ROBINS, Reverend Mr. Robert - 11/6/72
ROBINSON, Amos - 12/27/71
ROBINSON, Edward - 7/19/71; 1/29/73
ROBINSON, I. - 5/29/72; 6/19/72
ROBINSON, Ichabod - 1/12/70; 9/7/70
ROBINSON, Jack - 3/3/70; endnote 20
ROBINSON, John - 6/14/71
ROBINSON, Nicholas - 1/15/73
ROBINSON, Thomas - - 1/5/70

ROBINSON, Captain - 3/29/71
ROBINSON, Mr. - 10/22/73
ROCHFORD, Thomas - 4/9/73
ROCKWELL, Edward -2/21/72
ROCKWELL, Captain Samuel - 10/29/73
ROCKWELL, William 10/12/70
ROGERS, Alexander - 3/19/73
ROGERS, Daniel - 3/19/73
ROGERS, David - 7/17/72
ROGERS, Elizabeth - 3/20/72; 9/24/73
ROGERS, Gamiel - 9/24/73
ROGERS, James - 1/11/71; 6/5/72; 3/26/73
ROGERS, Capt. John - 1/5/70; 11/9/70; 3/19/73
ROGERS, Nathan - 12/14/70
ROGERS, Mrs. Sarah - 12/20/71
ROGERS, Stephen - 1/17/72
ROGERS, Dr. Theo.- 2/16/70
ROGERS, Uriah - 9/24/73
ROGERS, William - 12/20/71; 1/15/73
ROGERS, Zabadiah - 3/20/72
ROLLINS, Philip - 1/11/71
ROOT, Ephraim - 9/3/73
ROOT, Ezchiel - 7/9/73
ROSE, Joseph - 2/9/70; 5/7/73; 9/3/73
ROSE, Jr. Samuel - 5/7/73; 9/3/73
ROSE, Mrs. Sarah - 2/9/70
ROSS, Jeremiah - 2/16/70;6/7/71; 10/25/71; 1/15/73
ROSSETER, Asher-Sherman - 10/1/73
ROSSITER, Elnathan - 1/15/73; 3/5/73
ROSSITER, Rev. Mr.- 3/15/71; 10/11/71
ROTCH, Mr.- 12/24/73

ROWELY, Timothy - 1/11/71
ROWLANDSON, Mrs. Mary - 11/12/73
ROYCE, Mr.- 3/22/71
RUDD, Capt. Jonathan - 4/13/70; 12/14/70
RUGGLES, Rev. Mr. - 11/30/70
RUSSEL, Capt. Giles - 3/2/70; 1/15/73; 3/5/73; 7/9/73; 12/31/73
RUSSEL, William - 3/27/72
RUSTE, Daniel - 11/1/71

S
SABIN, Mrs. Mary - 10/1/73
SABIN, Seth - 10/1/73
SAFFORD, Solomon - 2/16/70
SAGE, Capt. Comfort .- 3/27/72;4/3/72; 5/15/72; 11/6/72
SALEM, Aaron - 11/9/70
SALTONSTALL,, Captain Dudley - 3/29/71; 4/10/72
SALTONSTALL, Col. Gurdon - 2/9/70 ; 4/13/70; 9/14/70; 9/6/71; 9/13/71; 10/25/71; 4/17/72; 4/30/73; 8/27/73; end note 55
SALTONSTALL, Miss Henrietta - 2/28/72
SALTONSTALL, Nathaniel - 1/5/70; 9/14/70
SALTONSTALL, Roswell - 7/2/73
SALTONSTALL, Winthrop -- 8/9/71 ;11/29/71; 12/6/71; 3/27/72
SAMBO - 5/4/70
SAMPSON - 8/31/70
SARGEANT, Jonathan - 11/26/73
SAUFLEY, Captain Nathaniel - 1/31/72

SAUFLEY, Mrs. - 1/31/72
SAY AND SEAL, Lord - 3/2/70
SCHINK, Paul - 1/11/71
SCOTT, Hannah - 3/8/71
SCOTT, Zebadiah - 3/8/71
SCOVEL, Elisha - 11/5/73
SCOVEL, John - 5/21/73
SCRANTON, Noah 10/12/70
SEABURY, Caleb - 6/26/72
SEABURY, Elisha - 6/26/72
SEABURY, Mrs. Elizabeth - 1/11/71
SEABURY, Deacon John - 1/11/71
SELDEN, Mrs. Ann - 7/23/73
SELDEN, Ezra - 8/16/71; 8/31/71
SELDIN, Samuel - 4/17/72
SEYMOUR, Miss Jane - 7/13/70
SEYMOUR Thomas - 7/13/70
SHAND, Capt.- 6/15/70
SHAPELY, Adam [see Shipley]- 5/3/7; 7/23/73 1
SHARPE, Benjamin - 1/5/70
SHAW, Jr., Nathaniel - 2/9/70;10/18/71; 11/1/71; 10/30/72
SHAW, Thomas - 11/26/73
SHEELS, James - 1/8/73
SHEFFIELD, Isaac - 1/15/73
SHELDON, Elisha - 10/25/71
SHELLS, James - 10/23/72
SHEPARD, Captain Isaac
SHEPARD, James - 10/26/70
SHERMAN, Daniel - 10/25/71
SHERMAN, David -8/9/71
SHERMAN, James - 10/1/73
SHERMAN, Roger - 10/25/71
SHIELD, James - 10/23/72
SHIPLEY, Adam [see Shapley]- 1/29/73
SHIPMAN, Captain Edward - 6/18/73

SHIPMAN, Nathaniel - 6/8/70
SHOULS, James - 1/5/70
SILLIMAN, Ebenezer - 10/25/71; 6/4/73
SIMONS, Jacob -
SIMONS, Jacob 10/12/70; 4/12/71
SIMPSON, John - 1/15/73
SISSON, Captain - 4/12/71
SISTAR, Gabriel - 11/19/73
SKINNER, Richard - 11/22/71
SKINNER, William - 9/14/70
SLATER, Zerubabel - 9/27/71
SLUMAN, Peter - 10/29/73
SMITH, Abiezer -4/20/70; 8/23/71
SMITH, Benjamin - 10/5/70
SMITH, Rev. Charles Jeffrey - 8/24/70
SMITH,, Charles - 7/9/73
SMITH, David - 6/8/70
SMITH, Duncan - 12/21/70
SMITH, Captain Hezehiah - 6/4/73
SMITH, Jabez - 5/4/70; 1/11/71
SMITH, James - 1/15/73
SMITH, Jedediah - 12/18/72
SMITH, John - 9/14/70; 3/6/72; 10/30/72; 1/22/73; 2/19/73; 3/5/73
SMITH, Jonathan - 12/27/71
SMITH, Nehemiah - 6/15/70
SMITH, Capt. Oliver - 1/15/73 12/3/73
SMITH, Peter - 6/18/73
SMITH, Phoebe - 1/22/73; 3/5/73
SMITH,Jr., Samuel - 5/28/73
SMITH, Thomas - 9/17/73
SMITH, Captain - 3/29/71
SNIDER, - 3/16/70
SNOW, Reverend Joseph - 3/19/73

SNOW, Miss Rebecca - 3/19/73
SOLOMON, Mr. - 12/4/72
SOUGHTON, Lemeul - 5/28/73
SOUTHWARD, William - 2/12/73
SPALDING, Captain Zechariah - 8/9/71
SPARROW, James - 5/24/71
SPENCER, Ichabod - 5/21/73
SPENCER, John - 12/3/73
SPENCER, Joseph - 1/11/71; 7/12/71; 10/25/71; 4/23/73
SPICER, Daniel - 7/10/72; 3/19/73
SPRAGUE, David - 7/12/71
SPRINGER, John - 3/27/72
SQUIRE, Capt. 10/12/70
ST. BARNABAS - end note 32
ST. PAUL - end note 32
STACY, Gideon - 3/12/73
STANLEY, Caleb - 9/3/73
STANNIS, William - 8/17/70
STANTON, Andrew - 3/9/70
STANTON, Capt. Phineas - 4/13/70; 11/8/71
STANTON, Lieut. Samuel - 3/9/70
STARK, Silas - 8/31/71
STARK, William - 7/12/71
STARKWEATHER, Seth - 10/1/73
STARR, Capt. Daniel - 11/15/51
STARR, Elihu - 4/3/72
STARR, Elisha - 10/29/73
STARR, Jonathan - 4/24/72; 6/18/73
STARR, Jr., Jonathan - 12/17/73
STARR, Joshua - 7/20/70; 6/4/73
STARR, Manuel - 1/5/70
STEDMAN, Deacon Thomas - 4/30/73

STEEL, Elisha - 9/3/73
STERNE, Thomas Smith - 8/9/71
STETSON, Lieutenant Eli - 7/31/72
STEVENS, John, - 8/14/72
STEVENS, Roswell - 6/18/73
STEVENSON, Allen - 9/14/70
STEWARD, William - 6/28/71
STEWART, Duncan - 3/16/70; 12/14/70; 6/14/71; 4/9/73
STEWART, Matthew - 3/16/70
STEWART, William - 12/6/71; 8/20/73
STILLMAN, Captain Allen - 3/22/71
STILLE, John - 2/28/72
STILLMAN, Capt. Samuel - 3/9/70; 3/22/71;
STILLMAN, Captain - 3/15/71
STOCKER, John - 3/27/72; 4/3/72
STOCKER, George - 2/5/73
STOCKING, Samuel - 7/24/72
STOCKWELL, Samuel - 3/27/72
STODDARD, Eleazer - 6/12/72
STODDARD, Ichabod - 5/17/71
STODDARD, Mark - 5/17/71
STODDARD, Robert, - 5/17/71
STONE, Caleb - 9/27/71
STONE, Nathaniel - 11/15/51
STORK, Moses - 9/14/70
STORRS, Aaron - 9/7/70
STORRS, Samuel - 6/12/72
STORY, Jonathan - 3/6/72
STREET, James - 1/25/71
STRONG, Asahel - 1/15/73
STRONG, Jedidiah - 6/5/72
STRONG, Nathan - 11/27/72
STRONG, Phineas - 4/13/70
STRONG, Thomas - 3/13/72
STRONG, Mr. - 9/17/73
SUZANNE - 4/30/73

SWADDEL, Samuel, - 1/25/71
SWAN, Robert - 6/26/72
SWIFT; Rowland - 9/17/73
SYBIL - 12/11/72
SYDELMAN, John - 2/19/73

T

TABOR, Capt. Jeremiah - 12/20/71
TAINTER, John -2/21/72; 1/15/73; 10/8/73 3; 12/17/73
TALBUT, Ebenezer - 4/9/73
TALBUT, Nathaniel - 4/9/73
TALCOTT, Captain John - 6/21/71
TALMAN, Samuel - 1/15/73; 1/22/73
TALMAN, Bethiah - 1/15/73; 1/22/73
TATSON, Warren - 12/6/71
TAYLOR, Benjamin- 6/22/70
TAYLOR Justus - 7/19/71; 2/5/73; 2/26/73
TAYLOR, , Pardon - 9/14/70
TAYLOR, Mr. - 1/5/70
TEAGUS, Jesse - 1/5/70; 5/4/70
TERELL, Thomas - 9/4/72
THOMPSON, Anne - 1/5/70
THOMAS, Elias - 11/12/73
THOMPSON, George - 5/4/70
THOMAS, James -1/25/71; 12/3/73
THOMPSON, Joseph 6/7/71
THOMPSON, Dr. James - 10/26/70; 5/15/72
THRALL, Joel - 8/21/72
THROOP, Capt. Dyar - 1/3/72 4/17/72; 4/30/73
THROOP, Rev. Benjamin - 7/27/70
THROOP, Reverend Mr.- 3/20/72 11/19/73

TIFFANEY, John - 9/17/73
TIFFANY, Timothy - 1/10/72
TILEY, Samuel - 12/27/71
TILLY, James - 7/20/70
TINKER, Mrs. Abigail - 10/29/73
TINKER, Nehemiah - 3/2/70
TINKER, Captain Sylvanus - 8/17/70; 10/29/73
TISDALE, Elkanah - 4/16/73
TOLES, Samuel - 6/26/72
TONEY - 4/30/73
TORRY, Miss Lucy - 12/7/70
TOWN, Joseph - 3/27/72
TRACY, Daniel - 3/3/70; 5/25/70; 2/1/71
TRACY, Elisha - 7/13/70; 3/20/72; 1/22/73
TRACY, Miss Hannah - 5/25/70
TRACY, Isaac - 5/25/70; 7/13/70; 3/20/72;1/29/73; 9/17/73
TRACY, Joseph - 1/5/70; 8/17/70
TRACY, Partial - 8/23/71
TRACY, Samuel - 9/13/71; 2/31/73
TRAPP, Caleb - 3/22/71
TREADWAY, Mr.- 11/1/71
TREAT, Samuel L.- 10/1/73
TREDWAY, Elijah - 10/29/73
TROWBRIDGE, Captain Joseph - 6/28/71
TROWBRIDGE, Mrs. Mary - 6/28/71
TRUMAN, Clark -9/27/71; 11/22/71
TRUMAN, Daniel - 8/14/72
TRUMAN, Eleaser - 11/22/71
TRUMAN, Thomas - 5/28/73
TRUMBULL, Jonathan - 10/25/71

TRUMBULL Jr., Jonathan - 1/25/71;10/11/7; 9/4/72 1
TRUMBULL, Joseph - 4/13/70; 1/25//71; 6/28/71; 6/28/71; 9/13/7; 6/4/73
TRUMBULL, Governor - 3/26/73
TRYON, Jeremiah - 9/3/73
TRYON, Skinner, John - 8/20/73
TRYON, Governor William - 4/19/71; end note 39
TUBBS,, Ezra - 2/1/71
TUBBS, Mr.- 10/19/70
TUCKER Jr, Ephraim - 9/28/70
TUCKER, Captain Stephen - 5/7/73
TUCKER, Mr. - 12/3/73
TUFF, John - 12/17/73
TURNER, Philip - 8/21/72
TURNER,, Samuel - 2/28/72
TUTHILL, Abia - 9/17/73
TUTHILL, Capt. Barnabas - 9/17/73
TUTHILL, John - 9/14/70
TUTHILL, Rufus -3/6/72
TYLER, Daniel - 8/31/70
TYLER, , Rev. Mr. John - 2/9/70; 5/25/70
TYLER, Capt. John,- 4/13/70
TYLER, Reverend Mr. - 8/23/71

U

UNCAS, Benjamin - 4/13/70
UNCAS Isaiah - 4/13/70
UNCAS, Sachem - 6/22/70; end note 24

V

VEIL, Stephen - 5/28/73
VELDALL, Dr. Anthony - 11/12/73

VINCENT, Widow - 12/11/72
VREDENBURG, Capt. John- 11/2/70; 7/31/72; 8/7/72

W

WADE, Elisha - 12/7/70
WADSWORTH, James 7/16/73
WAID, Roswel - 2/1/71
WAIT, Marvin - 6/15/70; 9/13/71; 12/18/72; 1/29/73; 7/23/73
WALES, Ebenezer - 11/5/73
WALES, John - 6/18/73
WALES, Nathaniel - 4/9/73; 6/4/73; 11/5/73
WALES, Jr., Nathaniel - 4/13/70; 6/22/70; 4/26/71; 9/13/71; 5/8/72;3/19/73;
WALES, Seth - 4/26/71
WALKER, Ebenezer - 5/8/72
WALKER, Robert - 10/25/71
WALKER, Doctor Thomas - 3/22/71
WALL, Henry - 1/10/72
WALTON, Oliver - 5/10/7
WALTON, Polly - 8/23/71 1
WALTON, Dr. William - 8/23/71
WALWA, Jr, Nathaniel - 6/18/73
WARD, Jr, John - 3/29/71
WARD, Sr., John - 3/29/71; 8/14/72
WARD, Capt.- 3/8/71; 3/22/71
WARNER, John - 3/27/72
WARWICK, Earl of - 3/2/70
WATER, Joseph - 6/22/70
WATERHOUSE, Mary - 1/11/71
WATERMAN, Andrew - 7/12/71
WATERMAN, Asa - 5/28/73
WATERMAN,Jr,. Asa - 7/2/73; 7/9/73
WATERMAN, Joseph - 8/7/72

WATERMAN, Thomas - 5/28/73
WATERMAN, Deacon - 3/9/70
WATERS, Abner - 7/12/71
WATERS, Jacob - 2/7/72
WATERS, Moses - 10/11/71; 2/7/72
WATKINS, Hugh - 5/28/73
WATKINS, William - 4/10/72
WATSON, James - 1/19/70; 12/14/70
WATT, Richard - 2/16/70
WATTER, Script - 4/23/73
WATTS, John - 11/27/72
WAY, Ebenezer - 8/31/71; 9/3/73
WAY, Joseph - 6/5/72
WAY, Mrs. Mary - 8/31/71
WEBB, Joseph - 11/5/73
WEBB, Samuel - 3/2/70; 3/9/70
WEEKS, Amos - 1/10/72
WEEKS, Ebenezer 10/12/70
WELCH, Rufus - 6/29/70
WELLES, Amos, - 7/12/71
WELLES, Captain - 9/13/71
WELLS, John - 9/14/70
WENTWORTH, Governor Benning end note 44
WEST, Joshua - 10/18/71
WEST, Nathaniel - 6/19/72
WEST, Zebulon - 6/22/70; 12/14/70
WESCOTE, Samuel - 6/1/70
WESCOTE, William - 12/17/73
WESTCOTT, Gideon - 1/15/73
WETMORE, Benjamin - 5/18/70
WHEAT, Samuel - 8/3/70; 9/21/70; 10/8/73
WHEELER, Coit - 3/26/73
WHEELER, Cyrus - 3/2/70
WHEELER, Job - 12/3/73
WHEELER, Mrs. Mercy - 2/16/70

WHEELER, Thomas - 2/16/70
WHEELER, William - 3/6/72
WHEELER Jr., Zaccheus - 10/18/71
WHEELOCK, R. - 12/14/70
WHEELOCK, Doct. - 12/14/70
WHISTON, Mr. - 2/15/71
WHITAKER D.D., Rev Nathaniel - 9/24/73
WHITE, Amos - 11/5/73
WHITE, Ebenezer - 4/30/73
WHITE ,Capt. Elijah - 4/11/73
WHITE, Capt. William - 9/14/70
WHITE, Rev. Mr.- 3/20/72
WHITEAR, John - 11/6/72
WHITING,, Mrs. Ann - 12/3/73
WHITING, Ebenezer - 8/7/72
WHITING, Colonel Nathan - 4/19/71
WHITING, Philenach - 1/11/71; 10/16/72
WHITING, Col. William - 2/16/70; 12/21/70; 1/11/71;10/16/72
WHITING, Deacon William - 12/3/73
WHITLEY; William - 12/3/73
WHITNEY, Rev. Mr.- 3/20/72; 4/17/72
WHITSEA, Elisha - 6/26/72
WHITTEMORE, Daniel - 7/12/71; 1/17/72; 5/29/72; 6/19/72; 7/31/72; 12/4/72
WHITTLESEY, Hez.- 4/13/70
WHITTEMORE, Mrs. Lady [Lydia] - 5/29/72; 6/19/72; 7/31/72
WICKHAM, Captain - 3/22/71
WIGGINS, James - 3/9/70; 5/3/71; 5/15/72
WIGHT, Joseph - 7/31/72
WILDS, Jonas 10/8/73

WILKINSON, Thomas - 8/7/72 ;7/31/72; 8/28/72
WILLES ,Thomas - 12/24/73
WILLIAM, Ann ,- 7/12/71
WILLIAMS, Charles -6/12/72
WILLIAMS, Col. Ebenezer - 4/13/70; 9/13/71; 9/4/72
WILLIAMS, Reverend Eliphalet - 10/30/72
WILLIAMS, Elisha - 3/19/73
WILLIAMS, Henry - 2/19/73
WILLIAMS, Jesse - 3/26/73; 12/3/73
WILLIAMS, John - 5/4/70;6/26/72
WILLIAMS, Jonathan - 9/14/70
WILLIAMS, Capt. Joseph - 8/24/70
WILLIAMS, Nathaniel - 2/23/70; 12/24/73
WILLIAMS, Samuel - 9/14/70; 11/22/71
WILLIAMS, Stephen. - 9/28/70
WILLIAMS, Thomas - 9/13/71; 2/5/73
WILLIAMS, William - 1/12/70; 4/20/70; 4/13/70; 9/7/70; 9/13/71; 11/15/71; 6/4/73
WILLIS, Samuel - 11/6/72
WILLOGHBY, Bliss - 9/14/70
WILLOGHBY, Joseph - 9/20/71
WILLSON, T.- 10/1/73
WINN, Captain - 10/4/71
WINSLOW, Job - 7/10/72
WINTER, Timothy - 11/13/72
WINTHROP,, Basil - 1/25/71
WINTHROP, John - 3/2/70; end note 16
WISE Jr,. Joseph - 1/5/70
WITE, James - 3/27/72
WOLCOTT, Alex - 8/27/73

WOLCOTT, Erastus. - 6/4/73
WOLCOTT, Oliver - 6/28/71; 10/25/71
WOLCOTTt, Simon - 12/21/70; 12/11/72; 12/3/73
WOOD, Simeon - 1/5/70
WOODBRIDGE, Dudley - 8/3/70
WOODBRIDGE,Ephraim - 4/30/73
WOODBRIDGE, Joseph - 9/14/70
WOODHOUSE, William - 1/25/71
WOODWARD, Benjamin - 3/2/70; 3/9/70
WOODWARD, Park - 1/15/73
WOODWORTH, Douglas - 1/15/73
WOODWORTH, Nathaniel - 6/14/71
WOODWORTH, Priscilla - 6/14/71
WOOMSLEY, William - 10/5/70
WORTHINGTON, Elias - 6/21/71; 10/8/73
WORTHINGTON,, Capt. William - 9/17/73
WRIGHT, Captain Dudley - 6/21/71
WRIGHT, Rev. Jabez - 10/11/71
WRIGHT, John - 2/9/70
WRIGHT, Joseph - 5/29/72

Z

YEAMANS, Daniel - 12/3/73
YEOMANS, Moses -8/9/71
YOUNG, William - 8/2/71

PLACE INDEX

Africa - 6/14/71
Albany - 7/9/73
Annapolis in Nova Scotia - 10/4/71
Antigua - 3/15/71; 4/12/71
Ashford - 1/4/71; 11/1/71 ; 4/10/72; 5/8/72; 6/12/72; 8/14/72; 6/18/73; 9/24/73
Atlantic Ocean - end note
Barbados - 3/9/70; 8/3/70 ; - 8/3/70; 10/9/72; 9/3/73
Beaver street New York - 2/19/73
Bethel - 3/8/71
Bethpage - 2/15/71
Block Island - 5/3/71; 1/10/72;5/7/73; 6/25/73
Bolton - 6/22/70
Boston -7/6/70; 7/13/70;7/20/70; 8/3/70;.8/10/70; 8/17/70; 8/24/70; 8/31/70; 9/7/70; 9/14/70; 9/21/70; 12/7/70; 12/21/70; - 3/16/70; 4/6/70; 5/25/70; 9/14/70; 10/26/70; 11/9/70; -3/29/71; 8/23/71; 9/13/71; 9/20/71; 10/18/71; 3/27/72; /10/72; 5/15/72; 10/16/72; 1/15/73; 6/4/73; 7/16/73; 9/17/73; 9/24/73; 10/1/73 ; 11/26/73; 12/3/73;12/10/73; 12/24/73; end notes 10, 31; 47, 53, 58
Branford - 1/19/70; 9/14/70; 9/14/70; 8/23/71
Bridgehampton - 6/15/70
Bristol - 10/25/71
Britain - end notes 2, 10, 58

Brookline - 1/15/73
Bucks County - 11/27/72
Cadiz - 10/18/71
Canaan, New Hampshire - 1/5/70; 5/21/73
Canada parish in Windham - 12/31/73
Canterbury - 1/5/70; 4/13/70; 8/3/70; 8/31/70; 11/9/70; 4/19/71; 9/13/71; 11/15/71;3/13/72; 11/13/72; 12/11/72;7/23/73; 8/20/73; 10/15/73
Canterbury Woods - 6/18/73
Capes of the Delaware - 11/5/73
Cape François - 5/3/71
Cape Hatteras - 4/12/71
Cape Nichola - 2/2/70; 7/27/70;7/27/70 ;3/15/71; - 3/29/71; 9/13/71; 9/11/72; end note 7
Cape Sable - 11/6/72
Carolinas - 9/10/73
Caribbean - end note 12
Caribean colonies - end note 17
Castle, Boston -12/10/73
Catskill Mountains - end note 37
Charleston - 10/29/73
Charleston, Rhode island- 11/12/73; 12/10/73; 10/30/72;
Charlestown, Boston - 6/14/71; end note 31
Chatham - 3/27/72; 12/25/72; 2/5/73 4/9/73; 4/30/73; 10/22/73; 10/29/73;
Chelmsford, Massachusetts - 8/9/71

Chelsea in Norwich [see also Norwich Landing]- 1/5/70; 2/16/70; 3/23/70; 6/29/70; 11/1/71; 5/29/72; 7/3/72; 6/25/73; 9/24/73; 11/19/73; 12/31/73; end notes 13, 19
Chester in Saybrook - 2/9/70
Chesterfield Society - 1/15/73; 2/26/73
Chesterfield Parish in Lyme - 5/14/73
Chesterfield Society in New London - 6/5/72
Clinton - 10/18/71
Colchester - 1/5/70; - 9/7/70; 9/14/70; 1/11/71; 2/1/71; 3/15/71; 5/10/71; 6/14/71; 6/21/71; 7/12/71; 8/9/71; 8/31/71; 11/1/71; 11/15/51; 2/21/72; 3/27/72; 5/15/72; 5/22/72; 6/5/72; 6/12/72; 7/10/72; 7/24/72; 9/25/72; 11/6/72; 11/13/72; 11/27/72; 12/11/72; 12/25/72
Colchester - 10/8/73; 11/5/73; 12/17/73; 1/15/73; 2/19/73; 2/26/73; 4/30/73; 5/7/73; 7/9/73; 7/16/73; 8/13/73; 8/27/73; 10/8/73; 11/5/73; 12/17/73
Conanicut Island, Rhode Island - 8/17/70
Concord, Massachusetts Bay - 8/13/73
Connecticut River - 3/9/70; 4/19/71; 5/31/71; 9/13/71; - 2/28/72; 3/27/72; 11/13/72; 1/15/73; 5/7/73; 5/21/73; 9/17/73; 11/12/73; 12/10/73; 12/31/73
Corn Hill, Boston - 3/16/70
Corwall. - 11/26/73
Coventry - 4/13/70; 7/19/71; 6/5/72; 9/4/72; 1/15/73; 5/7/73; 9/3/73
Coventry, Kent county, Rhode Island - 11/16/70
Danbury - 11/8/71
Davis Straits - 11/15/51
Delaware River - 7/13/70; 8/23/71
Derby - 11/2/70
Dock Square, Boston - 3/16/70
Dominica - 3/15/71; 6/4/73
Dr. Loring's Corner, Boston - 3/16/70
Duck Island - 5/31/71;-3/6/72 ; 3/26/73
East Branch of the Susquehanna; - 10/22/73
East Greenwich , Rhode Island - 11/9/70
East Haddam - 7/6/70; 8/10/70; 8/17/70; 1/11/71; 5/3/71; 5/24/71; 6/14/71; 7/5/7 ; 7/19/71; 11/22/71; 12/20/71 ;4/17/72; 7/10/72; 9/18/72 ;10/16/72;11/6/72; 11/27/72; 12/4/72; ;2/5/73; 2/12/73; 4/11/73; 4/23/73; 4/30/73; 5/21/73;7/23/73; 9/10/73; 9/24/73;-11/5/73; 12/3/73
East Haddam Landing - 8/17/70; 9/13/71
East Hampton - 3/9/70; 3/23/70; 7/6/70; 8/10/70;7/6/70; 8/10/70; 3/8/71; 6/26/72 ;12/11/72; 7/9/73; 10/29/73
East Hartford - 5/28/73
East Society in Lyme - 10/29/73
East Society in Norwich - 4/5/71; 7/31/72
East Windsor - 10/30/72;11/13/72

East Branch of the Susquehanna; - 10/22/73
East Hartford - 4/19/71; 5/1/72; 10/30/72; 5/28/73
East Haddam - 2/5/73; 2/12/73; 4/11/73; 4/23/73; 4/30/73; 5/21/73;7/23/73; 9/10/73; 9/24/73
Egg Harbor - 4/24/72
Eighth [h] Society, Norwich - 2/16/70; 3/3/70Elderkin's Bridge - 11/5/73
Enfield - 4/13/70; 2/12/73; 9/17/73
England - end note 8
Europe -8/9/71; 6/26/72 ; 9/11/72; 8/27/73
Eustatia - 3/22/71
Fairfield - 7/13/70; 11/6/72; 12/10/73; end note 44
Fairfield, New Hampshire - 6/5/72; end note 44
Faneuil Hall - 12/3/73
Faneuil Hall - 12/3/73
Farmington - 11/8/7; 7/16/73.
Ferry Wharf in New London - 8/9/71
Ferry Road -3/6/72
First Society in Ashford - 9/24/73
First Society in Chatham - 6/18/73
First Society in Lebanon - 4/16/73
First Society in Lyme,- 12/7/70; 5/7/73
First Society in New London - 4/19/71
First Society, Norwich - 1/5/70; 2/16/70; 4/3/72
First Society in Preston - 10/1/73
Fisher' Island - 11/2/70; 3/8/71; 4/24/72; 3/12/73; 4/2/73; ; 5/14/73; 9/3/73 ; 9/10/73; 10/1/73
Fishers Island Sound - 8/14/72
Flanders - 6/26/72
Florida - end note 53
Flushing on Otter Creek - 2/23/70; end notes 15, 38
Ford Way Board - 5/29/72
Fourth Meeting house in Boston - 12/24/73
Framingham - 3/16/70
France - 6/26/72
Gale's Ferry - 10/4/71; 5/28/73
Gardiners Island - 3/8/71
Gardiner's Point.-3/6/72
Gaspee Point- end note 45
Georgetown, Maryland - 7/23/73
Georgia - 7/2/73; - end note 53
Germany - 5/10/71
Glastonbury - 11/22/71; 5/7/73; 6/18/73; 11/5/73; 11/26/73
Goshen Parish Lebanon - 6/8/70; 9/13/71; 1/10/72; 3/27/72; 4/9/73
Grafton County, N. H- end note 44
Great Britain - 9/21/70; 9/28/70; 10/5/70
Great Wharf Bridge at Chelsea, Norwich - 12/31/73
Grenada - 8/31/70
Groton - 1/15/73; 1/22/73; 2/5/73; 3/12/73; 4/2/73; 4/30/73; 5/28/73;7/9/73; 9/17/73
Groton - 1/5/70; 2/9/70 ; 3/16/70;4/13/70;4/27/70 ; 5/4/70; 6/1/7; 6/22/70;6/29/70; 7/6/70;9/14/70; 12/21/70; 1/18/71; 2/22/71; 3/8/71;

3/15/71; 5/17/71; 6/28/71;
7/5/71; 7/12/71; 7/19/71;
7/26/71; 8/2/71; 9/6/71;
9/13/71; 9/20/71; -
11/15/51;1/17/72; 1/24/72;
1/31/72; 2/14/72; 4/17/72;
4/24/72; 5/15/72;
6/26/72;Groton 7/10/72;
9/11/72; 10/30/72; 12/11/72;
1/15/73; 1/22/73; 2/5/73;
3/12/73; 4/2/73; 4/30/73;
5/28/73;7/9/73; 9/17/73;
10/8/73
Guadalupe - 2/16/70; 3/29/71;
11/15/71; 4/10/72; 4/30/73
Guilford - 11/30/70; 3/22/71;
9/27/71; 11/22/71; 12/20/71;
1/10/72; 6/18/73
Haddam - 1/11/71
Haiti- end note 7
Halifax.- 6/14/71
Hanover,:Norwich - 2/16/70
Hanover, New Hampshire -
5/7/73; 5/14/73
Hartford county, - 12/14/70;
6/21/71
Hartford - 1/19/70; 5/18/70;
6/15/70; - 6/22/70; 7/13/70;
8/24/70;9/7/70; 10/26/70;
12/14/70; 2/1/71; 6/28/71;
7/19/71; 9/6/71; - 9/13/71;
1/10/72; -2/21/72; 2/28/72;
6/12/72; 7/17/72;12/4/72 ;
2/19/73; 3/19/73; 4/9/73;
8/20/73; 8/27/73; 9/3/73;
11/12/73; 11/19/73
Havana - 10/18/71
Hebron - 2/9/70; 6/22/70;
9/7/70; 7/12/71; 8/23/71;
3/13/72; 6/19/72; 8/21/72; -
11/6/72; 1/15/73; 3/19/73;
5/7/73; Hebron - end note 24
Hempstead Plain, - 2/15/71

Hispaniola -7/27/70; 3/29/71;
- 4/19/71; 1/8/73; 9/3/73
Hogs Neck, New London -
10/11/71
Hommocks, the - 5/14/73
Hudson River - 11/19/73
Huntington in the First
Delaware purchase - 8/6/73;
12/24/73
Ireland - 8/27/73
Isle of Mann - 10/25/71
Jamaica, - 4/24/72; - 5/1/72;
9/10/73
Johnson Hall, N.Y.- 9/17/73
Jordan Brook - 5/29/72; -
6/19/72
Keney's cove - 2/22/71
Kent - 12/14/70
Kent county, Rhode Island -
11/16/70;
Killingly - 5/4/70; 9/14/70;
1/11/71; 5/10/71; 6/7/71;
6/28/71; 6/26/72; 7/17/72
Killingworth - 5/4/70;
9/14/70;10/12/70; 3/8/71
King Street, Boston - 3/16/70
Lackwack Township -
4/5/71;end note 37
Lackawack township - 4/5/71;
Lancaster, Massachusetts -
11/12/73
Lebanon - 1/5/70; 1/12/70;
2/23/70; 3/2/70; 4/13/70;
4/20/70; 5/11/70; 7/6/70;
9/7/70; 9/14/70;
9/28/70;10/12/70 ;11/16/70;
11/23/70; 1/18/71; - 1/25/71;
3/22/71; 3/29/71; 7/5/71;
7/12/71; 8/9/71 9/13/71;
10/4/71; 10/11/71; 10/18/71;
11/1/71; 11/15/51; 11/22/71;
12/27/71; 1/3/72; 1/10/72;
1/17/72; 2/7/72; 3/13/72;

3/27/72; 5/29/72; 6/5/72;
6/19/72; 6/26/72; 8/21/72;
8/28/72; 9/4/72;
10/23/72;12/25/72; 3/19/73;
4/16/73; - 4/23/73;
5/7/73;6/25/73; 8/6/73;
8/27/73; 9/17/73;11/19/73;
12/3/73; end note 44
Lebanon Crank - 8/21/72;
5/28/73
Lebanon, Second Society - 1/22/73
Leicester - 11/26/73
Lichfield -3/27/72; 4/17/72;
6/12/72; 7/24/72; 10/30/72;
2/12/73; 4/9/73; 5/7/73
Litchfield County - 5/31/71
Lisbon - 2/2/70; 8/3/70;
7/19/71
Little Plain in Norwich - 4/13/70
Little Egg Harbor - 2/2/70
Liverpool - 12/20/71; 6/5/72
London - 12/21/70; 5/10/71;
6/28/71; 8/23/71; 10/4/71;
11/22/71; /3/72;
6/26/72;7/24/72; 8/28/72;
3/26/73; 4/30/73; 10/23/72;
12/3/73
Long Bridge, New London - 6/1/70
Long Island - 3/9/70; 3/23/70;
6/15/70 8/24/70; 9/14/70;
10/26/70; 11/16/70; 2/15/71;
3/8/71; 5/3/71; 6/7/71;
7/12/71; 10/18/71; 11/22/71;
11/29/71; 12/6/71;
12/27/7;4/24/72;
6/12/72;12/11/72 1; 1/15/73;
5/28/73; 7/9/73; 8/27/73;
9/24/73; 10/22/73
Long Island Sound -5/25/70;
3/8/71 ;10/15/73; 4/2/73;
7/9/73; end note 34
Long Meadow in Springfield - 2/26/73
Long Point at Stonington harbor - 5/4/70
Long Society: Norwich - 2/16/70
Lyme - 1/5/70; 1/12/70;
4/13/70; 4/20/70; 5/4/70;
5/25/70; 7/20/70; 8/3/70;
9/14/70; 10/19/70; 12/7/70;
1/11/71; 2/1/71; 2/22/71;
6/14/71; 6/28/71; 7/5/71;
7/19/71; 8/16/71; 8/31/71;
1/10/72; 2/14/72; 7/3/72;
10/23/72;10/30/72 ; 11/6/72;
11/27/72; 12/11/72 12/20/71;
12/27/71;1/1/73; 1/29/73;
3/5/73; 4/23/73; 5/7/73;
5/21/73; 9/17/73; 10/8/73; - 12/10/73; 12/31/73
Lyme, Chesterfield Parish - 3/26/73
Lyme Old Society - 10/26/70
Main Street, Guilford, - 11/30/70
Mansfield - 6/28/71; 11/8/71;
12/6/71; 2/7/72; 6/12/72;
7/31/72; 4/23/73; 5/28/73;
12/24/73
Marlboro's Society in Hebron - 6/18/73
Marlborough in Colchester - 2/9/70 ;5/22/72
Marshfield, Massachusetts - 3/2/70
Martha Vineyard. - 11/6/72;
11/13/72
Martinico - 10/25/71
Maryland - 7/2/73
Massachusetts Bay - 1/12/70
Massapeauge - 12/13/71;10/16/72

Middle Haddam - 9/17/73
Middletown -
Middletown, Rhode Island - 7/6
Middletown - 1/19/70; 2/2/70; 2/9/70; 2/16/70; 3/9/70; 6/22/70; 3/22/71; 7/19/71; 8/23/71;9/13/71; 10/18/71;1/31/72; 2/21/72; 3/27/72; 4/3/72; 5/15/72; 5/22/72; 1/6/72; 11/27/72; 12/25/72; 2/5/73; 2/12/73; 2/26/73; 4/30/73; 6/4/73; 10/22/73; 10/29/73; 12/17/73
Milford - 1/25/71; 11/8/71
Mill Cove - 11/23/70
Millick River - 4/9/73
Millington in East Haddam - 1/11/71; 10/4/71; 1/22/73; 1/29/73
Mississippi River - 8/27/73
Mohegan - 4/13/70; 9/14/70; 11/15/71; 1/10/72;6/26/72; 7/24/72
Montauk. - 3/9/70; 9/14/70; 6/25/73
Montauk Point - 8/27/73; 9/3/73
Mt Vesuvius - 8/31/71
Murray' Barracks, Boston - 3/16/70
Mystic meeting house - 7/9/73
Mystic - 5/4/70
Mystic River - 3/16/70; 2/22/71; 3/8/71
Nahactiuck River - 1/5/70
Namquit - 6/19/72
Naples - 8/31/71
Narragansett Beach.- 10/18/71
Nazareth in Voluntown.- 4/24/72
Netherlands Antilles - end note 12

New Bern - end note 39
New Concord, Norwich - 2/16/70;2/5/73 ;12/3/73
New England -8/3/70; 12/27/71; 5/15/72; 10/1/73; end note 25, 27
New Hartford - 9/25/72; 10/30/72
New Haven - 1/5/70; 2/23/70; 3/9/70; 5/4/70; 8/3/70; 9/21/70; 12/7/70; 1/25/71 ; 3/8/71;4/19/71; 5/3/71; 6/28/71; 8/9/71;8/31/71;9/13/71; 11/1/71;11/8/71; 5/7/73; 7/2/73; 8/13/73; 9/17/73; 11/12/73
New Jersey - 5/25/70; 4/5/71; 10/4/71; 10/18/71; 11/8/71; 12/20/71; 12/27/71;end note 31
New London - 1/5/70; 1/19/70; 1/26/70; 2/2/70; 2/9/70;2/16/70; 2/23/70; 3/2/70; 3/9/70; 3/16/70; 3/23/70; 4/13/70; 4/20/70; 5/4/70;5/11/70; 5/18/70;6/8/70; 6/15/70; 6/22/70; 6/29/70; 1/11/71; 1/18/71; 1/25/71; 2/22/71; -3/15/71; 3/22/71; 3/29/71;4/5/71; 4/12/71; 5/3/71; 5/10/71; 5/17/71;5/31/71; 6/7/71; 6/14/71; 6/21/71; 6/28/71;- 7/12/71; 7/19/71; 7/26/71; 8/2/71; -8/9/71; 8/23/71; 8/31/71; 9/6/71; 9/13/71; 9/20/71; 9/27/71; 10/11/71 ; 10/18/71;10/25/71; 11/1/71; 11/8/71; 11/15/51; 11/22/71; 11/29/71; 12/6/71; 12/13/71; 12/20/71; 12/27/71; 1/3/72; 1/10/72; 1/17/72; 1/24/72;

2/7/72; 2/14/72; 2/28/72;
3/13/72; 3/20/72; 3/27/72;
4/3/72; 4/10/72; 4/17/72;
4/24/72; 5/15/72; 5/22/72; ;
6/19/72 ; 6/26/72;
7/10/72;7/24/72 ; 7/31/72;
8/14/72; 8/21/72; 8/28/72;
9/4/72; 10/2/72; 10/9/72;
10/16/72; 10/23/72 ; 10/30/72;
11/6/72; 11/13/72; 12/4/72;
12/11/72;12/18/72; 12/25/72;
5/15/72; 9/18/72; 10/30/72;
1/1/73; 1/15/73;
1/29/73;2/5/73; 2/12/73;
2/19/73; 2/26/73; 3/5/73;
3/12/73; 3/19/73; 3/26/73;
4/2/73; 4/9/73;
4/30/73;5/7/73;5/14/73;
5/28/73; 6/4/73; 6/18/73;
6/25/73; 7/2/73; 7/9/73;
7/16/73; 7/23/73;; 8/13/73;
8/20/73; 8/27/73; 9/3/73;
9/17/73;
9/24/73;10/1/73;10/8/73;
10/15/73; 10/22/73; 11/12/73;
11/26/73; 12/3/73; 12/17/73;
12/31/73; end notes 10, 24, 31,
34, 55
New London County -4/26/71;
6/14/71; 2/14/72; 4/30/73
New London, Great Neck -
12/14/70; 1/18/71; 2/22/71;
4/19/71 ;4/10/72; 7/17/72;
8/14/72; 12/17/73
New London, North Parish -
1/12/70; 5/4/70;6/22/70;
11/16/70; 1/25/71; 3/8/71;
3/29/71; 7/19/71; 8/31/71;
9/6/71; 11/22/71; 2/28/72;
3/27/72, ; 8/21/72; 1/15/73;
3/5/73; 6/18/73; 6/25/73;
7/2/73; 11/12/73; 11/19/73
New Orleans - 4/19/71

New Providence - 3/16/70;
10/25/71
New York - 9/14/70; 10/12/70
; 10/26/70; 11/9/70;
11/23/70;12/27/71; 3/13/72;
4/10/72; 5/15/72; 6/5/72;
6/19/72;; 11/6/72; 11/27/72;
11/19/73; 12/3/73; 12/10/73
12/24/73; 12/24/73;1/8/73;
2/19/73; 4/30/73; end notes 15,
58
Newent, Norwich - 2/16/70;
3/15/71; 2/28/72; 3/27/72;
5/29/72; 7/17/72
Newport , Rhode Island -
7/6/70; 10/26/70; 11/2/70;
2/8/71; 2/15/71; 4/12/71;
4/24/72; 5/15/72; 6/19/72;
10/30/72; 1/15/73; 3/26/73;
5/7/73;7/9/73; 10/15/73,
12/17/73; end note 45
Niantic River - 2/22/71;
11/22/71; 2/19/73
North Branford - 11/5/73
North Carolina - 4/19/71;
9/13/71; 11/1/71; 12/3/73; end
note 39
North Parish, New London -
1/15/73; 3/5/73; 6/18/73;
6/25/73; 7/2/73
North River, N.Y.- 11/9/70;
7/31/72
North society, Lyme - 1/12/70;
7/27/70; 12/25/72; 2/12/73;
5/21/73
Northampton - 10/26/70
Norwalk - 10/23/72
Norwich -1/5/70; 1/12/70;
1/26/70; 2/2/70; 2/9/70
;2/16/70; 2/23/70; 3/2/70;
3/9/70; 4/6/70; 4/13/70;
5/4/70; 5/11/70 5/18/70;
5/25/70;6/8/70; 6/29/70; -

7/13/70; 7/20/70;
8/3/70;8/17/70; 8/24/70;
9/14/70; 9/21/70; 10/12/70;
11/9/70; 12/14/70; 12/28/70;
1/11/71; 2/1/71; 3/29/71;
4/12/71; 5/3/71; 5/31/71;
6/14/71; 6/28/71; 7/12/71;
8/2/71; 8/16/71; 8/23/71;
8/31/71; 9/13/71; 9/27/71;
10/4/71; 10/18/71;10/25/71;
11/8/71; 11/15/51; 12/6/71,
12/13/71; 12/27/71; 1/3/72;
1/31/72; 2/7/72; 2/14/72;
2/28/72; 3/20/72; 3/27/72;
4/3/72; 4/17/72; 4/24/72;
5/15.72; 6/19/72; 6/26/72
;7/10/72; 7/17/72; 7/31/72;
8/7/72; 8/21/72; 9/4/72;
10/2/72; 10/16/72; 10/23/72;
11/20/72;12/4/72; 12/11/72;
12/25/72; 1/1/73; 1/15/73;
1/22/73; 2/5/73; 2/12/73;
2/19/73; 3/5/73; 3/12/73;
3/19/73; 3/26/73; 4/2/73;
4/23/73; 4/30/73; 5/7/73;
5/14/73; 5/21/73; 5/28/73;
6/18/73; 7/2/73;7/9/73;
7/16/73; 8/6/73; 8/13/73;
8/20/73; 8/27/73; 9/10/73;
9/17/73; 10/1/73; 10/8/73;
10/22/73; 11/5/73; 11/12/73;
11/19/73; 11/26/73;
12/3/73;12/24/73; end note 13
Norwich East Society -4/3/72;
5/29/72;7/10/72
Norwich, First Society -
11/23/70; 3/26/73
Norwich Great Plain - 2/7/72
Norwich Landing [see also
Chelsea] - 2/9/70 ;2/16/70;
2/23/70; 3/2/70; 3/9/70;
3/23/70; 4/20/70 6/8/70 ; -
8/3/70; 8/17/70; 8/31/70;

1/18/71; 3/1/71; 3/22/71; -
5/17/71; 5/24/71; 6/28/71;
8/23/71; 9/20/71;10/4/71;
10/18/71; 12/20/71; 1/17/72;
1/31/72 1/31/72; 3/6/72 ;
3/27/72;4/24/72; 6/26/72;
7/10/72 ; 7/24/72; 10/2/72;
10/9/72; 10/16/72; 1/8/73;
1/15/73; 3/19/73; 4/9/73;
4/23/73;5/7/73; 5/28/73;
;7/2/73; 7/9/73; 7/23/73;
9/17/73;11/19/73; end notes
13,19
Norwich, North Plain -
11/15/51
Norwich River. - 7/24/72;
10/30/72
Norwich West Society -
12/24/73
Norwich, West Farms -
12/13/71; 1/10/72
Nova Scotia . - 8/17/70;
5/17/71; - 6/14/71; 8/23/71;
4/24/72; 10/2/72; 10/23/72;
4/9/73; 5/7/73; 7/2/73
Old Parish, Lebanon - 3/27/72
Otter Creek, N.Y. 2/23/70;
10/12/70
Oyster Pond - 3/23/70;
11/22/71
Oyster Pond Point - 1/19/70;
5/28/73
Palmer - 12/11/72
Paucatuck River - 3/9/70;
6/19/72
Peeling - end note 44
Pennsylvania - 11/27/72; end
note 8
Pequotanuck - 8/31/70
Philadelphia - 1/5/70; - 8/3/70;
9/28/70; 7/19/71; 12/13/71;
11/27/72; 7/2/73; 12/24/73;
end note 58

Piscataqua - 11/12/73
Pittsfield, Massachusetts - 7/9/73
Plainfield - 4/13/70; 8/10/70; 9/14/70; 7/12/71; 9/13/71; 11/15/71; 3/13/72; 11/6/72; 11/13/72; 1/1/73; 11/12/73
Plum Island - 1/19/70; 1/31/72; 3/6/72; 4/30/73
Plymouth. - 12/24/73
Point Judith 5/15/72
Pomfret -
Pomfret, - 1/5/70; 4/13/70; 7/20/70; 9/28/70; 10/12/70; 1/4/71; 8/9/71; 8/23/71; 9/13/71; 11/29/71; 12/27/7;1/10/72; 4/17/72; 9/4/72; 11/20/72;4/2/73; 7/30/73; 9/24/73; 10/29/73
Pomfret on Otter Creek, N.Y. - 10/12/70; 4/12/71; end note 38
Poquatanuk - 12/3/73
Poqutuck bridge - 4/23/73
Port au Prince - 7/27/70; 9/10/73
Post Road, - 10/26/70; 5/7/73;7/9/73
Poughkeepsie - 11/6/72
Preston: - 1/12/70; 2/9/70; 4/13/70; 8/3/70; 3/15/71; 5/10/71; 9/13/71; 3/13/72; 3/27/72; 5/15/72; 9/4/72; 2/5/73; 3/5/73; 3/26/73; 5/28/73; 8/6/73; 8/20/73; 9/17/73; 10/1/73; 11/26/73
Providence - 6/15/70; 10/11/71; 2/7/72; 1/15/73; 3/19/73; end note 45
Quebec - 2/1/71
Rhode Island - 3/3/70; 5/4/70; 8/17/70; 10/5/70; 10/26/70 11/9/70; 11/16/70 3/8/71; 12/20/71;- 3/12/73;

4/23/73; end note 45
Ripton - 10/15/73; 11/5/73
Rocky Hill - 6/21/71
Rope Ferry - 12/18/72
Roxbury - 11/26/73
Sag Harbor -3/9/70; 6/22/70; 4/5/71; 5/3/71; 6/14/71; 9/27/71; 5/15/72; 6/12/72 ; 4/9/73
Salem, - 3/5/73; 9/24/73
Salem parish in Colchester - 7/3/72
Santo Domingo . - 3/29/71; end note 7
Saybrook - 1/5/70; 4/13/70; 6/22/70; 7/20/70; 4/26/71; /31/71; 11/15/71; 1/10/72; - 2/28/72; 8/21/72; 10/23/72 ; 10/30/72; 11/6/72; 1/8/73; 1/15/73; 1/29/73; 3/26/73; 4/9/73; 6/18/73; 7/16/73; 8/27/73; 9/17/73; 12/3/73
Saybrook ferry. - 5/7/73
Scotland, British Isles - 10/26/70
Scotland Society, Windham - 1/5/70;10/12/70; 4/12/71; - 8/9/71; 9/6/71; 3/20/72; 3/27/72; 4/24/72; 6/26/72; 4/9/73; 6/18/73; 10/22/73; - 12/17/73
Second Society in Ashford. - 9/24/73
Second s Society, Lebanon - 8/21/72
Second Society, Windham - 4/30/7; 5/21/73 3
Shetucket River - 2/16/70; 2/28/72; 5/29/72; 10/8/73; end note 13
Simsbury - 1/19/70; 7/24/72
Sligo, Ireland - 12/11/72
Smith's Manor - 7/31/72

Smithfield - 8/23/71
Smithfield, Rhode island; - 5/70
Society of Brookline - 7/23/73
Society of Goshen - 1/25/71
South America - end note 1
South Carolina -10/25/71; 4/24/72; 6/26/72;9/18/72; 9/25/72; 7/23/73; end note 53
South East Pond - 10/8/73
South Haven, Long Island - 7/3/72
South Kingston, Rhode Island - 11/16/70
South Meeting House, Boston - 12/3/73
South Sea - 3/2/70
Southampton - 10/26/70; - 10/18/71; 5/15/72; 12/11/72; 4/30/73; 9/24/73
Southhold Point - 7/17/72
Southold, Long Island: - 1/5/70 ;1/19/70; 9/14/70; 4/5/71; 3/27/72; 5/28/73
Spain - 10/18/71
Springfield - 9/28/70; 11/13/72; 11/19/73
Statia - end note 12
St. Eustatia. - 2/9/70 ; 3/29/71; 1/15/73; end note 12
St. George's Manor - 6/7/71
St. Kitts. - 5/3/71; 10/9/72
St. Lawrence River - 2/1/71
St. Lucia - 3/9/70; 5/3/71
Sterling - 4/5/71
Stewart's farm - 2/22/71
Stockton - 7/30/73
Stoddard' Ferry -12/13/71; 3/6/72 ;5/15/72
Stonington harbor - 5/4/70; 1/10/72
Stonington - 1/5/70; 2/16/70;3/2/70; 3/9/70;

3/16/70; 4/13/70; -5/4/70; - 9/7/70; 9/14/70; 1/11/71; 2/15/71;3/29/71; 5/17/71; 5/31/71; 7/5/71; 7/12/71; 8/2/71; 10/11/71; 11/8/71; - 11/15/71; 1/10/72; -3/6/72; 6/26/72;7/10/72; 10/23/72; 1/15/73; 1/22/73; 2/5/73; 3/5/73; 3/19/73; 4/30/73; 6/18/73; 7/9/73; 9/17/73;10/22/73; 11/5/73; 11/12/73; 12/3/73; 12/17/73 12/24/73; 12/31/73
Stratford - 4/26/71; 8/9/71; - 1/17/72
Suffolk County 6/7/71; 5/15/72
Sullivan county - end note 37
Susquehanna Company - end note 8
Susquehanna territories - end note 8
Sussfield - 7/17/72
Taunton River - 4/24/72
Texas. - end note 53
Thames River.- 12/31/73; end note 13
Third Society of Windham,10/12/70
Thompson Parish in Killingly - 3/27/72
Tolland, - 12/14/70; 6/19/72; 9/3/73
Torrington - 8/21/72
Town Hill, New London - 2/16/70
Town Street, Norwich - 1/5/70
Town Wharf, New London - 3/16/70
Trinity, Martinico - 8/2/71
Turk's Island - 2/2/70; 3/29/71; 10/25/71
Virginia - 2/2/70; 4/12/71;

288

6/4/73; end note 53
Voluntown - 9/14/70; 2/28/72; 3/27/72; 1/22//73; 3/5/73
Wales - 3/3/70
Wallingford, - 11/2/70
Warwick, in the Susquehanna purchase - 12/3/73
Waterbury - 5/18/70; 8/31/70
Waterman's Point - 10/9/72
Wethersfield -
West Sheep Walk - 10/8/73
West Chester - 11/6/72
West Indies - 2/16/70; 12/21/70; 6/28/71; 7/19/71; 10/18/71; 11/1/71; 12/27/71; 2/28/72; 3/5/73; 3/12/73; 4/11/73; 5/7/73; 12/17/73
West Farms: Norwich - 2/16/70
West Parish, Saybrook - 5/31/71
West Sheep Walk - 10/8/73
Westerly - 5/4/70; 5/15/72; 10/23/72;6/4/73; 12/10/73
Westford in Ashford - 2/23/70
Wethersfield - 1/25/71; 3/22/71; 4/19/71; 6/21/71;5/1/72; 7/24/72 ;4/9/73; 4/30/73; 11/5/73; 11/12/73; -12/10/73; 12/17/73
White Beach, New London harbor - 2/19/73
William's Pasture - 3/16/70

Windham - 2/16/70; 3/2/70; 3/9/70; 4/13/70; 6/15/70; 10/5/70; 10/26/70; 12/14/70; 2/22/71; 4/26/71; 6/7/71; 7/26/71; 8/9/71; 8/16/71; 9/6/71; 9/13/71; 10/4/71;10/11/71; 11/15/71; 11/22/71; 1/17/72; 2/7/72; 2/21/72; 3/27/72; 4/17/72; 5/8/72; 5/15/72; 6/12/72; 6/19/72;8/21/72; 8/21/72; 9/4/72; 12/25/72; 1/1/73; 1/15/73; 2/26/73; 3/12/73; 3/19/73; 5/21/73; 6/18/73; 6/25/73; 8/6/73; 9/3/73; 9/10/73; 9/17/73; 9/24/73; 10/8/73; 11/5/73; 12/3/73; 12/17/73; 12/24/73; end note 8
Windsor - 6/21/71; 5/28/73
Woodberry - 10/11/71
Woodstock: - 4/13/70; 4/27/70; 6/1/70; 12/14/70; 9/13/71; 7/30/73
Woodstock, N. H.- end note 44
Woodstock Road - 11/20/72; 4/2/73
Wyoming - 8/3/70 ;2/22/71; 8/23/71
Wyoming Valley - end note 8
Yantic rivers - end note 13

GENERAL INDEX

Ames Almanac - 1/24/72
apples - end note 27
Backus Tavern - 3/22/71
Battle of Alamance - end note 39
Benjamin Bancroft & Sons - 1/5/70
Board of Commissioners at Boston - 1/15/73
Bolles Mill - 12/28/70Boston Massacre - 3/16/70; 11/9/70
Boston Tea Party - 12/24/73
branding - end note 21
brig *Betsy*, - 3/26/7 -
brig *Four Sisters* - 5/10/71
brig *Hero* - 6/26/72; 8/28/72; 9/3/73
brig *Mermaid* - *3/15/71*
brig *Nancy* -*3/6/72*
brig *Norwich Packet* - 1/15/73
brig *Royal* - 10/12/70
brig *Victory* - 6/5/72;
British Apollo - 7/19/71
Brooklyn Dodger - endnote 20
Bushnell and Amos - 3/13/72
Capt. Coit's tavern - 1/19/70
Captain Leffingwell's Tavern - 10/18/71
Carolina slaves - end note 53
Chelsea Bridge lottery - 8/7/72; 9/4/72; 2/5/73
Chickisaw - end note 53
China- end note 41
Christ Church ,New London - 5/25/70
Church & Hallam - 8/20/73
Church of Christ, Chelsea in Norwich. - 10/11/71
Clark Truman's Passage Boat - 3/9/70

coal - 10/22/73
codfish - 9/17/73
Committees of Correspondence and Inquiry - 6/4/73; end note 53
Committee of inspection - 6/15/70; 7/6/70; end note 14
Consumption - end note 3
cruiser *Snow* - 11/5/73
Dame schools - end note 42
Delaware companies - 1/22/72; 7/13/70; 8/6/73; 12/24/73; end note 8
Distill house, New London - 6/7/71; 4/24/72;7/2/73
dropsy - end note 40
drought - 10/1/73;10/22/73
ear cropping - end note 21
earthquake - 2/12/73
East India Company - 12/3/73; 12/24/73; end note 58
Ebenezer Fitch's Tavern.- 4/13/70
education - 12/3/73; end notes 25, 42
Episcopal church - 5/25/70
ferries - 1/18/71
Ferry House - 3/9/70; 4/13/70
First Church and Society of Wethersfield - 12/17/73
First Ecclesiastical Society in East Haddam - 10/16/72
First Church of Christ, East Haddam - 6/14/71; 11/6/72
First Continental Congress - end note 10
fish - 4/17/72
Fitch's Tavern - 3/9/70 -
floods - 1/19/70
Fordham'tavern - 3/9/70

Fourth Society in Hartford - 10/2/72
Freebetter's Connecticut Almanac - 10/22/73
fulling mills - end note 26
Furnace at Symsbury - 1/19/70
Gaspee Affair - end note 53
Gaspee - 9/27/71; 6/19/72; 1/15/73; 11/26/73; endnote 45
General Assembly - 3/9/70; 9/14/70; 9/21/70; 12/14/70; 12/21/70; 6/21/71; 9/13/71; 4/17/72; 2/5/73; 4/30/73 ;9/17/73; 11/26/73; 12/3/73; 12/10/73 6/12/72
Greeks - end note 3
Green & Spooner - 5/14/73; 10/22/73
Harris' sloop, -3/6/72
Harvard College - 9/17/73
Higgin's Wharf, Lyme
Himalayas - end note 41
HMS *Swan* - 4/2/73; 4/9/73
hogs - 12/31/73
House of Hanover - 3/16/70
House of Burgesses -
House of Burgesses - 6/4/73; end note 53
Hubbard and Greene - 5/24/71; 12/20/71
India - end note 41
Indian slaves - end note - end note 53
invention - 5/18/70
Jesuit Powder, - end note 1
Jesuit Bark - end note 1
Kennedy and Badger - 10/26/70
leather - end note 29
Ling fever - 9/6/71
London Coffeehouse Wharf- 9/3/73
London Packet -3/6/72

London Coffee House - 4/20/70; 10/12/70;7/19/71; 8/31/71; 9/13/71; 1/15/73; 5/14/73; end note 22
London Coffee House Wharf - end note 22
Lord, Durkee and Abel - 8/3/70
lottery - 8/7/72; 9/4/72; 2/5/73 8/27/73; 11/12/73; 12/31/73
mackerel - 9/20/71
mad dogs - 2/9/70;6/1/70; 6/15/70; 3/8/71; 7/19/71 ;end note 11
maple sugar - 6/8/70
Massachusetts Assembly - 11/5/73
measles -8/2/71; 9/25/72
Mermaid, the - 5/70
Mohegan Indians -
Mohegan Tribe - 4/13/70; 10/4/71
Nard oil- end note 41
Nepal. - end note 41
New London Gazette - 9/21/70; 3/22/71; 11/8/71;3/13/72; 3/5/73; 4/2/73; end notes 11, 21, 31, 39, 45, 46, 55, 58
New York Packet boat -3/6/72 s
New York College - 1/17/72
New London Ferry - 2/22/71
non importation agreement - 4/6/70; 6/15/70; 8/24/70; 9/21/70;9/28/70; end note 10
North Briton - 1/12/70
Norwich Meeting house - 4/20/70
Orations on the Beauties of Liberty or the Essential Rights of Americans - 7/2/73

Orphans Asylum Academy - 7/2/73
Packet ships - end note 2
Palmer worms - 7/13/70
Parliament - end note 58
passage boat - 4/13/70; -

Quorum - end note 43
rattle snakes - 8/21/72
Regulator War - end note 39
Regulators - 4/19/71; end note 39
right whales - end note 34
right hand of fellowship, the - end note 32
Ripley and Carey - 11/8/71
Robin passage boat - 5/3/71
salmon - 1/15/73
salt hay - end note 52
Say Brook ferry - 10/26/70
schooner *Pompey* 6/28/71
schooner *Two Brothers* - 7/2/73; 4/9/73
Schooner *Indian King*,- 10/2/72; 4/9/73; 5/7/73
Schooner *Liberty* - 2/9/70; 10/12/70
Second Church of Litchfield. - 10/30/72
Second Baptist Church, Boston - 7/2/73
Shaw's wharf -3/6/72
ship *Rosamond*, - 4/30/73
ship *Charming Nancy* - 9/10/73
ship *St. George* - 10/25/71
ship *London Packet*, 6/28/71
Sign Post, the - 9/24/73; 11/19/73
Six Nations - 8/3/70
sloop *Bridget* - 11/19/73
sloop *Britannia* - 7/2/73
sloop *Clarissa* - 12/27/71

6/22/70
Pennsylvania Proprietors - 8/3/70
perch -3/6/72
Peruvian Indians - end note 1
Potash - end note 23

sloop *Collin* - 3/15/71
sloop *Delight* - 10/4/71
sloop *Dispatch* - 8/17/70; 5/17/71; 8/23/71; 4/24/72
sloop *Esther* - 5/22/72
sloop *Fancy* - 2/2/70; 7/19/71
sloop *Fashion* - 3/8/71
sloop *Hannah* - end note 45
sloop *Lily* - 11/2/70
sloop *Nancy,*- 9/3/73
sloop *Patty* - 10/1/73
sloop *Phoenix* - 6/12/72
sloop *Ranger* - 6/4/73
sloop *Ruby* - 4/24/72
sloop *Sally* - 10/1/73
sloop *Swallow* - 4/12/71
small pox - 9/14/70; 11/23/70; - 1/25/71; 3/22/71; 5/31/71;8 /23/71;1/22/72; 3/6/72 ;4/10/72; 9/11/72; 2/5/73; 2/19/73;3/12/73; 3/26/73; 5/7/73; 7/2/73; end note 31
snow *Beggars Bennison*, - 9/18/72
snow *Peggy* - 2/2/70
snow *Tristman* - 6/15/70
Society for Propagating the Gospel - 1/17/72
Sons of Liberty - 4/6/70; end note 10
Spanish Indian slaves - end note 53
sperm whales - end note 34
Spikenard - end note 41
St. Vincent's. - 6/4/73
Stamp Act - 1/12/70; end note

292

10
Susquehanna Company -
2/2/70; 5/18/70; 7/27/70;
2/22/71; 6/7/71; 9/27/71;
2/21/72; 3/27/72; 3/19/73;
4/9/73
tea tax - 12/3/73; -12/10/73;
12/24/73
Tea Act - end note 58
Trinity Church in Pomfret -
8/23/71
tuberculosis - end note 3
Turlington's Balsam - 1/5/70
Walker's Jesuits drops -
1/5/70
Waters Tavern - 2/15/71
Webb's passage boat - 4/5/71

West Church, Hartford -
1/15/70
Whale and Cod fisheries -
12/21/70
whaling - 10/5/70;
10/12/70;3/15/71; 3/22/71;
3/29/71; 10/11/71;11/1/71;
11/15/51; end note 34
Whaling City - end note 34
whipping - end note 21
wool spinning - end note 28
worms 6/7/71
Yale college - 11/27/72
yellow fever - 8/2/71

Other Heritage Books by Richard B. Marrin:

Abstracts from the New London Gazette: *Covering Southeastern Connecticut, 1763-1769*

A Glance Back in Time: Life in Colonial New Jersey (1704-1770) As Depicted in News Accounts of the Day

Going to Court in Texas: Riding the Circuit, 1842-1861

The Paradise of Texas, Volume 1: Clarksville and Red River County, 1846-1860

Passage Point: An Amateur's Dig Into New Jersey's Colonial Past

Runaways of Colonial New Jersey: Indentured Servants, Slaves, Deserters, and Prisoners, 1720-1781

Other Heritage Books by Richard B. Marrin and Lorna Geer Sheppard:

Abstracts from the Northern Standard *and the Red River District [Texas]: August 20, 1842-August 19, 1848*

Abstracts from the Northern Standard *and the Red River District [Texas], Volume 2: August 26, 1848-December 20, 1851*